Researching Pedagogic Tasks

APPLIED LINGUISTICS AND LANGUAGE STUDY

GENERAL EDITOR

CHRISTOPHER N. CANDLIN

Chair Professor of Applied Linguistics
Department of English
Centre for English Language Education &
Communication Research
City University of Hong Kong, Hong Kong

For a complete list of books in this series see pages v–vi

Researching Pedagogic Tasks

Second Language Learning, Teaching and Testing

Edited by

MARTIN BYGATE
PETER SKEHAN
MERRILL SWAIN

An imprint of **Pearson Education**

Harlow, England · London · New York · Reading, Massachusetts · San Francisco
Toronto · Don Mills, Ontario · Sydney · Tokyo · Singapore · Hong Kong · Seoul
Taipei · Cape Town · Madrid · Mexico City · Amsterdam · Munich · Paris · Milan

Pearson Education Limited
Edinburgh Gate
Harlow
Essex CM20 2JE
England

and Associated Companies throughout the world

Visit us on the World Wide Web at:
www.pearsoneduc.com

First published 2001

ISBN 0-582-41482-2 PPR

British Library Cataloguing-in-Publication Data

A catalogue record for this book is available from the British Library

Library of Congress Cataloging-in-Publication Data

Researching pedagogic tasks: second language learning, teaching and testing/edited by Martin Bygate, Peter Skehan, Merrill Swain.
    p. cm. — (Applied linguistics and language study)
    Includes bibliographical references and index.
    ISBN 0-582-41482-2 (ppr)
    1. Language and languages—Study and teaching. 2. Second language acquisition. I. Bygate, Martin. II. Skehan, Peter. III. Swain, Merrill. IV. Series.

P51.R45   2000
418'.0071—dc21   00–058047

Set by 35 in 10/12pt Baskerville
Produced by
Printed in Malaysia, PA

APPLIED LINGUISTICS AND LANGUAGE STUDY

GENERAL EDITOR

CHRISTOPHER N. CANDLIN

Chair Professor of Applied Linguistics
Department of English
Centre for English Language Education &
Communication Research
City University of Hong Kong, Hong Kong

Error Analysis:
Perspective on Second Language
Acquisition
JACK C RICHARDS (ED.)

Contrastive Analysis
CARL JAMES

Language and Communication
JACK C RICHARDS *and*
RICHARD W SCHMIDT (EDS)

Reading in a Foreign Language
J CHARLES ALDERSON *and*
A H URQUHART (EDS)

An Introduction to Discourse Analysis
Second Edition
MALCOLM COULTHARD

Bilingualism in Education:
Aspects of Theory, Research and Practice
JIM CUMMINS *and* MERRILL SWAIN

Second Language Grammar:
Learning and Teaching
WILLIAM E RUTHERFORD

Vocabulary and Language Teaching
RONALD CARTER *and*
MICHAEL MCCARTHY

The Classroom and the
Language Learner:
Ethnography and Second-Language
Classroom Research
LEO VAN LIER

Listening in Language Learning
MICHAEL ROST

An Introduction to Second Language
Acquisition Research
DIANE LARSEN-FREEMAN
and MICHAEL H LONG

Process and Experience in the
Language Classroom
MICHAEL LEGUTKE *and*
HOWARD THOMAS

Translation and Translating:
Theory and Practice
ROGER T BELL

Language Awareness in the Classroom
CARL JAMES *and*
PETER GARRETT (EDS)

Rediscovering Interlanguage
LARRY SELINKER

Language and Discrimination:
A Study of Communication in
Multi-ethnic Workplaces
CELIA ROBERTS, EVELYN DAVIES *and*
TOM JUPP

Analysing Genre:
Language Use in Professional Settings
VIJAY K BHATIA

Language as Discourse:
Perspective for Language Teaching
MICHAEL MCCARTHY *and*
RONALD CARTER

Second Language Learning:
Theoretical Foundations
MICHAEL SHARWOOD SMITH

Contents

List of contributors

Martin Bygate, University of Leeds
Chris Candlin, City University, Hong Kong
Micheline Chalhoub-Deville, University of Iowa
Rod Ellis, University of Auckland
Pauline Foster, St. Mary's University College/King's College, London
Sharon Lapkin, Ontario Institute for Studies in Education
Tony Lynch, University of Edinburgh
Joan Maclean, University of Edinburgh
Virginia Samuda, Lancaster University
Peter Skehan, King's College, London
Merrill Swain, Ontario Institute for Studies in Education
Gillian Wigglesworth, Macquarie University

Publisher's Acknowledgements

We are grateful to the following for permission to reproduce copyright material:

W.J.M. Levelt and MIT Press for our Figure 2.1 from *Speaking: From Intention to Articulation* (1989); Iva Baltova for the 1994 'The Tricky Alarm Clock' drawings in Appendix 5.1 (in the context of the SSHRC grant awarded to Merrill Swain in 1993); Oxford University Press for our Figure 8.1, also reproduced as Figure 9.1, reproduced by permission of Oxford University Press from *A Cognitive Approach to Language Learning* by Peter Skehan © Oxford University Press 1998.

Whilst every effort has been made to trace the owners of copyright material, in a few cases this has proved impossible and we take this opportunity to offer our apologies to any copyright holders whose rights we may have unwittingly infringed.

Chapter 1

Introduction

Martin Bygate, Peter Skehan and Merrill Swain

TOWARDS A RESEARCHED PEDAGOGY

Pedagogy can be defined as 'intervention into thought and behaviour which is concerned to promote learning processes for intended outcomes'. By definition it therefore simultaneously involves decisions by teachers, action by learners and perceptible outcomes, both immediate and over time. Tasks are a central element of language pedagogy, and hence find themselves pivotally placed within this three-way relationship: their design can affect their use by teachers in the classroom, the actions of learners and the performance and learning outcomes. This book explores that relationship.

Pedagogy has been studied for centuries. However, much of that study has been based on principle, prescription and analogy. In contrast, a researched pedagogy (Leung, 1993) scrutinises pedagogic activity to assess its modes of implementation, its operation and its outcomes. This volume builds upon a growing number of previous publications to bring together a series of studies which investigate tasks in this way. Overall this is a very long-term project. A volume such as this can only sample a small range of tasks, in a limited number of contexts, with relatively few students, under a restricted range of conditions. There is a substantial range of pedagogic activities that remain to be researched, in a vast range of circumstances. In contrast, then, this collection makes a small contribution to the field. Yet this is the only way for progress to be made: pedagogy needs to be founded on systematic as well as enlightened observation. Systematic contributions will often be small, but no less valuable for that.

In fact, research into pedagogic tasks is one of a growing number of areas of empirical research which have emerged since the early 1980s. One of the basic functions of empirical research into language pedagogy is arguably feedback to the teaching profession, so that, as Brumfit argued 'we are able to attempt to assess the effectiveness of our educational system', and in order to receive 'information about alternatives to traditional methods, so that the alternatives can be introduced, in some systematic way, into the system' (Brumfit, 1980: 132). Following the discrediting of the large-scale experimental research projects of the 1960s and early 1970s (see, for example, Brumfit,

1980; Howatt, 1984; Ellis, 1985; Johnson, 1996), the 1970s had seen a highly significant period of largely conceptual research in language teaching. This culminated in a series of landmark publications (such as Stevick, 1976; Wilkins, 1976; Widdowson, 1978, 1979; Munby, 1978; Brumfit and Johnson, 1979; Breen and Candlin, 1980; Canale and Swain, 1980).

Three particular themes were to permeate subsequent thought. First, communicative language teaching was explicitly a post-method approach to language teaching (see notably Brumfit and Johnson, 1979; and Brumfit, 1988), in which the principles underlying the use of different classroom procedures were of paramount importance, rather than a package of teaching materials. Second, the most fundamental element of the approach was its explicit emphasis on the role of authentic communication within classroom contexts. Third, the measure of effectiveness was no longer simply the ability to use language accurately (Widdowson's 'usage', 1978); it became the ability to use language accurately and appropriately in communicative contexts. These three themes had a strong influence on the nature and scope of subsequent empirical research, providing a justification for a narrowing of the focus from the earlier concern with the impact on learning of whole methods or courses, to the impact on learning of particular activities or interactions.

MULTIPLE PERSPECTIVES ON TASKS: TEACHING, LEARNING AND TESTING

The three themes have had a major impact upon the nature of language teaching. One aspect of this impact has been the growing importance attached to the use of tasks within language pedagogy (Prabhu, 1987), a change which has led to a burgeoning of activity around task-based concepts. This, in turn, has resulted in the problem that the term 'task' is interpreted in a number of different but systematic ways by different groups of people. The purpose of this section is to explore some of these multiple interpretations with a view to disentangling the different viewpoints, and locating them in characteristic different contexts. Misunderstandings arising from the different perspectives may thus be more readily identified, and even avoided.

As a starting point, it is useful to focus on two groups who have each appropriated the term 'task' for their own purposes: these are communicative language teachers, and second language acquisition (SLA) researchers. Earlier approaches to communicative language teaching, developing ideas originating in discourse analysis, pragmatics and sociolinguistics, suggested that requiring learners to express meanings would be an effective underpinning principle to motivate foreign language learning (Brumfit and Johnson, 1979). A wide range of imaginative classroom techniques were consequently developed in the 1970s and 1980s to implement such an approach, and provided teachers with a much greater range of activities on which they might draw, either as supplementary materials functioning in an adjunct manner to a main coursebook, or as materials that could be integrated into main coursebooks.

Earlier interpretations of such activities represented them as methods of promoting interaction so that learners could express meanings in natural ways. Terms such as information gap activities (Harmer, 1991) or jigsaw activities (Geddes and Sturtridge, 1978) were used to capture how learners were required to use language for communicative purposes. As time went on, such activities were described increasingly as *tasks*, and attempts were made to develop methodologies and principles by which such tasks could be used effectively. In this way, the idea of task has, for many people, superseded the term *communicative language teaching* and portrays what happens when meaning-based language teaching is carried out systematically and as an alternative to instruction which focuses on form**s** (Long and Robinson, 1998). Significant publications of this sort are Prabhu (1987), who has articulated the feasibility of using a task-based approach to underpin an actual curriculum in India, and Willis (1996), who has put forward a set of principles by which tasks may be developed and used by teachers, building upon the production of a coursebook series (Willis and Willis, 1988). One might also draw attention to writers on process syllabuses (e.g. Breen, 1984) and project work (Fried-Booth, 1986), who have shown how tasks can be integrated into alternative frameworks for organising foreign language instruction.

The contrasting perspective on tasks has come from the work of SLA *researchers*. As the inadequacy of input as an explanatory construct to account for second language development became apparent (Swain, 1985), SLA researchers, too, began to focus on interaction and the output it triggered as causative influences on second language development. Theoretically, the viewpoint that interaction promoted negotiation for meaning, and that such negotiation provided ideal circumstances for SLA to proceed became, and remains, influential (Long, 1989; Long and Robinson, 1998). It was argued that such negotiation enables acquisitional processes to be catalysed, and that sustained development results. Negotiation itself is thought to ensure that there is a focus on form during the interaction, so that learners are provided with feedback to precisely those points of the interlanguage system which are malleable and ready to change. Swain (1985) extended this interpretation to theorise how output itself pushes learners to reflect upon language form so that interlanguage change is more likely.

Arising from such theoretically motivated concerns, researchers came to use the concept of task to account for the manner in which interaction was more or less likely to provoke negotiation for meaning, and published accounts of how different task features might be associated with such performance differences. Long (1989), for example, in an influential article, argued for the use of what he termed 'closed' tasks (e.g. agreeing on the objects needed in a survival scenario, i.e. *requiring* agreement on the outcome) rather than 'open' tasks (e.g. a discussion, where no required agreement is inevitable). Equally importantly, such theoretical accounts were matched by a strong commitment to empirical research. The claims about different task properties were seen as requiring empirical confirmation: simply making claims about the desirability of one task over another was regarded as vacuous – the claim had to be translated into empirical operationalisations and confirmation. As a result, a range of studies was published, and a range of empirical techniques was developed.

The two approaches, although sharing the concept of task as central, use this concept to address different problems. The pedagogic approach presents the problem as one of understanding how the behaviour of the teacher can be made more effective and how learners can interact with tasks more effectively. Any solution to this problem is likely to involve teachers, course designers, and materials writers drawing on their teaching experience to understand task properties and produce effective examples of tasks. This is essentially a pragmatic response to characterising and working with tasks. The research approach presents the problem as one of how tasks may be used as a device to uncover the effective engagement of acquisitional processes. Tasks, in this account, are a window enabling fundamental issues to be studied more effectively. In this approach the role of theory is more prominent, as is an explicit concern with methods of inquiry. Data gathering and data analysis are themselves of interest, as the methods by which hypotheses and interpretations are substantiated.

It is also possible to view tasks in terms of different groups of users. This focuses more on the context of task use, rather than the manner in which tasks are investigated. In this respect, one can explore whether a concern with tasks relates to:

• the activity of the teacher;
• the process of learning and the role of the learner;
• the assessment of learning.

In the first of these cases, one would be looking at the decisions to be made about teaching tasks. The decisions might be for pedagogic action, or for data gathering or theory testing, but they would, ultimately, relate to pedagogic activities. In the second case, the emphasis would be on what happens from the learner's perspective. This would lead to an emphasis on what changes might take place in the learner's interlanguage; what processes might be operative to facilitate desirable change, and how the learner might respond to, or even choose, a task. Finally, assessment implicates tasks as testing devices and explores what can be said about the nature of learning and of performance as seen through task-based measurement formats.

The two dimensions at work here – manner of working with tasks (pragmatic vs research) and user groups and contexts (teachers, learners, assessment) – interact. A matrix (Figure 1.1) begins to make this clear. The pragmatic vs research dimension distinguishes between informal, practical decisions on the one hand, and the theoretical, systematic, evidence-based decisions on the other. Then, one can consider that the vertical dimension focuses on what the decisions in each case will be about, and who will make them. Hence the first row is concerned with tasks as the unit of decision-making for instruction (which can be approached either in terms of practical decisions, or research decisions). The middle row is concerned with tasks as the vehicle for the learner and learning, so that decisions relate to effectiveness for each *focus*

	Pragmatic/pedagogic	**Research**
Teachers and teaching	• Task as a unit of work in a scheme of work • Interlinked activity sequences developing thematic unit • Methods of involving learners • Deliberate starting point for unknown direction or explorations	• Task as researchable unit • Neat, cross-sectional approach • Relatively brief time interventions • Focus on the isolation of variables • Search for 'effects' through manipulation

Learners and learning	• Learner orientation and autonomy
	• Task reinterpretability
	• Interactive development through collaboration of groups of learners
	• Authenticity of response
		• Extent to which learning processes are catalysed
		• Identification of theorised methods of operationalising constructs and measuring dependent variables
		• Research designs to probe:
		  – salient task variables
		  – salient task conditions

Testing	• Formative evaluation • Provision of structured feedback on communication • Reactive, unstandardised and individual based	• Summative evaluation • Task as format • Comparability and standardisation • Issues in performance assessment

Figure 1.1   Two dimensions underlying the study of tasks

of these cases. The last row is concerned with decision-making about learning and achievement, whether these are informally conducted, or whether the decision is linked to systematic research.

Each of the cells in Figure 1.1 is worth further discussion. In the *pragmatic/pedagogic* teachers and teaching cell of the matrix (i.e. top left) it can be seen that the focus for task concerns teacher decision-making about instructional issues. A first point here is that, given the different ways tasks are used, there is a wide range of activity in this cell. First of all, there is the issue of *what* a teacher considers a task to be. This may simply involve a task as an element in a scheme of work. In such a case, 'task', for the teacher, may be synonymous with a relatively self-contained activity (Nunan, 1989). But teachers may also use tasks in longer sequences of instruction, and so a teacher might consider the term 'task' to include a wide-ranging extended pedagogic plan or scheme of work. This might comprise a task cycle, as described by Willis (1996), which could extend over a few lessons, giving them unity, and possibly focus on particular areas of language. In such cases, it may be the teacher's intention, while the extended task is running, to provide principled support and feedback to induce learners to interpret tasks according to some pre-existing pedagogic plan. Alternatively, a task might be a theme which generates a whole series of lessons, in which case the teacher might well have in mind that longitudinal development on the part of learners should be fostered, and achieved, while only one (extended) task is being accomplished. In fact, 'task' viewed in this way bears a strong resemblance to project work (see below). Indeed, to extend this teacher perspective on tasks, one might even think of a task as an activity initiated by a teacher in full knowledge that the development of the task will require him or her to relinquish control, as learners together, and in conjunction with the teacher, 'take possession' of the task. In this view, the task would be a teacher-oriented device to engage learners in a worthwhile set of linked activities.

But in all these cases, it should be said that the purpose of using tasks is to engineer satisfactory pedagogic activities and outcomes. For example, a (self-contained) task may be chosen to 'Machiavellise' the use of a particular structure – cf. Loschky and Bley-Vroman's (1993) *necessary* condition for a structure–task pairing. This may be done unavoidably, through task design (Fotos and Ellis, 1991) or it could be that the task prepares the ground for teacher activity to draw attention to form–meaning linkages (see Samuda, Chapter 6 in this volume). Alternatively, a task may be chosen simply to promote language use in a general performance area, such as fluency, or some aspect of communicative competence. It might even be that the teacher's purpose is to galvanise learners so that they spend more time focused on language precisely because a task is a more motivating activity than (say) a substitution exercise. In this case, the purpose of the task will be to catalyse general learning, and even the amount of time that is spent. In effect, this brings us close to the rationale for using tasks within project work: the initial task is merely a starting point. It is the structure it provides for teacher–student interaction that is the key to future development and exploitation, as learners take the original task in unforeseen directions.

If we turn next to the *research* cell of the teachers and teaching row, we can see a very different set of considerations. Here, *task* is conceptualised as a focused activity which is used because it will generate data of interest to the researcher. The interest may arise from theoretically motivated questions, such as the role of negotiation for meaning in promoting change in an interlanguage system, or the allocation of attention within an information-processing paradigm and the associated questions regarding performance dimensions. Equally, the interest could be derived from pedagogy, in which case many of the questions raised in the previous section could be reinterpreted to make them susceptible to research. Studies might pursue the comparative usefulness of different task types in achieving certain pedagogic goals, or the motivating qualities of tasks with different characteristics.

Very importantly, flowing from this starting point, some other features of tasks-as-research unit follow. For example, it is much less likely that the task will lead to extended work of the sort that is central to many pedagogic–pragmatic interpretations of task. Rather the researcher will probably want to gather data using a cross-sectional research design, with neatly organised groups of subjects, chosen to be as equivalent as possible. It is also likely that the conditions of task implementation will satisfy conditions of standardisation, and, as a result, some degree of ecological validity is likely to be lost. The search, in other words, is for experimental effects, and it is likely that if a quantitative approach is taken, the conventions of statistical evaluation (significance levels, testing of hypotheses, falsifiability) will be applied. If, in contrast, a more qualitative approach is used, it is likely that transcript data from relatively small groups of learners over brief time intervals will be examined, and explanations and interpretations devised accordingly. In any case, there is likely to be some connection, in the evaluation phase, with underlying theory to account for the results that will have been obtained. The motivation to do research, in other words, will cause slightly different questions to be raised, as well as investigative conditions used, such that the capacity to use research results to make pedagogic recommendations will not be straightforward. The precision of doing research (and the pursuit of internal validity) may compromise the ease with which claims can be made about real-world settings (and the pursuit of external validity).

The pragmatic–research distinction also applies to the learners and learning row from Figure 1.1. Here, where the *pragmatic/pedagogic* interpretation applies, the emphasis is likely to be on the way in which the learner influences the choice, nature and interpretation of a task. Task choice is connected with issues in learner autonomy and reflects the way in which, in some pedagogic approaches, learners have a strong influence on which tasks are completed, and when (Breen, 1987). But even when a task is chosen (or imposed by the teacher), there is still the issue of what the learner makes of that task. Learners are perfectly capable of reinterpreting tasks, in such a way that the carefully identified pedagogic goals are rendered irrelevant as a learner invests a task with personal meaning, and takes it away from the teacher's expected path (Duff, 1993). It can even be the mark of a good task that learners are pushed in to this type of reaction. Developing this point, it may be the case that *groups* of learners reinterpret tasks in a collective manner, reacting to one another's contributions to take the task in unforeseen (but possibly more interesting) directions. As a result, the contributions that they make may have a more authentic quality, since the meanings that are being expressed may no longer be within the parameters set by the task designer, but may instead reflect the current interests and personalities of the learners. That such tasks may then be more stimulating for learners connects interestingly with situated interpretations of foreign language learning motivation (Dörnyei, 1996).

Turning next to the *research* perspective on learners and learning, we see yet another picture. Once again, we need to consider the questions which motivate the research, as well as the research methodologies that are used. Regarding research questions, the problems are interestingly different. Where learning itself is concerned, research will draw upon theories of second language development, expressed in terms of structural development or processes of change, to formulate questions for which task-generated data are relevant. Such questions might propose how particular interaction and task types or conditions for task implementation might be more supportive of interlanguage change. They may also explore how form–function relationships may be brought into prominence, or how interlanguage change may be nurtured and consolidated. In all these cases, the challenge will be to propose research methodologies which can enable internal processes to be addressed through external, publicly analysable evidence.

Where learners themselves are concerned, research questions are more likely to focus on the acceptability of tasks to learners, and the potential that different task types have to catalyse extending and involving learner performances. There are also issues of learner motivation to be examined.

The previous *research* cell in our matrix, that for teachers and teaching, emphasised systematic inquiry, probably within a limited time-frame. Similarly, with learners and learning, it is likely that a research perspective will identify particular research problems as worthy of investigation and, as a result, introduce a focus into the research which causes a loss of ecological validity. In the case of teaching, relatively general manipulations of instructional activity may be operative. In contrast, with learners and learning, the emphasis is more likely to be on detailed analysis, with careful examinations of task performance, and scrutiny of such performance for specific evidence of learning processes. Operationalisation of measurement is more likely to be at a premium, and it may be that there is also a greater focus on the effects of different task characteristics and task conditions on the nature of the performance which results. The research designs which are used may, as a result, be further away from classroom realities, even to the extent of a reliance on laboratory-oriented research settings.

We turn now to the testing row. From a *pragmatic/pedagogic* perspective, the emphasis is on the use of information as a contribution to pedagogic decisions. This implies the use of tasks to provide formative information, during instruction, so that learners and teachers are better informed about the progress that has been made. It may also involve the use of tasks to generate feedback on communication, i.e. not simply to decide whether learning has taken place, but to provide diagnostic information to indicate to learners where their strengths and weaknesses lie and how they might be improved. One can imagine, in this respect, choosing and using tasks so that they provide better quality information to learners than would be available either by using alternative testing formats, or by using teacher judgements which may not benefit from the known qualities of using particular tasks to deliver useful information. One might add here that although tasks play a central role in much communicative teaching, the development of reliable task-based assessment techniques is woefully inadequate. This is one of the areas most in need of future attention.

We turn finally to the *research* perspective on using tasks for assessment. Here the focus is on how tasks can be used for summative evaluation, i.e. how tasks can be used to make reliable, valid and useful decisions about the level of achievement and proficiency of learners. The assumptions here are that:

• tasks are necessary for assessment since they create the required conditions for effective decisions about communicative *performance*;
• nonetheless tasks can introduce measurement bias if they are not based on known properties;

- examining how tasks can work effectively requires a research perspective which subjects candidate assessment tasks to some sort of scrutiny to establish that they are functioning in the way that is intended.

Activity in researching tasks from this perspective would lead to studies which treat 'task' as potential artefact, and explore the systematic influences that might follow from task choice and conditions of task use. The findings from such research will help to establish the way particular task choices or conditions might cloud the assessment decision that is made, i.e. cause the 'score' that is assigned to be partly or wholly a property of the task decisions that are made, rather than candidate ability.

DEFINING TASKS

Most attempts to define the concept of task have taken a context-free approach. Such attempts have often proved unsatisfactory since they inevitably have a limited range of application. To take a slightly different approach, we can now use the multiple perspectives on tasks from the previous section to reopen the way tasks can be defined. A sampling of definitions from the literature is a useful starting point. For example, and in chronological order:

> A task is a piece of work undertaken for oneself or for others, freely or for some reward. Thus examples of tasks include painting a fence, dressing a child . . . In other words, by 'task' is meant the hundred and one things people *do* in everyday life, at work, at play, and in between. (Long, 1985)

> A piece of work or an activity, usually with a specified objective, undertaken as part of an educational course, at work, or used to elicit data for research. (Crookes, 1986)

> An activity which required learners to arrive at an outcome from given information through some process of thought and which allowed teachers to control and regulate that process was regarded as a 'task'. (Prabhu, 1987)

> Any structured language learning endeavour which has a particular objective, appropriate content, a specified working procedure, and a range of outcomes for those who undertake the task. 'Task' is therefore assumed to refer to a range of workplans which have the overall purpose of facilitating language learning – from the simple and brief exercise type, to more complex and lengthy activities such as group problem-solving or simulations and decision-making. (Breen, 1987)

> A piece of classroom work which involves learners in comprehending, manipulating, producing or interacting in the target language while their attention is principally focused on meaning rather than form. (Nunan, 1989)

> A task [is] any activity in which a person engages, given an appropriate setting, in order to achieve a specifiable class of objectives. (Carroll, 1993)

... we define a *language use task* as an activity that involves individuals in using language for the purpose of achieving a particular goal or objective in a particular situation.   (Bachman and Palmer, 1996)

Tasks are always activities where the target language us used by the learner for a communicative purpose (goal) in order to achieve an outcome.   (Willis, 1996)

A task is an activity in which

- meaning is primary
- learners are not given other people's meanings to regurgitate
- there is some sort of relationship to comparable real-world activities
- task completion has some priority
- the assessment of the task is in terms of outcome.   (Skehan, 1998)

This range of task definitions has been provided because the definitions are interestingly similar but also interestingly different. There is a sort of inclusive definition, such as that provided by Skehan (1998) which tries to embrace most (but not all) of the characteristics included in other definitions. But many of the definitions contain distinctive emphases. Some (e.g. Long) emphasise the real-world relationship for an activity to qualify as a task, while others (Carroll, Willis, and Bachman and Palmer) downplay this slightly, but still focus on the achievement of an *objective* where the emphasis is on meaning, not language. Most of the remaining definitions mention tasks in relation to classrooms. Some, such as Prabhu, Nunan and Crookes, also emphasise the outcome-linked nature of an activity, but clearly indicate that there is room for teacher intervention and possibly control. Others, principally Breen in this case, broaden what it is possible to include within a task to embrace most of what goes on within a language-learning classroom, with or without an emphasis on meaning.

In some ways, Breen's definition here is the broadest of them all, since it allows a very wide range of activities to be included, even those with some degree of an explicit focus on form. Slightly paradoxically, therefore, Breen (1987), in the context of describing process syllabuses, provides a radically different approach to characterising tasks. Most of the other approaches predicate some degree of control in task use, either through pedagogically motivated task choices, or through pedagogically motivated predictions as to the language which will be generated by the task activity. Breen (1987), in contrast (and see also Candlin, 1987), discusses the way in which pedagogic frameworks can give learners control over the original choice of task, *and* over the ways in which tasks are developed. In other words, far from expecting control over task use, Breen is proposing that it is a beneficial quality of language-learning activities if they can give learners room to reinterpret what is required, and take the activity in unforeseen, but satisfying, directions. To put this another way, Breen is arguing that a workplan which the teacher thinks will be implemented rigidly and exactly as planned is a delusion: real classrooms, he argues, never follow pre-ordained paths, and are the better for it.

This insight of Breen's also leads into another important issue in characterising task: the time-frame within which the task operates. Most of the definitions that we have surveyed, even those which are focused on pedagogy, implicitly focus on establishing a threshold of 'taskiness', so that one can decide whether a particular activity qualifies for the description 'task'. But if there is a pedagogic dimension to the way a task is used, there is also a concern with the sequence of activity under the broad rubric of 'task'. In other words, different developmental courses can be charted for a given task which might have radically different effects upon what happens to the 'starting task'. This, coupled with Breen's claim that tasks are invariably reinterpreted, raises something of a contrast between the circumscribed, focused task, where control and prediction of language are major issues, and the more open task, which is susceptible to development over time, as well as change to suit learner need.

The most effective response to this situation is perhaps to state the obvious: definitions of task will need to be different for the different purposes to which tasks are used. Indeed, the range of definitions we have already seen may need to be extended to take account of the different emphases which reflect the different uses of task. We can start with a fairly basic, all-purpose definition, and then see how this needs to be supplemented:

> *A task is an activity which requires learners to use language, with emphasis on meaning, to attain an objective.*

If we were to try to adapt this definition to make it more directly relevant to the pragmatic/pedagogic, teaching cell from, it might need to be modified to read:

> *A task is an activity, susceptible to brief or extended pedagogic intervention, which requires learners to use language, with emphasis on meaning, to attain an objective.*

If instead, while staying with the pragmatic/pedagogic column of Figure 1.1, one moved to adapt the definition for learners and learning, it might need to be changed to read:

> *A task is an activity, influenced by learner choice, and susceptible to learner reinterpretation, which requires learners to use language, with emphasis on meaning, to attain an objective.*

Finally, in the pragmatic/pedagogic column, we can consider a definition of task that might be appropriate for testing and assessment purposes:

> *A task is an activity which requires learners to use language, with emphasis on meaning, to attain an objective, and which is chosen so that it is most likely to provide information for learners which will help them evaluate their own learning.*

We can now turn to the second, research-oriented column. Two points are worth making at the outset. First, in contrast to the other column, not all tasks are connected to pedagogy. It may be the case that tasks are used for research in order to gain a better understanding of pedagogy. There may be occasions when tasks are a suitable vehicle for researchers to investigate other issues of interest, such as the nature of performance, or the competence–performance relationship. On occasions, studies focusing on such issues may have an indirect relationship to pedagogy, but there may be occasions when there is little connection whatsoever. Second, in contrast to most of the pedagogic perspectives, there is likely to be a much greater concern to achieve control over what happens with tasks, since it is in the nature of research (or at least, quantitative research), to achieve some degree of precision and control of variables in establishing causality in the effects which may be found.

With these factors in mind, we can try to adapt the basic definition for the research column applied to the teachers and teaching row:

> *A task is a focused, well-defined activity, relatable to pedagogic decision making, which requires learners to use language, with emphasis on meaning, to attain an objective, and which elicits data which may be the basis for research.*

In contrast, when we move to the learners and learning row, it would be more appropriate to suggest that:

> *A task is a focused, well-defined activity, relatable to learner choice or to learning processes, which requires learners to use language, with emphasis on meaning, to attain an objective, and which elicits data which may be the basis for research.*

Finally, we come to the research perspective on testing and assessment. For this, the definition might be adapted as follows:

> *A task is a contextualised, standardised activity which requires learners to use language, with emphasis on meaning, and with a connection to the real world, to attain an objective, and which will elicit data which can be used for purposes of measurement.*

This definition brings out that the purpose of choosing a task for testing is to identify a data elicitation procedure of known qualities, and which meets the criterion of communicativeness that is attractive in all task-based work. The overriding purpose is to identify a data elicitation method which is as transparent and as fair as possible.

Clearly, *task* will mean slightly different things to different groups. What the different definitions (and the characterisations from the previous section) emphasise is that there is scope for misunderstanding between the different groups. Researchers may frequently prefer tasks which are rather static in nature, precisely because this provides them with a dependable unit on which they can hang their research. They may research such a task through quantitative or qualitative methods, but they will want the focus and circumscribed nature that the research-oriented definitions provide. In contrast, tasks approached from a teaching perspective may well be dynamic and extended – qualities that may be most desired by task users. The lack of standardisation that results may cause difficulty for researchers, but the potential that such tasks have for development may be exactly what makes them attractive. It may be necessary, therefore, to have greater clarity about the definition of task that applies in different circumstances. This will allow greater harmonious coexistence between the different groups, and enable each of them to be more appreciative of the others, as well as avoid applying inappropriate standards for task evaluation.

THE PEDAGOGIC VALIDITY OF THE RESEARCH CONTEXT

Given this volume's focus on research-based studies, there are a number of general issues that bear on the place and conduct of task-based research. Most broadly, in this respect, Freedman (1971) argued for large numbers of small-scale studies of particular pedagogic approaches. Brumfit, in contrast, suggested the running of more loosely controlled experiments, 'but which are closely related to actual teaching situations, using typical teachers, in typical conditions, and on a very large scale' (Brumfit, 1980: 135). These views were early signals of a re-centring of language teaching research in which a central factor is the pedagogic validity of the research context.

The question of the pedagogic validity of task research has been a consistent matter of contention. The questions of the early 1970s remain (as reflected in the recent papers by Crookes, 1997, and Ellis, 1997):

- What is the pedagogic validity of research that has been carried out in non-classroom settings?
- What is the validity or reliability of research that has been carried out in such settings?
- To what extent can single-shot studies, whether small scale or large scale, carry conviction if they remain without replication in other contexts or by other researchers?

Hence, it is perhaps understandable that while most of the studies in this volume are classroom-based, questions can still be asked about the typicality of these classroom contexts. More generally, the view proposed here argues for the acceptance of the importance both of *case studies*, which enable micro-genetic analyses of transcript data, and of *group studies*, which tend to depend for their arguments on generalisations based on relatively large sets of pooled data.

The research into task-as-pedagogic unit can be generalised into three main areas of concern:

- the impact of task design and task conditions on performance;
- the impact of task selection and use on learning;
- the relationship of tasks to underlying processing factors.

Regarding the first of these, the issue of task design and performance has as priority the identification and separating out of underlying features of tasks which are capable of impacting on the content and complexity of learners' language and of their language processing (Bygate, 1999). This issue can be summarised as emphasising the construct validity of tasks and their conditions of use, and is clearly important for test design, materials design, materials implementation and syllabus development.

The second concern – the dynamic issue of the impact of task selection and use on language learning – focuses rather on the ways in which performance can effect changes in competence. This is being theorised in a number of ways – for instance, in terms of a task's capacity to focus learners' attention on, and facilitate their retention of, specific features of language (e.g. Swain, 1985, 1995; and Ellis in this volume); or in terms of the ways tasks and task conditions can lead learners to adjust their focus of attention between accuracy, fluency and complexity (Skehan, 1998). Both concerns engage our conceptualisation of the underlying construct of task performance. In the absence of a fully developed theory of the complexities of task performance (which would entail a multi-level account, capable of showing the ways in which learners' capacities develop simultaneously on a range of levels), empirical research must simplify the construct. Hence the different aspects of language and language processing focused on by the various contributors to this volume, and the partial views they reflect.

The third area of concern, that of the relationship between tasks and underlying processing factors, includes issues such as:

- The impact of the conceptual content of tasks.
- Parameters of task design in terms of their likely impact on aspects of language processing.
- The nature of the interactive dimension of different tasks.
- The nature of comprehension processing.
- The ways in which interaction on tasks can focus learners' attention on form–meaning relations during lessons.

The connection between processing and learning is also pursued in a number of different ways, such as studies which consider the manner in which comprehension processing relates to the acquisition of new language, and studies which explore how task performance itself might develop over time.

AN INTRODUCTION TO THE VOLUME

We can now draw upon this discussion to locate the contributions to the book. All the contributions take a research perspective to tasks, but they do so in different areas, with sets of papers emphasising teaching, learning and assessment respectively. In Part I, chapters by Bygate, Ellis and Foster address issues connected with task pedagogy from teaching perspectives. In each case, the focus is on understanding the predictable qualities that different sorts of tasks may have, and the methodological approach is to study manipulations in task qualities and relate these to the sort of performance that results.

Bygate, in Chapter 2, explores how second language speakers can learn to use what they know in more effective ways. He draws upon Levelt's theory of speech performance, and its proposed components of a conceptualiser and a formulator to explore how meaning and form can be contrived to be in productive balance. He reports on a study in which task repetition and task type are the experimental variables, and in which he shows how the opportunity to repeat a task enables learners to access more demanding language more readily.

Ellis (Chapter 3), like Skehan in Chapter 8, reviews a *series* of studies, rather than reporting on just one. In this way, he is able to propose more wide-ranging generalisations for the theme of the research: the use of non-reciprocal tasks in language learning. After proposing interesting justification for researching non-reciprocal tasks, he draws upon theories of the role of input and output in second language learning to underpin a series of studies exploring the respective contributions and value of unmodified, premodified and interactionally modified input. He also explores how output itself has an important part to play in second language development.

In Chapter 4, Foster reports on a study of the effects of planning on the lexicalised language used in a decision-making task. After reviewing the literature on the use of formulaic language, she explores how learners and native speakers use prefabricated chunks differently under planned and unplanned conditions. She shows that the two groups respond to the opportunity to plan in different ways, which one group uses lexicalised chunks more under planned conditions, and the other less. The study also makes important contributions to the identification of chunk-based language in spoken performance.

Part II of the book focuses on the nature of learners and learning. Two of the chapters have a clear focus on the way teachers may try – either through the activities that are used or through the nature of teacher–student dialogue while a task is being done – to bring form and function into clear and interesting relationship. Swain and Lapkin (Chapter 5) explore the consequences for learners of using particular types of pedagogic tasks. They give learners dictogloss and jigsaw tasks to complete, and then explore the potential these tasks have for focusing learners' attention on gaps in their interlanguage, and for stimulating collaborative dialogue to repair these gaps. The approach is Vygotskyan in nature, in that it explores how potentially productive encounters are exploited by learners *when they work together* in an effective manner. The study uses both quantitative and qualitative data analyses to compare the usefulness of the two types of task in question.

Samuda (Chapter 6) explores what teachers can do to help learners notice relevant form–meaning mappings while carrying out tasks in class. She is concerned with ways that teachers can make form–meaning connections more salient without compromising the communicative nature of the encounter. She distinguishes between knowledge-activating and knowledge-constructing tasks, and shows how teacher behaviour can produce input-enhancement for learners, in which teachers, in the context of knowledge-activating tasks, can build upon what learners already know by 'leading from behind'. The emphasis in this study is on how a careful task choice can lead students, under teacher-supported conditions, to 'mine' tasks to achieve such initial noticing, but then also to reflect upon the form–meaning mappings concerned, as well as consolidate use of the forms in question. Samuda relates this work to current activity with recasts and shows how what she terms interweaves and precasts can impact upon language learning.

Lynch and Maclean (Chapter 7) take a slightly different approach to researching tasks within the context of teaching. Like Bygate in Chapter 2, they also research the effects of task repetition, but are more concerned with exploring how learners, within an intact class, can be provided with a task susceptible to repetition which is an entirely natural part of the teaching plan. They report a case study from a medical English ESP programme. Participants (oncologists and medical specialists), while preparing to make conference presentations, were required to interact with one another, either as 'authors' of posters, or as questioners of the authors of posters. Pairs of students constructed posters based on a short article (with a different research article for each pair). One of each pair then 'visited' the other posters in the class while the other member stayed behind and 'received' visitors. (Then roles were reversed.) In this way, repetition was naturally built into an activity for the poster 'host', as a series of visitors arrived. Lynch and Maclean were able to study the language development and the self-perceptions of language improvement over a cycle of several 'hostings'.

The final set of chapters focus on tasks as a vehicle for assessment. In Chapter 8, Skehan, like Ellis, reports on a metastudy, but this time in the area of testing. He draws upon a series of research studies into tasks to search for generalisations on the effects of different task characteristics on performance. Drawing on a model of oral language assessment, he shows how tasks are not neutral devices to elicit rateable performance, but rather they introduce artefactual influences such that certain sorts of task predispose performance in certain directions. Task performance is measured in this study by detailed indices based on transcripts. Even so, the connection to actual testing situations is clear. Ratings assigned in such situations might not reflect candidate ability as much as the consequences of the particular task type that was used.

Wigglesworth (Chapter 9) also reports on a study of the effects of task characteristics on performance. Although this is only one study, conducted in the context of migrant education in Australia, it is a complex study, in which a number of different task characteristics – e.g. presence or absence of pre-task planning, and task structure – are investigated. Wigglesworth uses a number of methods of assessing performance. Unlike Skehan, she does not uses detailed, transcript-based measures, but instead relies on three sources of evidence: direct ratings of performance, logit scores based on an item response analysis (which takes into account relative difficulty of tasks), and candidate reactions to the different tasks used. Like Skehan in Chapter 8, the conclusion is that tasks introduce systematic variance into the testing enterprise: their characteristics inevitably introduce systematic effects upon performance.

In Chapter 10, Chalhoub-Deville discusses fundamental concepts in task-based assessment, and also reports on an empirical study. She explores the relevance for testing of the concepts of learner-centredness, contextualisation, and authenticity, and shows how these three concepts can profitably be applied to some common oral language assessment frameworks. Drawing on this discussion, she then adopts the less frequently used statistical technique (in task and testing research) of multidimensional scaling to examine the extent to which three popular formats in oral assessment might contain format effects which intrude into the neutrality of the measurement of oral language that results. In a similar way to Skehan and Wigglesworth, she is able to show that the choice of assessment procedure, itself conceptualised in terms of task, introduces unwanted variance into measurement.

The three chapters in the testing section show that the two areas of language testing and task-based instruction, although rarely brought together, have much to offer one another. Testing contributes interesting statistical techniques, often designed to identify difficulty. Task researchers similarly are interested in the concept of difficulty, but often approach it in a more conceptual manner. As seen from the chapters in this volume, the combination of task-derived theorising, and testing-derived measurement rigour can make major future contributions.

CONCLUSION: PEDAGOGY AND RESEARCH

There are a number of potential problems in the relationship between pedagogy and research which have been the focus of concern in the literature. The main problems can be seen as different facets of the overriding concern of relevance. These include issues such as:

- The focus of the research – whether it meets the priorities of teachers.
- The way the research is problematised or conceptualised – that is, whether it is conceptualised and analysed in ways which make sense to teachers.
- The applicability of the research – that is, whether teachers can use it.

The purpose of publishing such a volume is to try to put the work to the test of relevance, and to find ways in which future work could get closer to meeting each of the three criteria and, as a result, show how research can relate to pedagogy.

The focus of research into tasks is inevitably going to be partial, and reflect the interests of each investigator. But then, the priorities of different teachers will not coincide either, as different classroom realities are responded to. We can only propose that the themes of the different chapters do relate to priorities that are operative for a great many teachers. Frequent questions which are posed in teachers' seminars concern how tasks may be chosen and used, as well as what language different task choices are likely to predispose. The range of studies here provide some clues for teachers who are seeking to make task selection and task implementation decisions based on principle, with chapters on issues such as task repetition, planning, task choice, and how to bring form into focus.

The way that tasks are problematised can also be a barrier for teachers-as-consumers of research, since, as the section on task definition earlier in this chapter makes clear, it is all too easy for teachers to feel somewhat disenfranchised because task researchers have pursued internal research validity at some expense to the directness of connections with real classrooms. Yet the studies in the present collection mostly take, as task-to-be-researched, a range of activities which would not look out-of-place in any communicative classroom. Indeed, most tasks were chosen for their very ordinariness, providing them with strong claims for classroom relevance. In addition, there are contributions, especially in Section Two, which foreground the role of the teacher, e.g. the chapter by Samuda. These show what scope there is for teacher decisions while a task is running, and how the role of the teacher in task-based learning is only now being clarified.

In assembling this collection, the editors are aware that the contributions vary in the extent to which they meet the criterion of relevance. We are confident that all the chapters meet the criterion of applicability. Whether in the areas of teaching, testing, or learning, the theme of each chapter has, we believe, practical relevance to the classroom, whichever the theme: negotiating from meaning to form; the carousel; task repetition; the role of planning time; formulaic language; focus on form during comprehension and negotiation tasks; and task complexity. What is less certain is that teachers will have already spontaneously chosen these issues as relevant issues, or whether they will wish to think about them in the ways outlined in these pages. At the least, this volume provides a series of argued insights into the impact of tasks on language learning, and so contributes to development in the understanding of theory and practice.

Collections of research articles can often appear to reflect a troubling lack of consensus between the authors. Whichever designs are used, they seem to imply disagreement with other types of design: this might suggest a war of conflicting approaches in which alliances – between authors represented within the same volume, or between individual authors within the volume and other groups of researchers – vie to gain control over the terrain. This volume has not been assembled on this assumption. Many of those publishing group comparative studies in this volume have also used case studies on other occasions, and will do so again. The volume, therefore, represents a range of understandings of (a) the nature of task-based language, language processing, and language learning, (b) the tasks that can be usefully researched and (c) the ways in which those tasks can be studied. In so doing, it continues a long-standing tradition in the human sciences in general, and in education in particular, of attempting to discover how human events relate to learning – however chaotic they may appear to be (Dewey, 1910; Bruner, 1966).

REFERENCES

Bachman, L. and Palmer, A. (1996) *Language Testing in Practice*. Oxford: OUP.
Breen, M. (1984) Process syllabuses for the language classroom. In C.J. Brumfit (ed.) *General English Syllabus Design*. ELTDOCs 118. Oxford: Pergamon.
Breen, M. (1987) Contemporary paradigms in syllabus design (Parts 1 and 2). *Language Teaching*, 20: 91–2 and 157–74.

Breen, M. and Candlin, C. (1980) The essentials of a communicative curriculum in language teaching. *Applied Linguistics*, 1 (2): 89–112.

Brumfit, C. (1980) *Problems and Principles in English Language Teaching*. Oxford: Pergamon.

Brumfit, C. (1984) *Communicative Methodology in Language Teaching*. Cambridge: CUP.

Brumfit, C. and Johnson, K. (1979) *The Communicative Approach to Language Teaching*. Oxford: OUP.

Brumfit, C. (1988) Applied linguistics and communicative language teaching. In W. Grabe (ed.) *Annual Review of Applied Linguistics: Communicative Language Teaching*. New York: Cambridge University Press.

Bruner, J. (1966) *Towards a Theory of Instruction*. Harvard: Harvard University Press.

Bygate, M. (1999) Task as context for the framing, re-framing, and unframing of language. *System*, 27: 33–48.

Canale, M. and Swain, M. (1980) Theoretical bases of communicative approaches to second language teaching and testing. *Applied Linguistics*, 1 (1): 1–47.

Candlin, C. (1987) Towards task based language learning. In C. Candlin and D. Murphy (eds) *Language Learning Tasks*. Englewood Cliffs, NJ: Prentice Hall.

Carroll, J.B. (1993) *Human Cognitive Abilities*. New York: Cambridge.

Crookes, G. (1986) *Task classification: a cross-disciplinary review*. Technical Report No. 4, Deparment of ESL, University of Hawaii at Manoa.

Crookes, G. (1997) SLA and language pedagogy: A socioeducational perspective. *Studies in Second Language Acquisition*, 19 (1): 93–116.

Crookes, G. and Gass, S. (eds) (1993a) *Tasks in a Pedagogical Context: Integrating Theory and Practice*. Clevedon, Avon: Multilingual Matters.

Crookes, G. and Gass, S. (eds) (1993b) *Tasks and Language Learning: Integrating Theory and Practice*. Clevedon, Avon: Multilingual Matters.

Dewey, J. (1910) *How We Think*. London: Heath & Co.

Dörnyei, Z. (1996) Moving language learning motivation to a larger platform for theory and practice. In R.L. Oxford (ed.) *Language Learning Motivation: Pathways to the New Century* (pp. 89–101). Honolulu: The University of Hawai'i Press.

Duff, P. (1993) Tasks and interlanguage performance: An SLA research perspective. In G. Crookes and S. Gass (eds) *Tasks and Language Learning: Integrating Theory and Practice* (pp. 57–95). Clevedon, Avon: Multilingual Matters.

Ellis, R. (1985) *Understanding Second Language Acquisition*. Oxford: Oxford University Press.

Ellis, R. (1997) SLA and language pedagogy: an educational perspective. *Studies in Second Language Acquisition*, 19 (1): 69–92.

Fotos, S. and Ellis, R. (1991) Communicating about grammar: A task-based approach. *TESOL Quarterly*, 25: 608–28.

Freedman, E. (1971) The road to Pennsylvania – Where next in language teaching experimentation. *Audio-visual Language Journal*, 9 (1). (In C.J. Brumfit (1980) *Problems and Principles in English Teaching*. Oxford: Pergamon.)

Fried-Booth, D. (1986) *Project Work*. Oxford: Oxford University Press.

Geddes, M. and Sturtridge, G. (1978) Jigsaw listening. *Modern English Teacher*, 6 (1).

Harmer, J. (1991) *The Practice of English Language Teaching*. London: Longman.

Howatt, A. (1984) *A History of English Language Teaching*. Oxford: Oxford University Press.

Johnson, K. (1996) *Skill Learning and Language Teaching*. Oxford: Blackwell.

Leung, C. (1993) The coming crisis of ESL in the National Curriculum. *British Association for Applied Linguistics Newsletter*, 45: 27–32.

Long, M. (1985) Input and second language acquisition theory. In S. Gass and C. Madden (eds) *Input and Second Language Acquisition*. Rowley, Mass.: Newbury House.

Long, M. (1989) Task, group, and task-group interaction. *University of Hawaii Working Papers in English as a Second Language*, 8 (2): 1–26.

Long, M. and Robinson, P. (1998) Focus on form: theory, research, and practice. In C. Doughty and J. Williams (eds) *Focus on Form in Classroom SLA*. Cambridge: CUP.

Loschky, L. and Bley-Vroman, R. (1993) Grammar and task-based methodology. In G. Grookes and S. Gass (eds) (1993b).

Munby, J. (1978) *Communicative Syllabus Design*. Cambridge: Cambridge University Press.

Nunan, D. (1989) *Designing Tasks for the Communicative Classroom*. Cambridge: CUP.

Prabhu, N.S. (1987) *Second Language Pedagogy*. Oxford: OUP.

Skehan, P. (1998) *A Cognitive Approach to Language Learning*. Oxford: Oxford University Press.

Stevick, E. (1976) *Memory, Meaning, and Method*. Rowley, Mass.: Newbury House.

Swain, M. (1985) Communicative competence: Some roles of comprehensible input and comprehensible output in its development. In S. Gass and C. Madden (eds) *Input in Second Language Acquisition*. Rowley, Mass.: Newbury House.

Swain, M. (1995) Three functions of output in second language learning. In G. Cook and B. Seidlhofer (eds) *Principle and Practice in Applied Linguistics* (pp. 245–56). Oxford: Oxford University Press.

Widdowson, H.G. (1978) *Teaching Language as Communication*. Oxford: Oxford University Press.

Widdowson, H.G. (1979) *Explorations in Applied Linguistics*. Oxford: Oxford University Press.

Wilkins, D. (1976) *Notional Syllabuses*. Oxford: Oxford University Press.

Willis, D. and Willis, J. (1988) *COBUILD Book 1*. London: Collins.

Willis, J. (1996) *A Framework for Task-based Learning*. London: Longman.

Willis, J. and Willis, D. (1996) *Challenge and Change in Language Teaching*. London: Heinemann.

Part I

TASKS AND LANGUAGE PROCESSING

The three chapters in this part all report on task-based studies which are experimental in nature, in that each uses a careful research design and emphasises a quantitative methodology (although each also draws upon qualitative data). They also have in common that they each investigate the operation of one or more central aspects of language processing in relation to second language acquisition. In this respect, the three papers make a much needed contribution to our understanding of how the use of tasks can be exploited to engage different psycholinguistic processing mechanisms to promote development. Each of the studies grounds its concerns in a guiding literature and examines task performance in light of that literature.

For Bygate, the emphasis is on models of speech performance, particularly that of Levelt. The chapter explores the possibility that teachers' choice of task type could be deliberately targeted to provide learners with systematic practice, in particular by aiming to develop learners' capacities to deal with particular task types. This provides the backcloth for an investigation of the effects of repetition on task performance. In contrast, Ellis considers the impact on noticing and recall of different input channels and of different qualities of input. He draws upon the extensive literatures on input, modification of input, and output effects to explore how comprehension, acquisition, and performance are affected by a range of experimental pedagogic manipulations. He offers extensive detailed justification for the use of non-reciprocal tasks in terms of this literature, showing that input issues are susceptible to investigation with such tasks, but that interactive tasks may well have stronger effects than one-way tasks. In Chapter 3, Foster shares Bygate's concern with the processing of language output in task contexts. She reports on a study which connects with the literatures on planning and on lexicalised language, showing how, when native and non-native speakers carry out a production task, they rely upon lexicalised language in different ways under different conditions. As in the case of the other two chapters in this part, this study is unusual within the literature on task-based learning in that it uses output data to infer patterns in the processing of spoken language – in this case to suggest differences in the speech processing of native and non-native speakers.

All the studies use careful research designs, with comparisons of different experimental conditions undertaken so that revealing insights about performance will emerge. In each case, variables are identified and manipulated, often with precise research questions so that data can be approached predictively. For Bygate the variables concern repetition itself, task comparison (narrative and interview), as well as practice on task types (to explore whether practice can develop a performance capacity which generalises across different tasks of the same type). Ellis, reporting a meta-analysis (see Skehan in Chapter 8 for another meta-analysis) of a series of linked studies, explores how manipulations of input and interactive conditions produce both predictable and unexpected effects on comprehension and learning. Focusing on lexical acquisition, he also shows how different word features have different patterns of effects on comprehension and acquisition. Foster examines the effects of two variables – pre-task planning time and native vs non-native speaker interlocutors – on task performance. This combination of a task condition variable and a person variable, linked to the need to identify formulaic language in speech performance, breaks new ground. The use of native-speaker baseline data in task research is rare, and so the comparison between the task effects which override the native/non-native contrast, and those differences in speakers' reliance on the use of lexicalised language sequences under planned vs unplanned conditions, has implications for pedagogy and for models of native-speaker speech performance.

All three chapters, then, contribute in novel ways to our understanding of how learners' involvement in tasks can affect their language processing, and hence learning capacity. In contrast with a data-driven approach to data-analysis, all three chapters are theory-driven, often drawing on theories from outside SLA in order to understand language processing and development. However, it is worth pointing out that because the three chapters report on experimental studies, it is incumbent on each to make connections back to pedagogy and to the language classroom. Each author does this, and brings out how the findings concerned could have important practical implications. But it is interesting to see how this is done. The advantages of control and precision, not to mention effective pursuit of theory-motivated questions, do not come without cost, at least in terms of the lack of evidence linked to classrooms themselves. However, it is clear that the phenomena that the authors study are certain to occur in classroom contexts, and hence the authors can argue persuasively that their studies are not research for the sake of it, but can make the connection back to the real world, and so inform language-teaching decisions.

Chapter 2

Effects of task repetition on the structure and control of oral language

Martin Bygate

INTRODUCTION

The central challenge for language teaching is to develop learners' communicative language ability through pedagogic intervention. However, because this involves a number of distinct processes, different kinds of learning activities may each help to develop a learner's ability to use the language, albeit in different ways. This chapter[1] explores one likely influence on development, that of learners' repeating a task or practising a type of task.

Communicative language ability centrally involves the ability to use formal linguistic resources (vocabulary, idiomatic expressions, grammatical features, phonological features) to express ideational, interpersonal and discoursal meanings, in order to achieve communicative goals in real contexts. Learners must therefore internalise the patterned relationships existing in the target language between form, meaning and use to develop not only that ability, but also the capacity to use those resources in real contexts and in real time. Much recent work has concentrated on the challenge of getting learners to engage successfully in the processes of identification and internalisation of new language (e.g. Doughty and Williams, 1998; VanPatten, 1996).

However, second language development also involves developing learners' capacity to use resources already available to them, and there are at least two main reasons for believing that this is important. Firstly, experience of language production enables learners to identify gaps in their knowledge of the language, and to prepare their own knowledge base for reception of new language (Swain and Lapkin, 1995). In other words, using language exposes the gaps in the learners' knowledge. Secondly, it has been shown quite consistently (Harley and Swain, 1984; Swain, 1985) that substantial exposure to meaningful samples of the language is not sufficient to ensure native-like output. It is true that carefully contrived focus on the receptive processing of meaningful forms of the language might help to improve the quality of learners' language production. However, as soon as the learners' store of internalised language needs to be accessed in the service of their own improvised output, previous functional storage of the language becomes subjected to new processing demands. Hence output practice is needed to enable learners to cope with these demands in order to integrate language knowledge into productive use.

The focus of this chapter is then on output and language development. However, as in other types of language practice, a central issue concerns the extent to which form and meaning can be interrelated, and the ways in which learners can be led to work on this interrelationship in the language classroom. This issue will be discussed more fully in the following section.

THEORETICAL BACKGROUND TO THE STUDY

Processing theories of language development highlight the multi-level nature of second language development, and in particular the cognitive processing demands on developing the ability to use a second language. Related accounts of this issue are offered by Crookes (1989), Johnson (1996) and Skehan (1994), and this is also illustrated in Levelt's (1989) account of language processing (see Figure 2.1).

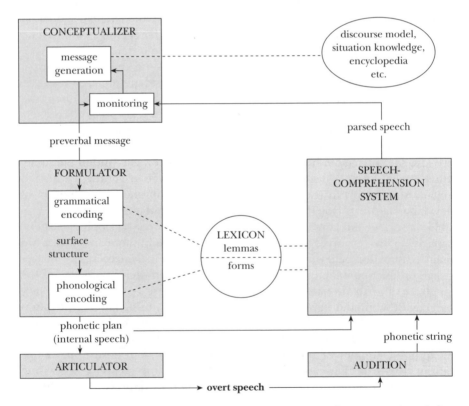

Figure 2.1 A blueprint for the speaker. Boxes represent processing components; circle and ellipse represent knowledge stores.

Levelt's model includes both comprehension and production, but this account will concentrate on the production phases. According to the model, language use implies three related phases of processing – conceptualisation, formulation and articulation – which is broadly consistent with other models (e.g. Garrett, 1981; Garman, 1990; Smyth et al., 1987).

Conceptualisation is concerned with the macro-planning of the direction and phases of the discourse, and with planning the conceptual – referential, interpersonal, illocutionary and, where relevant, perlocutionary – content for each message. Conceptualisation draws on a general knowledge store and a discourse knowledge store. A pre-planned message is then provided by the conceptualiser as input to the formulator. The formulator is thought of as drawing on a lexical store, a grammatical store, and a syllabary in order to express the intended message, by accessing, grouping and ordering morphemes and collocational chunks. The output of the formulator is a phonological plan, priming the speaker for the articulation of the utterance. Articulation itself is the process whereby the prepared string is physically produced, including the interweaving of selected patterns of stress, rhythm and intonation.

Levelt sees the internal operations of each phase as occurring autonomously, each one however providing input for the following one. The whole is supervised by a monitor, located in the conceptualiser. This checks on the appropriacy of the content of the intended message, the phonological production, and the actual output. The monitor can also operate on potential formulations, checking them for appropriacy and accuracy, and providing re-formulations prior to production (Faerch and Kasper, 1983; Dörnyei and Kormos, 1998). The monitor operates covertly – that is, prior to or during articulation – as well as overtly, following articulation (Laver, 1970; Morrison and Low, 1983). In producing a second language, then, speakers have to integrate their perceptions of formulation possibilities with their articulation and with a broader communicative intention.

Within this whole process, second language speakers have to sort out the relationship between the conceptual content of their messages and the formulation possibilities that they are aware of. They have to do this under the time pressure created by the pressing need to articulate a message. In meeting this challenge there are two ways in which (a) speech production can be expected to be taxing, and (b) communicative production can help language development. Initially, learners have to prepare specific messages and find some way of formulating them, prior to articulation. There is, then, a broad planning process, in which learners need to identify appropriate message content, and connect it to formulation and articulation processes. As the connections between these phases of processing are established, there is within the area of formulation a second necessary level of processing, in which the nature of language itself poses more specific problems. It is not the purpose of this chapter to explore linguistic problems in depth, but it is relevant to the argument to relate the broad communication process just outlined with more specific linguistic issues. Two particular characteristics of language are worth mentioning.

Firstly, language use involves establishing and working with form–meaning relations (Lightbown, 1998; Widdowson, 1978). Within the context of an emerging message, speakers need to track down appropriate morpholexical items from memory. Here recall is needed. Also, however, matching judgements need to be made to ensure that relevant items are used, or adapted in order to be interpreted by listeners as conveying the intended message (Bygate, 1999; Doughty and Williams, 1998). Secondly, in developing a more target-like use of the language, speakers need to manage two particularly problematic aspects of languages: anomalousness, that is, the irregularity of natural languages (Bolinger, 1975; Chafe, 1968; Westney, 1994) and redundancy, that is, the relative unimportance of some of the features of languages for communicating specific messages (George, 1972; VanPatten, 1996). These characteristics of language imply problems at the point where the novice second language speaker has to convert specific meaning intentions into formulations, under that pending pressure of intended articulation. The time available for sorting through possible meaning–form pairs, and for checking on redundant or anomalous features, is tight: communicative language processing could easily result in a reduction of work at the point of formulation, in order to achieve rapid completion of the speaking process. Yet what is wanted is what Lightbown (1998) calls the 'continuous integration' of form and meaning.

To summarise, second language production is bound to place strains on learners in terms of their managing form–meaning relations, according to target norms, and while processing messages. Yet this is the object of language learning. A central issue for language teaching, then, is how to provide learners with learning experiences which will better enable them to relate form to meaning while they keep control of the anomalies of the language they are learning. That is, communication demands exert pressures on a learner's capacity to deal with these cognitively difficult issues – to identify relevant forms for the speaker's meaning; to identify the anomalies within the regularities; and to pay attention to what is redundant even though it is often not crucial to the communication of meaning.

It is relevant to the study of the development of oral skills to consider how the parts of this model may affect the fluency and focus of attention of a second language learner. Assuming that a speaker is familiar with a topic, and is familiar with how to segment the topic conceptually for speech production, their main task is going to be to find appropriate formulations, and articulate them. Attention then can be concentrated on the selection, assembly and articulation of language, doing this against, as it were, a stable mental representation of the information to be conveyed. Even if the information is familiar, on the first occasion of speech production on the topic, substantial effort is likely to be expended on the task. If however the information is not familiar, or if the speaker has to struggle to assemble relevant information in order to carry out the task, clearly his or her attention is going to be divided between message content and formulation. In either case, at a first attempt, VanPatten's (1996) observation about input processing is also likely to apply to speech production: a speaker's focus is more likely to be on non-redundant, lexical features, and is less likely to be available for processing of relatively redundant features.

On subsequent occasions, a speaker is going to be able to draw on the conceptual structuring of the information and on encodings which they had previously used, benefiting potentially in one or more of three particular ways: they may simply become more fluent in terms of speed and general smoothness of delivery since the processes of formulation and articulation of the necessary language are likely to be easier in various ways. Alternatively, the speaker may not gain much in fluency, but might pay more attention to the precision of the language selected, whether in terms of the accuracy with which the intended meanings are conveyed, or in terms of the extent to which production matches the norms of the target language (a possibility also outlined in Foster and Skehan, 1996, and in Skehan in this volume). A third possibility however exists – the speaker might choose to build on the routines established previously to produce a more complex or more sophistic-ated formulation of the message. In other words, repetition of the task may give rise to changes in performance, in terms of fluency, accuracy and/or complexity. This is because, on subsequent occasions, a speaker's attention may be freer to focus on relatively redundant forms in order to improve accuracy or increase complexity. At the very least, speakers should be able to improve their fluency. In other words, repetition of the task may give rise to changes in performance, in terms of fluency, accuracy and/or complexity (see also Lynch and Maclean in this volume).

Empirical background to the study

In a pilot case study (Bygate, 1996), I found evidence that repetition of a task affected accuracy in some interesting ways, which were consistent with this account. Without any prior warning, or indication that the task was to be repeated, and without any use of or reference to the task in class, on repeat-ing a video narrative task a speaker showed striking adjustments to the way she spoke. In particular, her lexical selection, her selection of lexical colloc-ates, her selection of grammatical items, and her ability to self-correct were better, in the judgement of a number of experienced judges, on repetition of the task. This performance would be consistent with the processes outlined above: on the first performance, the speaker is likely to have been more taxed by the task of holding meanings in memory, transferring the mean-ings into words and articulating them, under time pressure; on the second performance, the speaker is likely to have been able to take advantage of the familiarity with the content, and with the processes of formulating the mean-ings, so as to have been able to devote a bit more capacity to the lexico-grammatical selection.

Of course change in performance on a given task is not of itself evidence of overall language development: language development requires learners to be able to generalise from specific learning events in order to apply new understandings to the communication of other messages. Hence, change in the ability to handle a specific task is not a sufficient gauge of development. Yet even so, in terms of providing a learning context, repetition of similar tasks is more likely to provide a structured context for the mastery of form–meaning relations than is a random sequencing of tasks. Development of performance on specific tasks is therefore of interest in its own right, and this is the theme of the study reported in this chapter.

Previous studies have shown a rehearsal effect in connection with other procedures. Planning – mental rehearsal of the message and its formulation prior to communication – has been shown to have an effect on second language performance by Crookes (1989), Foster and Skehan (1996), Skehan and Foster (1997) and Wigglesworth (1997) variously affecting complexity, fluency and accuracy. Skehan and Foster (1997) have shown that benefits from planning can favour one of the dimensions (e.g. complexity) to the detriment of one of the others (e.g. accuracy). Plough and Gass (1993) explore the impact of topic familiarity on speakers' willingness to negotiate meaning. While these studies provide support for the theoretical basis of this chapter, they focus on a different issue. Plough and Gass are concerned with content familiarity but not with familiarity derived from using it in the context of a specific task. Also, their dependent variables are not the language used on the task, but the extent to which the speakers negotiate misunderstandings. The planning dimension is perhaps closer to the focus of this study. However, planning does not constitute quite the same process as repetition: it does not relate rehearsal to actual enactment of the task. Rather the key performance is related to preparation in the learner's short-term memory rather than in long-term memory, whereas task repetition involves relating the new performance to information kept in the long-term memory (LTM) store. Ellis (1987) showed that recycling of task content across a series of tasks affected performance in terms of accuracy. However, this study compared performance on an unrehearsed oral task with performance on a second oral task which had been preceded by written output of the material. Once again, short-term memory processes were involved, with the additional complication that rehearsal was confounded with the mode of processing, the preparatory phase of the second oral task involving writing. Other pedagogic procedures tap the rehearsal dimension in which the initial focus can be on meaning rather than form: the dictogloss procedure (see Swain and Lapkin, in this volume) clearly involves repeated use of conceptual content, during which earlier formulations can be revised and new content recovered, and then expressed; Willis's (1996) approach to task-based lessons is centred on an input–rehearsal–performance cycle, in which learners improvise their response in groups prior to a public performance of the task, though this involves referring learners initially to native speaker modelling of the performance; Allwright's 'draft–redraft' approach to teaching writing seems to exploit the same dimension (Allwright et al., 1988). However, none of these approaches involves exploitation of rehearsal in terms of real task repetition – that is, the kind experienced by learners when they find themselves repeatedly in highly similar communication situations, and with the opportunity to build on their previous attempt at completing the task. There are two distinct but related ways in which repetition might have an effect on performance.

Firstly, experience of a particular communication task on one occasion can help learners to carry out the *same* task on a subsequent occasion. This proposition assumes that part of the work of conceptualisation, formulation and articulation carried out on the first occasion is kept in the learners' memory store and can be reused on the second occasion, thereby freeing up some of the learners' capacity to pay attention to other aspects of the task, particularly in the processes of formulation and articulation. The effects predicted in this study are for changes in the fluency, accuracy and complexity of students' performance.

Secondly, work on a particular *type* of communication task helps learners to deal with new versions of that task type. This proposition depends on assumptions made by psycholinguists (e.g. Levelt, 1989) and discourse/conversation analysts (e.g. Gumperz, 1983), ethnomethodologists (e.g. Roberts et al., 1992) and SLA theorists (e.g. Selinker and Douglas, 1985) that experience of handling discourse types is stored in long-term memory, contributing to communicative competence, and affecting the effectiveness with which a speaker carries out a task. This would make sense if it is understood that different examples of the same task type share certain characteristic discourse features, such as elements of narrative structure, or argumentational structure, that is, schematic properties of the discourse. Familiarity with a task type could be expected to affect the capacity available for attending to formulation and articulation, in the sense that familiarity with a particular task type will result in differences in performance on familiar and unfamiliar types of task.

Finding systematic effects would provide a basis for the repeated pedagogic use of unscripted speaking tasks to lead learners to shift attention from conceptualisation to formulation and articulation, so as to encourage the 'integration of form and meaning'. The study also enables investigation of Foster and Skehan's 'trade-off effect' (Foster and Skehan, 1996).

To summarise, task repetition is relevant to a conception of pedagogy in which meaningful activity is construed as central. The fundamental question is how pedagogy can enable learners to internalise and exploit a language for their own communicative purposes, and in doing this, to sort out and integrate their perception of the complexities of the language system (such as the form–meaning relations, and the redundancy and anomalous nature of language) within specific communications. It may be that this problem is fundamental to many areas of education; it is certainly central to teaching and learning of language for use. The issue is whether the repeated use of the same and similar communication tasks can affect processing in such a way as to be capable of fostering language development. This is studied in the following section.

THE STUDY

The aims of the study were to test an aspect of the general assumption – implicit in communicative approaches to language teaching – that engagement in a communication task can of itself create conditions for learning.

Research questions

The study focused on three questions:

1. Would there be significant differences between performances on a task type practised over a 10-week period, compared with performance on a type of task that had not been practised ('task-type practice')?
2. Would there be significant differences between a repeat performance of a task performed 10 weeks earlier, and performance on a new task ('task repetition')?
3. Would there be significant overall differences between performances on the two types of task ('task effect')?

Participants

Participants were 48 overseas NNS students at the University of Reading, who were invited to participate in the study in exchange for feedback at the end of the project on their oral performance, and a small fee. Controlling for proficiency, students were randomly allocated to one of the three conditions, 16 in each: control; narrative; interview (for definitions of the groups, see 'Tasks' and 'Design' below). Level of proficiency was assessed through preliminary interviews administered by an experienced tester using the widely used International English Language Testing System (IELTS) oral proficiency bands developed by the University of Cambridge Local Examinations Syndicate (UCLES) for testing the proficiency of students intending to undertake university study through English as a second language (see Weir, 1990, for definitions of the bands). *t*-tests were used on the three measures of performance (accuracy, fluency and complexity) at the start of the study on a narrative and interview task to test for significant differences between the groups. No differences were found in five out of the six comparisons; the only difference being that the interview group paused significantly more than the other groups on one of the two tasks. In all other respects the performances of the three groups were not significantly similar.

Tasks

Two sets of tasks were designed for the study: a 'narrative' set and an 'interview' set. Both sets were designed so that the six versions of each one followed a standard pattern, in terms of interviewer procedure (e.g. greeting and closing), sequencing of any subcomponents of the task, types of stimulus, and types of requirement placed on the student (e.g. in terms of question types). For example, all the interviews were structured around pictures reflecting some aspect of life in Britain (food, dress, buildings), and all interviewees were first asked to comment on what struck them about the pictures, how they saw the pictures, and whether and in what ways the pictures showed images that were different from or similar to what they would be likely to see in their own country.

The narratives were based on short video extracts from a range of *Tom and Jerry* film cartoons, controlled for length. This topic was chosen partly because (a) it was expected to be reasonably though not intimately familiar to all participants, irrespective of country of origin; (b) it was expected that the content would constitute a feasible but significant processing load in terms of organising it for discursive output; and (c) the cartoons lacked dialogue, thus avoiding the risk of participants' performance being influenced by their listening comprehension, or of participants focusing on the dialogue rather than on the events. Subjects were asked to watch the extracts in the presence of the researcher, and then recount what the episode consisted of.

Participants were questioned in such a way as to give the impression that the focus of the task was on content, rather than expression. Procedures for each task type were identical, whether the specific version of the task was new or repeated. The stimulus materials were shown to experienced language teachers to check for consistency, practicality and face validity. They were then piloted to ensure that they generated adequate quantities of talk.

Design

Three groups were used in this study. All did the time 1 and time 5 tasks. Two of the groups were experimental groups (e-groups). Each e-group worked on one of the task types over the 10-week period, one on narrative tasks (narrative group) and the other on interview tasks (interview group). A control group (c-group) received no treatment over the same 10-week period, apart from encountering the tasks at times 1 and 5. The design is charted in Table 2.1.

Table 2.1   Design of the study

Group	Treatment 1	Treatment 2			Data
	Time 1				Time 5
	Week 1	Week 3	Week 5	Week 7	Week 10
Narrative group	Nar. 1 Int. 1	Nar. 2 & 3	Nar. 3 & 4	Nar. 4 & 5	Nar. 1 & 6 Int. 1 & 6
Interview group	Nar. 1 Int. 1	Int. 2 & 3	Int. 3 & 4	Int. 4 & 5	Nar. 1 & 6 Int. 1 & 6
Control group	Nar. 1 Int. 1				Nar. 1 & 6 Int. 1 & 6

At the start of the study, participants were all recorded on one narrative and one interview task. The two experimental groups were then recorded on a fortnightly basis undertaking either two narrative or two interview tasks, according to group. At the tenth week, all participants were given two interview tasks and two narrative tasks, which form the database of this study. One of each of the tasks was a repetition of the task they had undertaken at the start of the study. Half the participants did the narrative tasks first; the other half did the interview tasks first. To avoid an immediate practice effect, both on task type and on the familiar/new version of the tasks, the order of the presentation of the new and familiar tasks of each task type was also reversed for half the participants (see Table 2.2).

Table 2.2   Sequencing of time 5 tasks across total population

Repeated nar.	New nar.	Repeated int.	New int.
New nar.	Repeated nar.	New int.	Repeated int.
Repeated int.	New int.	Repeated nar.	New nar.
New int.	Repeated int.	New nar.	Repeated nar.

No tuition or feedback was provided before or during the study in relation to the tasks or to the students' performance, the aim being to gather purely task-based effects. Since the participants were attending British university degree courses, they all had extensive communication practice in English throughout the period of the study.

Research question 1 was studied by comparing the performances of the two experimental groups on the task types they had worked on with those they had not worked on. Research question 2 was studied by comparing the repeated performance of the 'narrative 1' and 'interview 1' tasks at time 5, and the new versions of the two types of task (narrative 6 and interview 6). Research question 3 was investigated by studying the differences at time 5 between performances on the interview and on the narrative tasks. The data could therefore be structured in a $3 \times 2 \times 2$ statistical design. This is represented in Table 2.3, along with the questions relating to each comparison.

Table 2.3   Design of the data analysis

	Group (= task type exposure)	Task repetition	Task type
Narrative group	Nar. vs Int.	Nar. 1 vs 6	Nar.
Interview group	Int. vs Nar.	&	vs
Control group	Nar. vs Int.	Int. 1 vs 6	Int.
Questions	Did each e-group perform better on the task type they had worked on, and the control group no better on either?	Did the participants perform better on the repeated number 1 than the new number 6 tasks?	Was there an overall difference between the performances of the participants on the two types of task?

Effects were studied through an ANOVA repeated measures design. To narrow down the effects on the experimental groups, the ANOVA analysis was also run on a $2 \times 2 \times 2$ design, omitting the c-group. Post-hoc t-tests were run to locate the precise effects.

Independent variables

- *Task-type practice.* The independent variable '*task-type practice*' relates to the treatments, which involved 10 weeks' exposure to either narrative or interview tasks (e-groups), compared with no exposure (control group).
- *Repetition.* This variable contrasts performance of a repeated or new version of a task. This was operationalised by having the participants repeat a version of each task type which they had originally performed 10 weeks earlier at the start of the study. Performance was compared with performance on a new version of the same task type.
- *Task type.* This explored the effect of task type (narrative or interview) ('task type') on language. The purpose was to explore whether the two task types led to differences in language production.

The effects of these variables were studied in the data collected at time 5, and through the interactions between *task-type practice* and *task* ('task-type practice $\times$ task'); and between *task-type practice* and *repetition* with a specific task ('task-type practice $\times$ repetition'). A 'task-type practice $\times$ task' interaction would be the stronger exposure effect since it would imply generalisation of the effect of exposure to more than one task of the same type. A 'task-type practice $\times$ repetition' interaction would imply that exposure to a task type would have a different impact on performances on repeated or new tasks – for instance, exposure to the task type helping performance on a repeated version of a task more or less than performance on a new version of the task. This would suggest a more complex effect of task practice.

Data

The data consisted of recordings of time 5 performances of one repeated and one new version of each of two task types (narrative and interview) by three groups (two experimental and one control group). Correlations of participants' scores on the three measures were checked across the six tasks (three versions of each of two task types), yielding 45 comparisons. This enabled an assessment of the consistency of performance of individual students in relation to the group. A preliminary analysis showed that only one of 18 correlations was non-significant. Nine correlations were low, but eight were between 0.59 and 0.82. This provides evidence that participants' performances on the three target measures remained consistent. It is worth noting that five lower correlations occurred on comparisons of performance across task type, and four between performances on the first and last presentation of the task type. This indicates a very high residual stability in task performance at a given time and across similar task types, and a significant stability even across different task types and at different times. This is of interest since it confirms a consistency of performance. Also, the high correlation between performances of similar type provides further empirical support for the notion of task type in terms of speaker performance.

Dependent variables

Dependent variables were selected which focused on three potential qualities of the participants' speech: fluency, accuracy and complexity. Skehan (1998, and this volume), Skehan and Foster (1997), Ellis (1987) and Crookes (1989) have all used measures focusing on combinations of these features. Although these are clearly only general aspects of the data, and are not sensitive, for instance, to the nature of the features of complexity or the aspects of language which speakers produce accurately and fluently, they nonetheless provide a reasonable basis for assessing the general impact of tasks on participants' talk. The measures were operationalised as follows.

Fluency

Fluency was calculated in terms of the number of unfilled pauses per *t*-unit – that, is, the higher the number, the less fluent the talk. This is just one of a number of possible measures of fluency (see Lennon, 1990, for a detailed study of measures of pausing).

Accuracy

Accuracy was reflected by calculating the incidence of errors per *t*-unit – the higher the number, the less accurate the language. Other studies have analysed the number of error-free *t*-units (e.g. Foster and Skehan, 1996). It was thought that by reducing the number of errors recorded, this latter measure might reduce discrimination between participants, and that error per *t*-unit, being more detailed, would be more sensitive. In the absence of fuller research into the validity and effectiveness of the two measures, it was felt that it would be useful in terms of research methodology to investigate the effectiveness of using errors per *t*-unit as the accuracy measure. Note that accuracy was analysed for only 30 participants in all, 10 from each group.

Complexity

Complexity was measured in terms of number of words per *t*-unit – the higher the number, the more complex the language. This measure reflects an ability to combine a number of lexical items around syntactic structures. To some extent this might be thought of as a covert fluency measure, since, given the limitations on short-term memory, the ability to access lexical items while holding a syntactic structure in short-term memory (STM) is partly a function of speed of lexical and syntactic access. However, number of words per *t*-unit reflects more than just speed: it also involves the extent to which lexical accessing can be managed according to basic syntactic parameters – that is, a cognitive capacity. Other possible measures of complexity include *c*-units, subordination and verb-argument structure. *c*-units (used by Foster and Skehan, 1996; and Skehan and Foster, 1997 – see Crookes, 1990, for a definition) were not used for this study, on grounds that the narrative tasks were likely to involve relatively little use of non-finite *c*-units compared with the interview task, and that analysis of *c*-units was therefore likely to yield a predictable and uninteresting finding. A *t*-unit was defined as a finite clause together with any subordinate clauses dependent on it.

Hypotheses

It was hypothesised that each of the three independent variables would significantly affect the data. Firstly, it was hypothesised that task type (narrative vs interview) would differentially affect performance in terms of fluency, accuracy and complexity, giving rise to less fluent and less accurate performance, but conceivably bringing about more complex output (H1). This was predicted on the basis that the narrative tasks – which the reader will recall involved watching and then recounting a video sequence – were expected to carry a greater cognitive load, principally in terms of memory load; in terms of the expected cognitive processing and sorting of the input data; and given the fact that the interlocutor was provided no interactive support.

Secondly, it was hypothesised that task repetition would affect performance, giving rise to greater fluency, accuracy and complexity (there was no reason to expect the dependent variables to be affected differently on this variable) (H2). This was expected on the grounds that, through prior completion of the tasks, speakers would have already carried out a good bulk of the cognitive processing required to complete the task, and that this might provide a degree of task priming, enabling greater accuracy and greater complexity on the second occasion.

Thirdly, it was hypothesised that task-type practice – the treatment conditions – would affect subsequent performance on the task types, helping the experimental groups over the control group, and differentially helping the experimental groups in their performances on the task type they had practised. The prediction was that exposure to narratives would correlate with an increase on all dependent variables on the narrative tasks, and that exposure to interviews would correlate with a similar increase in performance on the interview tasks (H3).

To summarise, the hypotheses were:

H1 Narrative tasks would give rise to less fluent and less accurate, but more complex, output.

H2 Task repetition would affect performance, giving rise to greater fluency, accuracy and complexity on repeated versions of tasks.

H3 Task 1. type practice would affect subsequent performance on the task types.

Table 2.4 Descriptive statistics

	N-group		I-group		C-group	
	Mean	**s.d.**	**Mean**	**s.d.**	**Mean**	**s.d.**
Pauses per t-unit ($n = 48$)						
Familiar narrative	2.38	0.72	2.92	1.53	2.28	0.91
New narrative	2.49	0.78	2.71	1.31	2.08	1.02
Familiar interview	3.40	0.67	4.00	1.31	3.07	0.92
New interview	3.34	0.73	3.28	1.34	2.66	0.74
Accuracy ($n = 30$)						
Familiar narrative	1.33	0.14	1.32	0.22	1.24	0.14
New narrative	1.36	0.28	1.27	0.17	1.34	0.33
Familiar interview	1.45	0.36	1.29	0.24	1.32	0.16
New interview	1.45	0.57	1.06	0.28	1.29	0.47
Words per t-unit ($n = 48$)						
Familiar narrative	10.89	3.14	10.83	3.19	11.25	3.54
New narrative	10.39	2.64	9.84	2.58	10.49	3.54
Familiar interview	12.50	3.76	12.58	3.76	12.26	2.72
New interview	12.58	3.27	11.26	3.06	11.28	2.21

RESULTS

Descriptive statistics appear in Table 2.4, and in Table 2.4a (reliability/validity correlations) in Appendix 2.1; results of the ANOVA (repeated measures) appear in Table 2.5 for all three groups, and in Table 2.6 for the two experimental groups; results of *t*-tests comparing scores on task type, and familiar and unfamiliar versions of the tasks, appear in Tables 2.7, 2.8, 2.9 and 2.10.

Correlations were checked for consistency of performance across tasks (see Table 2.4b in Appendix 2.1). There are high correlations on the six cross-task comparisons for fluency. On the other hand, there are high correlations for complexity between tasks of the same type, but lower correlations across tasks of different types. Correlations on the accuracy measure are significant, though low, across tasks of the same type, and across familiar versions of the different task types, but totally absent across *different* task types and *unfamiliar* tasks. To summarise, the fluency correlations suggest considerable consistency of performance, while correlations on the complexity and accuracy measures suggest that consistency is strongest across tasks of the same type or on familiar tasks.

Turning to the study of main effects (Tables 2.5 and 2.6), highly significant results were found for the independent variables 'task type' and 'repetition' on the fluency and complexity measures. A trend towards a task-type effect was found on the accuracy measure for the narrative group. A study of within-task correlations for the whole of the sample revealed very limited evidence for trade-off effects, in that there were virtually no negative correlations

Table 2.5　ANOVA results (repeated measures design) (for three groups)

Measure/factor	SS	DF	MS	F	Sig. of F
Pauses per t-unit (48 cases)					
Task type	31.72	2	31.72	77.81	0.000
Repetition	3.02	1	3.02	15.79	0.000
Group × repetition	2.02	2	1.01	5.26	0.009
Group × task type	0.79	1	0.79	0.27	0.604
Errors per t-unit (30 cases)					
Task type	0.00	1	0.00	0.00	0.994
Repetition	0.03	1	0.03	0.54	0.468
Group × repetition	0.19	2	0.09	1.78	0.188
Group × task type	0.27	2	0.13	1.27	0.296
Words per t-unit (48 cases)					
Task type	102.44	1	102.44	11.49	0.001
Repetition	26.52	1	26.52	9.64	0.003
Group × repetition	7.54	2	3.77	1.37	0.265
Group × task type	8.46	2	4.23	0.47	0.625

Table 2.6　ANOVA results (repeated measures design) (for the two experimental groups)

Measure/factor	SS	DF	MS	F	Sig. of F
Pauses per t-unit (32 cases)					
Task type	24.57	1	24.57	58.63	0.000
Repetition	1.56	1	1.56	9.39	0.005
Group × repetition	1.93	1	1.93	11.58	0.002
Errors per t-unit (20 cases)					
Task type	0.00	1	0.00	0.01	0.935
Repetition	0.08	1	0.08	1.71	0.207
Group × repetition	0.13	1	0.13	2.87	0.107
Group × task type	0.27	1	0.27	2.68	0.119
Words per t-unit (32 cases)					
Task type	97.28	1	97.28	33.86	0.000
Repetition	14.83	1	14.83	5.92	0.021
Group × repetition	7.16	1	7.16	2.86	0.101

between scores on the three measures. I will now report the results in more detail, followed by a discussion of the findings. Note that *Group* is not included as a main effect since the task-type practice effect is best detected as an inter-action with task type.

I will discuss each of the main effects in turn, starting with task type. This variable is clearly associated with a highly significant effect on fluency and complexity, although, as with the other independent variables, not at all on accuracy. Relating this to the high correlations reported earlier between performances on similar task types (see p. 36), this clear task-type effect adds empirical support to the argument that tasks differ in the impact they have on language performance. However, the direction of the finding is contrary to the one predicted in H1. *t*-tests for the whole sample show significantly less fluency and greater complexity on the interview tasks than on the narrative tasks. It appears on this basis that fluency and complexity correlate: speakers pause more and produce more complex utterances in similar circumstances, and this is more likely to occur when being interviewed. At the same time, this result provides some evidence of a trade-off effect. The overall result here suggests that cognitive content – the influence hypothesised as crucial in narrative output – is not the only active influence: the interpersonal dimension of the communication found in interview tasks may have an impact on the way speakers process language, since it is unlikely that the cognitive content of the interview *requires* more pausing than on the narrative. More likely, the interpersonal aspect of the speech events had an effect – either through the interlocutor causing the speaker more unexpected on-line processing, or perhaps sanctioning more pausing, and thereby encouraging more attention on the part of speakers to develop the complexity of their utterances. This is consistent with arguments that propose that a dialogic dimension to communication helps speakers to structure their utterances.

t-tests were run to compare the means of complexity, accuracy and fluency scores across the two task types, and confirm the pattern. These are reported in Table 2.7.

Table 2.7   Paired *t*-test for differences in performance across task type

Variable	Task	Number of pairs	Mean	*t*-Value	*df*	2-tailed sig.
Fluency	Int.	48	3.29	8.90	47	0.000
	Nar.		2.48			
Accuracy	Int.	30	1.31	−0.01	29	0.994
	Nar.		1.31			
Complexity	Int.	48	12.08	3.43	47	0.001
	Nar.		10.62			

A comparison of *t*-test scores group by group shows that most of the variance is accounted for by the experimental groups (see Table 2.8). The interview group showed significant differences across task type on all three measures, less fluency on the interview tasks going together with greater complexity and greater accuracy. The narrative group showed significant differences in performance on two of the three measures, again less fluency accompanying greater complexity on the interview tasks. Finally, the c-group performed differently on only one measure, with less fluency occurring in the interview tasks. (See Skehan, this volume, for a meta-analysis of several task studies which draws similar conclusions.) That is, all groups were significantly

Table 2.8   Paired *t*-test for group-wise comparisons across task type

Variable	Task	No. of pairs	Mean	*t*-Value	*df*	2-tailed sig.
Interview group						
Fluency	Int.	16	3.64	4.06	15	0.001
	Nar.		2.81			
Accuracy	Int.	10	1.17	−2.29	9	0.048
	Nar.		1.30			
Complexity	Int.	16	11.91	3.62	15	0.003
	Nar.		10.33			
Narrative group						
Fluency	Int.	16	3.37	8.61	15	0.000
	Nar.		2.43			
Complexity	Int.	16	12.54	4.66	15	0.000
	Nar.		10.64			
Control group						
Fluency	Int.	16	2.86	4.43	15	0.000
	Nar.		2.17			

NB: $n = 16$ for fluency and complexity measures; $n = 10$ or accuracy measures.
Significant differences only are shown.

less fluent on the interview tasks; the narrative and interview groups were significantly less fluent and more complex on the interview tasks; and the interview group was also significantly more accurate on the interview task. The c-group is least open to the task-type effect.

Turning to the second independent variable – specific task repetition – ANOVA shows a significant effect on the fluency and complexity measures, although once again not on participants' accuracy. The reader will recall that the repeated tasks had been previously encountered 10 weeks earlier. The evidence from this result is that the impact of that earlier experience of the task carried over across the 10 weeks to significant effect, irrespective of participants' subsequent exposure to the task types. This finding is consistent with hypothesis 2. A post-hoc paired *t*-test of the differences between measures on familiar and new tasks for all participants was significant (see Table 2.9).

Table 2.9   *t*-Tests for paired samples (all subjects): repeated–new, by task

Measure	Task version	No. of pairs	Mean	S.D.	*t*-Value	*df*	2-tailed sig.
Fluency	Int. repeated	48	3.49	1.05	4.40	47	0.000
	Int. new		3.09	1.00			
Complexity	Int. repeated	48	12.44	3.38	2.07	47	0.044
	Int. new		11.79	2.89			
Complexity	Nar. repeated	48	10.99	2.94	2.42	47	0.019
	Nar. new		10.24	2.90			

This shows that repetition was significantly related to differences in complexity on both types of task, but not accuracy. Fluency was significantly affected on the interview task but not on the narrative task. This suggests that repetition of a specific task provides a basis for more complex production of language, accompanied, at least on the interview task, by a significant increase in pausing.

In order to narrow down further the source of the variance, differences of means between repeated and new versions of tasks were submitted to a *t*-test for paired samples on a group-wise basis, and significant and near-significant results are reported in Table 2.10.

Table 2.10   Groupwise *t*-tests for paired samples: repeated/new by task

Measure	Task version	No. of pairs	Mean	S.D.	*t*-Value	*df*	2-tailed sig.
I-group							
Fluency	Int. repeated	16	3.40	1.31	4.43	15	0.000
	Int. new		3.28	1.34			
Accuracy	Int. repeated	10	1.29	0.24	2.52	9	0.033
	Int. new		1.06	0.27			
Complexity	Int. repeated	16	12.58	3.76	2.03	15	0.060
	Int. new		11.26	3.06			
Complexity	Nar. repeated	16	10.83	3.19	1.79	15	0.093
	Nar. new		9.84	2.58			
C-group							
Fluency	Int. repeated	16	3.02	0.91	2.71	15	0.016
	Int. new		2.66	0.74			

Table 2.10 shows that the bulk of the variance in performance on repeated and new tasks can be attributed to the performance of the Interview group on the interview task. Two of the three comparisons result in significant differences, fluency and accuracy being less on the repeated task, and the third comparison – complexity – narrowly missing significance, with the higher score for complexity occurring on the repeated task. Together the three measures suggest that gains in complexity are paid for by a loss in fluency and accuracy on repeated tasks. This suggests once again a trade-off effect. On the narrative task with the same group, comparison on one measure – complexity – approaches significance ($p = 0.093$), once again the higher score being generated on the repeated version of the task. For the c-group, a significant difference was found on just one score, the fluency score on the interview task, again more pausing occurring on the repeated version of the task. No significant differences were found in the data from the narrative group. The variance that is found, then, suggests a consistent effect on the interview tasks for the interview specialist group, the repeated version generating more pausing, less accuracy and greater complexity. It is as though the dominant concern of speakers on the repeated interview task is to take advantage of the repetition of the topic to develop more complex responses,

sacrificing fluency and accuracy in the process. The performance of the narrative group follows a similar pattern, although when taken on its own it fails to reach significance. This overall result is consistent with hypothesis 2.

We now turn to the effect of the task-type practice variable on performance and discuss, first, the issue of the effects of exposure to a task type in relation to performance on the two types of task. Disappointingly, the interaction between group and task is not significant on any of the three measures. In other words, practice on narrative tasks did not help the narrative specialist group on the two post-test narrative performances when compared with their performances on the interviews, and the same held for the interview group: performance on the two post-test interviews was not significantly different from performance on the post-test narratives. Hence the study provides no clear evidence that practising a task type will have a facilitating effect on the future performance of any other tasks of the same type. This and other results are discussed more fully in the following section.

There was, however, a partial task-type practice effect. This can be noted in the highly significant interaction between repetition and task-type practice on fluency: participants were significantly more fluent on repeated versions of a type of task to which they had been exposed than on repeated tasks to which they had not been exposed over the 10 weeks. Although the results for this interaction do not reach significance for complexity or error, there is nevertheless a pattern towards an interaction on both these measures.

These results, however, may have been diluted by the less homogeneous performance of the c-group. Attempting to track down the task-type practice effect more closely, an ANOVA analysis was therefore run, omitting the control group (which in any case had had no exposure to the tasks and therefore were not centrally relevant to the study of a task-type practice effect). Omission of the c-group resulted in F scores for accuracy and complexity which were closer to significance, 2.86 (sig. of F: 0.101) and 2.87 (sig. of F: 0.107) respectively. This suggests an underlying trend, in line with hypothesis 3, of an increase in fluency, accuracy and complexity as a result of task-type practice. When considered together with the significant effect on the fluency score, these results then are consistent with the hypothesis that task-type practice has a capacity to affect performance on practised tasks at least when the test task is repeated, but not on novel tasks of the same type. What may be happening is that performance on a repeated task is primed by some kind of build-up from the experience of attending to tasks of the same type.

Relative accuracy on interview and narrative tasks on the part of the two groups was studied more closely through the group-wise *t*-test for paired samples (see Table 2.4). The interview group produced significantly more accurate performances on the interview tasks than on the narrative tasks, the control and narrative groups showing no significant difference between task performances on this measure.

As expected from the earlier analyses, there is no overall difference in accuracy. However, repeated versions of both types of task generated more words per *t*-unit, and the repeated interview task also generated significantly more pausing. This supports the hypothesis that repetition affects performance on both types of task although not in all aspects of performance.

Finally, testing out the trade-off effect through correlations, results were at best weak and positive, and the only ones were for complexity and pausing (0.27 ($p < 0.067$) between the measures on the new narrative task, and 0.26 ($p < 0.079$) on the new version of the interview task). While the trade-off effect is supported in the ANOVA results, the lack of negative correlations over the whole sample seems to mitigate the arguments in support of the pervasiveness of the effect.

DISCUSSION

The results reported above are reasonably clear cut. Firstly, the data show a consistency in participants' performances relative to each other across different tasks. This is a reassuring background against which to discuss other effects, since it is to be expected that participants' relative proficiency should remain broadly – though not completely – stable in different circumstances. Secondly, the study provides confirmation that different versions of the same type of task can have consistent effects on performance. This provides strong empirical evidence of the existence of 'task types' (see Bygate, 1988, for an earlier empirical study that provided further evidence of this issue). This is important, since it reminds us that there is reason for language professionals to be rational in the way they select tasks in terms of the types of language processing that they are likely to encourage. The main focus of this study, however, has been on the effects of task-type practice and task repetition. In this regard results are encouraging, although there are complex tones to the picture that emerges.

Firstly, there is a strong effect for task repetition. One brief encounter with a task 10 weeks earlier seemed to have been sufficient to affect subsequent performance of the same task. It is hard to escape the conclusion that this can only be an effect of highly contextualised cognitive rehearsal, releasing spare capacity on the part of the speaker to increase fluency or complexity. This is a remarkable effect for such a brief speech event, first encountered so long ago, and since then followed by a huge number of subsequent language experiences in the students' daily lives, many of them presumably far more memorable than this. The pedagogic implications of this context-bound phenomenon are worth further exploration.

Secondly, while the strong 'task-type practice' hypothesis is not supported (the task-type practice × task interaction did not have a significant impact), a weaker effect does seem to have emerged. This was measured in the interaction between task-type practice and repeated task: while not all results reached significance, those that did were supported by other results showing strong trends in the same direction, suggesting that performance on repeated tasks is affected by interim exposure to other tasks of the same type. Hence the notion of 'discourse competence' – the capacity to process certain types of discourse more easily than others – does appear to have some empirically identifiable psychological reality, although according to this evidence it is not as strong as initially hypothesised. Possibly for the fuller effect of task-type practice to emerge, more – or more massed – task exposure might be needed. It is also possible that, at the levels of proficiency of these particip-ants, a ceiling was reached on these task types, although this is perhaps less likely given the range of participants' levels. Further, a possible weakness in the design was that the interview task, while realistic, may have been already too commonly experienced by the participants for additional massed exposure to make much difference to their performance. The trends within the data set need to be interpreted against the fact that this occurred within the con-text of massive daily second language experience, and on a task which was probably not particularly unusual for them.

The final issue concerns the accuracy results. There is evidence within the data that speakers' accuracy can be affected by task practice, at least within the confines of the interview task. Why, though, was this aspect of their per-formance less open to influence from task-type practice or task repetition than fluency or complexity? It is possible that the measure of 'errors per *t*-unit' was too conservative: it might be more important for studies of perform-ance to assess the extent to which speakers manage to produce error-free *t*-units than to compute the total number of errors that they produce. Under the 'errors per *t*-unit' method of scoring, one or two more exploratory but error-strewn utterances can compromise an otherwise error-free performance. Additionally, it is possible that accuracy is a more complex phenomenon: for instance, the capacity for self-correction might need to be distinguished to indicate degrees of accuracy on the part of speakers. This possibility needs to be left for future study. However, the lack of correlations on this measure leaves us with no clues to the way in which error may be affected by task practice. Theoretically it seems unlikely that error is beyond the scope of task practice, given the effects that the study produced on the other two measures, and given the earlier work of Skehan and Foster (1997) and Ellis (1987).

CONCLUSION

The two key findings among these results have potentially important ped-agogical implications. The first is that the data provide empirical evidence that memory of a previous encounter with a task as much as 10 weeks earlier can have an effect on unscripted performance. This finding is consistent with that outlined in an earlier pilot study (Bygate, 1996). The importance of this cannot be overstated. It suggests that previous experience of a task is avail-able for speakers to build on in subsequent performance. In other words, it is possible to harness earlier work on a task to elaborate more complex and/or more fluent performance. The reason for this is likely to be that some at least of the cognitive work undertaken on a previous occasion to internalise the information, to organise it prior to verbalisation, and to verbalise it is still accessible during the repeated performance, and frees up capacity for new cognitive searches. Although more accurate performance was not found in this study (possibly because of the selection of over-conservative measures of accuracy), given the findings in Bygate (1996), the results that *are* produced by the study suggest that accuracy should be open to a similar effect, perhaps under different conditions of performance. Perhaps the effect depends on students' allocation of attention (Skehan, 1998). In any event, teachers and students might be usefully encouraged to exploit task repetition to enable them to focus their attention closely on the relevant form–meaning relations. In particular, the evidence strongly supports the view that previous experience of a specific task aids speakers to shift their attention from processing the message content to working on formulations of the message.

The evidence also provides some support for the view that experience of a task type affects subsequent performance in the same way: the interaction between the variables of task-type practice and repetition on the fluency measure suggests that although task-type exposure does not affect performance on all tasks of the same type, there may be a residual gain which can be found from task-type exposure when a specific task is repeated.

Communication is spontaneous and to some degree improvised, and this quality of language use certainly needs to be practised in classroom pedagogy. And yet to provide speaking practice only under these conditions runs the risk that learners will constantly be improvising, constantly experimenting with new forms, but also constantly doing so while having to pay some considerable attention to the content of what they want to say. A basic challenge to language teaching is to provide students with practice at improvising the expression of their meanings, so that they get better at the task. Selecting and reusing tasks systematically would seem to be an important way of helping students to do this.

ACKNOWLEDGEMENTS

I am particularly grateful to David Perry for his work in the phases of design and data collection, and to Jane Wagstaff for her transcription and analysis. Acknowledgements are also due to Gin Samuda, Peter Skehan and Merrill Swain for comments on earlier drafts of the work.

NOTE

1. The research reported in this chapter was made possible through an initial grant from the Centre for Applied Language Studies at the University of Reading, and the ESRC (Award No. R000221941).

REFERENCES

Allwright, R.L., Woodley, M.-P. and Allwright, J.M. (1988) Investigating reformulation as practical strategy for the teaching of academic writing. *Applied Linguistics*, 9(3): 237–58.

Bolinger, D. (1975) Meaning and memory. *Forum Linguisticum*, 1: 2–14.

Bygate, M. (1988) *Linguistic and strategic features of the language of learners in oral communication exercises.* Unpublished PhD thesis, University of London.

Bygate, M. (1996) Effects of task repetition: appraising the developing language of learners. In J. Willis and D. Willis (eds) *Challenge and Change in Language Teaching* (pp. 134–46). London: Heinemann.

Bygate, M. (1999) Task as context for the framing, reframing and unframing of language. *System*, 27: 33–48.

Chafe, W.L. (1968) Idiomaticity as an anomaly in the Chomskyan paradigm. *Foundations of Language*, 4: 109–27.

Crookes, G. (1989) Planning and interlanguage variation. *Studies in Second Language Acquisition*, 11: 367–83.

Crookes, G. (1990) The utterance, and other basic units for second language discourse analysis. *Applied Linguistics*, 11: 183–99.

Dörnyei, Z. and Kormos, J. (1998) Problem-solving mechanisms in L2 communication: a psycholinguistic perspective. *Studies in Second Language Acquisition*, 20: 349–86.

Doughty, C. and Williams, J. (eds) (1998) *Focus on Form in Classroom Second Language Acquisition*. Cambridge: CUP.

Ellis, R. (1987) Interlanguage variability in narrative discourse: style-shifting in the use of the past tense. *Studies in Second Language Acquisition*, 9: 12–20.

Faerch, C. and Kasper, G. (eds) (1983) *Strategies in Interlanguage Communication*. Harlow: Longman.

Foster, P. and Skehan, P. (1996) The influence of planning on performance in task-based learning. *Studies in Second Language Acquisition*, 18: 299–324.

Garrett, M.F. (1981) Levels of processing in sentence production. In B. Butterworth (ed.) *Language Production*, Vol. 1. *Speech and Talk*. London: Academic Press.

Garman, M.A. (1990) *Psycholinguistics*. Cambridge: CUP.

George, H.V. (1972) *Common Errors in Language Learning*. Rowley, Mass.: Newbury House.

Gumperz, J. (1983) *Discourse Strategies*. Cambridge: CUP.

Harley, B. and Swain, M. (1984) The interlanguage of immersion students and its implications for second language teaching. In A. Davies, C. Criper and A. Howatt (eds) *Interlanguage*. Edinburgh: Edinburgh University Press.

Johnson, K. (1996) *Language Teaching and Skill Learning*. Oxford: Blackwell.

Laver, J. (1970) The production of speech. In J. Lyons (ed.) *New Horizons in Linguistics* (pp. 53–75). Harmondsworth: Penguin.

Lennon, P. (1990) Investigating fluency in EFL: a quantitative approach. *Language Learning*, 40(3): 387–417.

Levelt, W.J.M. (1989) *Speaking: From Intention to Articulation*. Cambridge, Mass.: MIT Press.

Lightbown, P. (1998) The importance of timing in focus on form. In C. Doughty and J. Williams (eds), pp. 177–96.

Morrison, D.M. and Low, G. (1983) Monitoring and the second language learner. In J.C. Richards and R.W. Schmidt (eds) *Language and Communication* (pp. 228–50). Harlow: Longman.

Plough, I. and Gass, S.M. (1993) Interlocutor and task familiarity: Effects on inter-actional structure. In G. Crookes and S.M. Gass (eds) *Tasks and Language Learning*, (pp. 35–56). Clevedon, Avon: Multilingual Matters Ltd.

Roberts, C., Jupp, T. and Davies, E. (1992) *Language and Discrimination*. London: Longman.

Selinker, L. and Douglas, D. (1985) Wrestling with context in interlanguage theory. *Applied Linguistics*, 6: 190–204.

Skehan, P. (1994) Second language acquisition strategies, interlanguage develop-ment and task-based learning. In M. Bygate, A. Tonkyn and E. Williams (eds) *Grammar and the Language Teacher* (pp. 175–200). Hemel Hempstead: Prentice Hall.

Skehan, P. (1998) *A Cognitive Approach to Language Learning*. Oxford: OUP.

Skehan, P. and Foster, P. (1997) Task type and task processing conditions as influ-ences on foreign language performance. *Language Teaching Research*, 1(3): 185–211.

Smyth, M.M. et al. (1987) *Cognition in Action*. London: Lawrence Erlbaum Associates.

Swain, M. (1985) Communicative competence: Some roles of comprehensible input and comprehensible output in its development. In S. Gass and C. Madden (eds) *Input in Second Language Acquisition*. Rowley, Mass.; Newbury House.

Swain, M. and Lapkin, S. (1995) Problems in output and the cognitive processes they generate: a step towards second language learning. *Applied Linguistics*, 16: 371–91.

VanPatten, B. (1996) *Input Processing and Grammar Instruction*. Norwood, NJ: Ablex.

Westney, P. (1994) Rules and pedagogical grammar. In T. Odlin (ed.) *Perspectives on Pedagogical Grammar* (pp. 72–96). Cambridge: CUP.

Weir, C.J. (1990) *Communicative Language Testing*. Hemel Hempstead: Prentice Hall.

Widdowson, H.G. (1978) *Teaching Language as Communication*. Oxford: OUP.

Wigglesworth, G. (1997) An investigation of planning time and proficiency level on oral test discourse. *Language Testing*, 14: 85–106.

Willis, J. (1996) *A Framework for Task-based Learning*. London: Longman.

APPENDIX 2.1

Table 2.4a   Comparability of groups at the start of the study

Measure	Group	No. of cases	Mean	s.d.	*t*-value	d.f.	Levene's test of var. 2-tail sig.	*F*	Sig.
Control–Narrative groups									
Task: Interview									
Accuracy	C-group	10	1.25	0.09	−2.13	18	0.047	9.75	0.006
	N-group	10	1.51	0.38					
Fluency	C-group	16	2.68	0.77	−2.46	30	0.020	0.354	0.56
	N-group	16	3.29	0.63					
Complexity	C-group	16	11.67	0.45	−0.58	30	0.57	2.04	0.16
	N-group	16	12.13	0.65					

Table 2.4a   (*cont'd*)

Measure	Group	No. of cases	Mean	s.d.	*t*-value	d.f.	Levene's test of var. 2-tail sig.	F	Sig.
Control–Narrative groups									
Task: Narrative									
Accuracy	C-group	10	1.31	0.16	−1.05	18	0.31	6.92	0.02
	N-group	10	1.44	0.36					
Fluency	C-group	16	3.07	0.91	−1.15	30	0.26	2.02	0.16
	N-group	16	3.40	0.67					
Complexity	C-group	16	12.26	2.71	−0.21	30	0.84	1.33	0.25
	N-group	16	12.50	3.76					
Narrative–Interview groups									
Task: Interview									
Accuracy	N-group	10	1.51	0.38	1.44	18	0.17	5.22	0.035
	I-group	10	1.33	0.15					
Fluency	N-group	16	2.30	0.63	0.34	30	0.74	1.53	0.23
	I-group	16	3.20	0.84					
Complexity	N-group	16	12.13	2.59	0.52	30	0.61	1.91	0.177
	I-group	16	11.72	1.81					
Task: Narrative									
Accuracy	N-group	10	1.45	0.36	1.14	18	0.27	1.86	0.19
	I-group	10	1.29	0.24					
Fluency	N-group	16	3.40	0.67	−1.62	30	0.11	7.77	0.009
	I-group	16	4.00	1.31					
Complexity	N-group	16	12.50	3.76	−0.06	30	0.95	0.023	0.88
	I-group	16	12.58	3.76					
Control–Interview groups									
Task: Interview									
Accuracy	C-group	10	1.25	0.09	−1.32	18	0.20	2.54	0.13
	I-group	10	1.33	0.16					
Fluency	C-group	16	2.68	0.77	−1.84	30	0.075	0.30	0.58
	I-group	16	3.20	0.84					
Complexity	C-group	16	11.67	1.82	−0.08	30	0.94	0.006	0.94
	I-group	16	11.72	1.81					
Task: Narrative									
Accuracy	C-group	10	1.32	0.16	0.26	18	0.796	2.97	0.10
	I-group	10	1.29	0.24					
Fluency	C-group	16	3.07	0.92	−2.31	30	0.028	2.39	0.13
	I-group	16	4.00	1.3					
Complexity	C-group	16	12.26	2.71	−0.27	30	0.78	0.90	0.35
	I-group	16	12.58	3.76					

Table 2.4b   Correlations of dependent variables across tasks

Repeated/new narratives

	Accuracy	*Fluency*	*Complexity*
Accuracy	0.38		
	p < 0.038		
Fluency		0.77	
		p < 0.000	
Complexity			0.73
			p < 0.000

Repeated/new interviews

	Accuracy	*Pauses*	*Words-p.t-unit*
Accuracy	0.40		
	p < 0.028		
Fluency		0.81	
		p < 0.000	
Complexity			0.70
			p < 0.000

Repeated narrative/repeated interviews

	Accuracy	*Pauses*	*Words-p.t-unit*
Accuracy	0.58		
	p < 0.001		
Fluency		0.64	
		p < 0.000	
Complexity			0.41
			p < 0.004

New narrative/new interview

	Accuracy	*Pauses*	*Words-p.t-unit*
Accuracy	−0.09		
	p < 0.63		
Fluency		0.79	
		p < 0.000	
Complexity			0.37
			p < 0.010

New narrative/repeated interview

	Accuracy	*Pauses*	*Words-p.t-unit*[*]
Accuracy	0.16		
	p < 0.394		
Fluency		0.76	
		p < 0.000	
Complexity			0.28
			p < 0.057

Repeated narrative/new interview

	Accuracy	*Pauses*	*Words-p.t-unit*
Accuracy	0.25		
	p < 0.175		
Fluency		0.69	
		p < 0.000	
Complexity			0.49
			p < 0.000

Chapter 3

Non-reciprocal tasks, comprehension and second language acquisition

Rod Ellis

INTRODUCTION

Tasks can involve varying degrees of reciprocity. Reciprocal tasks are tasks that require a two-way flow of information between a speaker and a listener; they are speaking tasks. Non-reciprocal tasks require only a one-way flow of information from a speaker to a listener. This distinction, however, is best viewed as reflecting a continuum rather than a dichotomy as the extent to which the participants in a task are required to interact can vary. At one end of the continuum are tasks that are entirely non-reciprocal in that they do not permit learners any opportunity to interject whatsoever even if they do understand (e.g. a non-interactive lecture), while at the other end are reciprocal tasks that can only be accomplished successfully if the particip-ants interact to ensure mutual understanding (e.g. an information-gap task where the information has been split among the learners). In between, there are tasks that provide the learners with some negotiation rights but these are restricted (e.g. an interactive lecture where students have the opportunity to interrupt the lecturer). This chapter is concerned with tasks that are either entirely non-reciprocal or that allow relatively limited opportunities for two-way interaction. Where the learner is the addressee, such tasks are, in fact, listening tasks. Where the learner is responsible for communicating the in-formation, they are speaking tasks.

There are two good reasons for examining non-reciprocal tasks. The first is that, in general, they have been somewhat neglected in the pedagogic literature on tasks. For example, the tasks described in Klippel (1984) or in Nunan (1989) are all reciprocal tasks. So too are the tasks typically referred to in the task-based research literature (e.g. Crookes and Gass, 1993; Skehan, 1998). This emphasis on reciprocal tasks in teaching and research, however, is not reflected in common definitions of a 'task'. Skehan (1996), for example, defines task as 'an activity in which: meaning is primary; there is some sort of relationship to the real world; task completion has some priority; and the assessment of task performance is in terms of task outcome'. Such a defini-tion, of course, is just as applicable to listening non-reciprocal tasks as it is to speaking reciprocal tasks.

The second reason is that, from the second language acquisition (SLA) researcher's perspective, non-reciprocal tasks have an enormous advantage; they make it possible to investigate not only the kind of processing that results from performing a listening task but also what learners actually acquire from the performance. There is now a very considerable literature examining the kinds of language learners produce when they undertake different kinds of tasks under different conditions (as will be seen, for example, after reading the other chapters in this book). However, this literature has not addressed directly what effect learner performance has on acquisition, and there are good reasons for this. First, it is unlikely that a single task (or even a short series of tasks) will result in measurable changes in general language skill (e.g. fluency). Second, it is extremely difficult to devise tasks that make it obligatory to use some specific linguistic feature, the acquisition of which might be measurable. Loschky and Bley-Vroman (1993) have pointed out that, while it may be possible to construct tasks that make it 'natural' or 'useful' for learners to employ a specific feature, it is almost impossible to ensure that the feature is 'essential'. As a result, researchers such as Skehan (1998), who are interested in the relationship between production on a task and language acquisition, have not been able to examine the relationship empirically (i.e. they have not investigated what effect performing a task has on a learner's interlanguage system). They have invoked theoretical arguments to make claims about the possible effects that certain types of task-derived production might have on learners' interlanguage development without examining whether these effects actually occur. Non-reciprocal tasks, in contrast, do provide a means by which researchers can directly investigate the relationship between task performance and acquisition. As Loschky and Bley-Vroman have observed, comprehension tasks allow for the input to be scripted in such a way that it contains particular linguistic features, the learners' acquisition of which can be tested on completion of the task. Thus such tasks make it easier for the researcher (and the teacher) to investigate whether any acquisition takes place as a result of learners performing them.

This chapter, then, differs from most of the others in that it not only examines tasks that are essentially non-reciprocal, but also examines the relationship between task design on the one hand, and acquisition as well as language use (comprehension) on the other. It also differs from other chapters in the theoretical basis of the research reported. While researchers such as Skehan have drawn on output theories of one kind or another, the research in this chapter is based mainly on the input theories of Krashen and Long. In the section that follows, an example of the kind of non-reciprocal task used in the research is provided and discussed. The theoretical basis of the research is then outlined and a summary of the findings of a series of studies is given. Finally, some of the implications for task-based teaching are considered.

AN EXAMPLE OF A NON-RECIPROCAL TASK

All the tasks used in the research were similar to the task used in Pica et al. (1987) and consisted of:

- structured input (i.e. input that had been specially designed to include specific linguistic features – vocabulary items);
- a non-verbal device (i.e. a diagram).

In each task, the structured input took the form of a series of directives requesting the learners to carry out a series of actions. These actions involved the learners in identifying the referents referred to in the directives and shown in an array of pictures, and then indicating the correct position of the referents in a matrix diagram. Such tasks are examples of what Widdowson (1978) has called information-transfer tasks, in that they require learners to transfer information from one modality (linguistic) to another (diagrammatic). They are also examples of what Pica et al. (1993) have called one-way information-gap tasks.

Figure 3.1 (overleaf) shows the pictorial materials for the task used in Ellis et al. (1994). In this task, the directives consisted of instructions about where to place a series of objects in a diagram of a kitchen. The following is an example of one of the directives:

(1)　Can you find the scouring pad? Take the scouring pad and put it on top of the counter by the sink – the right side of the sink.

For this directive, the students had to identify the scouring pad in the series of small pictures and then write the number of the picture in the correct position in the matrix diagram of the kitchen.

This kind of task has a number of advantages. First, as pointed out above, it enables the researcher to incorporate specific linguistic features into the input (hence the term 'structured input'). In the research to be summarised below, the linguistic features were lexical items (such as 'scouring pad') which, as shown by prior testing, the learners did not know. Second, it is possible to manipulate the input in different ways in order to test the effect that various input modifications have on comprehension and acquisition. For example, the directive shown above is an example of 'baseline input' (i.e. the kind of input that native speakers provide when they talk to other native speakers). In another version of the same task, the directive consisted of 'premodified input' – that is, the baseline input had been modified prior to the learners' performing the task in accordance with how native speakers address learners. The modified directive, corresponding to (1) above, took this form:

(2)　Can you find the scouring pad? A scouring pad – *scour* means to clean a dish. A scouring pad is a small thing you hold in your hand and you clean a dish with it. Take the scouring pad and put it on top of the counter by the sink – on the right side of the sink.

A third advantage of this kind of task is that it contains a built-in measure of learners' comprehension. Comprehension is demonstrated if a learner can indicate the position of the correct object on the matrix picture. This obviates the need to design a separate test to ascertain whether learners have understood the directives.

The tasks used in the studies varied in a number of ways. First, the *content* of the tasks differed. The content of the above task was 'kitchen objects', that

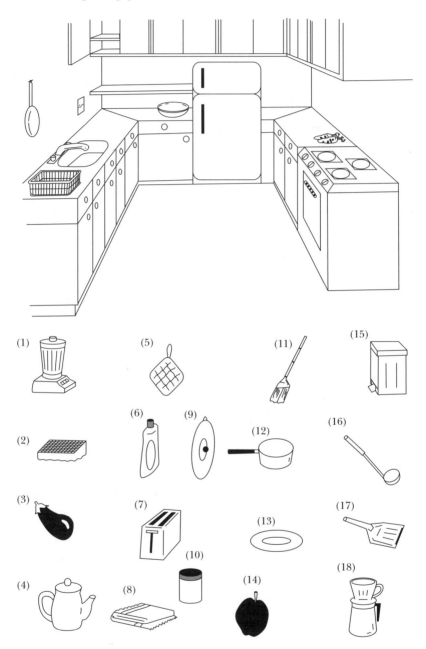

Figure 3.1   Materials used in the listening task

of the task in Ellis and Heimbach (1997) was 'bugs and birds' while in Ellis and He (1999) it was 'furniture'. Another difference concerned the *response manner*. In Ellis et al. (1994) and He and Ellis (1999) the learners were adolescents or adults, who were able to respond to the directives by writing the numbers of the pictures into the matrix picture. In Ellis and Heimbach (1997), however, the learners were young children, for whom such a response might have been problematic. In this case, therefore, the learners were provided with separate cards which they picked up and placed manually on the matrix diagram. More significantly from a theoretical point of view, the tasks differed with regard to their *interactivity*. In all the studies, some learners were not allowed to interact when they listened to the directives, even if they did not understand them, while other learners were allowed (indeed, encouraged) to interact by requesting clarification. One of the purposes of the study, in fact, was to compare comprehension and acquisition under these two conditions. Finally, the tasks differed in terms of the *input source*. In Ellis et al. (1994) and in Ellis and Heimbach (1997) the source of input was the classroom teacher (i.e. the learners functioned as listeners). However, in one of the conditions studied in Ellis and He (1999), the source of the input was the learners (i.e. learners addressed the directives to each other). As we will see later, where there was interactivity and, in particular, where the learners acted as the source of the input, the tasks became more reciprocal in nature. However, because the degree of interactivity was still restricted by the inherent structure of the tasks, they remained essentially non-reciprocal in type. Table 3.1 summarises the main design features of the tasks.

Table 3.1   Main design features of the non-reciprocal tasks used in the studies

Study	Content	Response manner	Interactivity	Input source
Ellis et al. (1994)	Kitchen; objects found in a kitchen	Students write numbers of pictures of kitchen objects in a matrix picture of a kitchen	Students permitted to signal non-comprehension in one of the task conditions but not in other two	Teacher
Ellis and Heimbach (1997)	Bugs and birds, cages	Students place small cards with pictures in a diagram of coloured cages	Students interact with teacher in pairs and in small groups	Teacher
Ellis and He (1999)	Furniture; apartment	Students write in numbers of pictures of furniture in a plan of an apartment	Students permitted to signal non-comprehension in two of the task conditions but not in the other	Teacher in two of the conditions; fellow students in the third condition

The tasks were designed to test specific hypotheses relating to L2 comprehension and acquisition. In the next section, the theoretical basis of these hypotheses is discussed.

INPUT, INTERACTION AND LANGUAGE ACQUISITION: THE THEORETICAL BACKGROUND

A number of researchers have argued that acquisition occurs incidentally when learners are able to comprehend the input to which they are exposed. Krashen (1985, 1994) has argued that the 'fundamental principle' of L2 acquisition is that 'acquisition', which he defines as the subconscious process of internalising new linguistic forms and their meanings, will occur automatically if learners receive comprehensible input. According to Krashen's Input Hypothesis, learners need (1) access to comprehensible input and (2) a low affective filter that makes them open to the input in order to acquire. Krashen identifies two primary ways in which input is made comprehensible. Firstly, speakers employ 'simplified registers' when speaking to learners. These registers provide learners with the kind of 'modified input' illustrated in the previous section. They involve what Krashen (1981) refers to as 'rough tuning', i.e. pitching the input at a level that enables the learner to understand, but also containing some linguistic forms that the learner has not yet acquired. Secondly, listeners can use contextual information to help them decode input containing unknown linguistic forms and thereby comprehend and acquire them.

The idea that comprehension is crucial for acquisition also underlies Long's Interaction Hypothesis (see Long, 1983), according to which:

- comprehensible input is necessary for acquisition; and
- modifications to the interactional structure of conversations which take place in the process of negotiating solutions to communication problems help to make input comprehensible to the learner[1] and, thereby, potentially enable learners to process linguistic forms that are problematic to them.

Interactional modifications can be triggered in a number of ways (see, for example, Varonis and Gass, 1985). In the case of the interactions arising from the kind of task described above, the trigger was a directive which a learner failed to understand, often because he or she did not know a key lexical item. The indicator of non-understanding took the form of a clarification request and the teacher's response usually involved some attempt to define the meaning of the key lexical item. Here is an example, taken from Ellis et al. (1994):

(3)   T: We have an apple. And I'd like you to put the apple in the sink. (Trigger)
       S: What is the sink? (Indicator)
       T: Sink is a place to wash dishes. It's a hole where you wash dishes. (Response)

Such negotiation provides the learners with information that may help them to acquire new language. For example, in the àbove exchange, learners are given the opportunity to learn the meaning of 'sink'. Such interactions, assuming they engage the learner in message-oriented communication, involve *incidental* rather than *intentional* acquisition (Schmidt, 1990). Of course, they may also result in some kind of deliberate attempt on the part of the learner to memorise the new items.

There are a number of objections to the central claim advanced by Krashen and Long – namely, that acquisition will occur naturally if learners understand what is said to them. One obvious objection is that neither Krashen nor Long specify what is meant by 'comprehension'. As Anderson and Lynch (1988) point out, comprehension involves degrees of understanding. At one end of the continuum is total non-comprehension (i.e. the listener does not even hear what is said), while at the other is successful comprehension (i.e. the listener has attended to the message fully and is able to construct a coherent interpretation). Intermediate levels of comprehension arise when the listener can hear words but cannot fully understand them, or can hear them and has some rather imprecise idea of what they mean, or is able to hear and understand what has been said but has 'switched off', so the input goes in one ear and out of the other. A key question, not addressed by either Krashen or Long, is: What degree of comprehension is necessary for acquisition to take place?

Other applied linguists have pointed out that there is a theoretical need to distinguish input that functions as intake for comprehension and input that functions as intake for learning. White (1987), for example, argues that the kind of simplified input that works well for comprehension may be of little value for acquisition because it deprives learners of essential information about the target language. This is not a strong argument, however, because it views simplified registers as static. In fact, research has shown that such registers are progressively complexified in accordance with the language proficiency of the learners (see, for example, Henzl, 1979). It would seem likely, then, that simplified input does not totally deprive learners of the input that is crucial to acquisition, but rather systematically supplies them with input that is more and more linguistically complex. If one assumes that this input is one step ahead of learner syntactic processing, then, it may serve as the ideal source of input that Krashen claims it to be.

A stronger criticism of the Input and Interaction Hypotheses can be found in Sharwood-Smith's (1986) argument that there are two ways of processing input, one involving comprehension and the other acquisition. He argues that acquisition only occurs when learners discover that their original surface structure representation of the input does not match the semantic representation required by the situation. It will not occur if learners rely purely on top-down processing by utilising non-linguistic input to infer what is meant; extensive bottom-up processing is also needed. In other words, comprehension is necessary but not sufficient for acquisition to take place. Faerch and Kasper (1986) offer a similar view, arguing that interactional input modifications will only lead to acquisition if learners recognise that a 'gap' in understanding is the result, not of the interlocutor's failure to make herself understood, but of the learner's own lack of linguistic knowledge. They also point out that not all communication problems, even when fully negotiated, will contribute to acquisition.

A further challenge to the position adopted by Krashen comes from recent work on the role of consciousness in language acquisition. Krashen has consistently argued that acquisition is a subconscious process (i.e. learners are not aware of what they attend to in the input or of what they acquire). Schmidt (1990, 1994), however, has argued persuasively that what he calls 'noticing' is a conscious process. Furthermore, he claims that 'noticing' and 'noticing-the-gap' (i.e. identifying how the input to which the learner is exposed differs from the output the learner is able to generate) are essential processes in L2 acquisition. He refers to a diary study of his own learning of Portuguese in Brazil to demonstrate that in nearly every case new forms that appeared in his spontaneous speech were consciously attended to previously in the input (see Schmidt and Frota, 1986). Schmidt's position is clearly incompatible with that of Krashen. However, a role for consciousness would seem to be implicit in Long's Interaction Hypothesis if it is assumed that one of the principal functions of interactional modifications is to draw the learners' conscious attention to the linguistic properties of the input and how these differ from the properties of the learners' output (Ellis, 1995). In fact, Long (1996) is explicit in acknowledging the consciousness-raising function of meaning negotiation.

Information-processing models of L2 acquisition also distinguish the processes responsible for comprehension and acquisition. Robinson (1995), in a review of these models, identifies two general types. Filter models view information as being processed serially and attention as selective. Capacity models allow for the parallel processing of information with the possibility of allocating attention to two tasks simultaneously. The research considered in the next section is based on a capacity model. That is, the listener is credited with the potential to attend simultaneously to both message and to code and thus be capable of engaging in processing for comprehension and processing for acquisition. However, such dual processing only becomes possible when learners can draw on automatised knowledge of the L2. As VanPatten (1989) has pointed out, tremendous demands are placed on learners' information-processing systems when listening. The controlled processing required to extract meaning from input may prevent learners from attending to form or, conversely, the effort expended in attending to form may make the extraction of meaning problematic. Less proficient learners, therefore, may be faced with a choice – to attend to message content or to focus on the linguistic code. However, as they become more proficient and are able to engage in automatic processing, dual attention becomes more possible.

The assumption that language acquisition is entirely input-driven has also been challenged. Swain (1985, 1995) has suggested that learner output also has a role to play. Like others, she notes that learners can comprehend input by means of 'semantic processing' and thus avoid having to attend to linguistic form. She argues that when learners are 'pushed' to produce output that is concise and appropriate, they are forced into making use of the kind of 'syntactic processing' needed for acquisition. In this way, they may come to 'notice the gap' between the forms they use in their output and the forms present in input. In other words, output works together with input, the former serving as a cognitive trigger for the kind of input processing needed for acquisition. It would follow from Swain's position, that when learners have the opportunity to produce target items they are more likely to acquire them.

This theoretical background suggests a number of key questions which can be investigated by means of tasks that involve minimal reciprocity. These questions are:

1. What kind of input (simplified or interactionally modified) works best for comprehension?
2. What kind of input (simplified or interactionally modified) works best for acquisition?
3. What is the relationship between comprehension and acquisition? For example, are learners more likely to acquire new words if they understand the directives in which they are embedded?
4. What are the features of modified input that promote comprehension and acquisition?
5. Does the opportunity to produce target forms promote their acquisition?

In the following section, these questions are examined in relation to the comprehension and acquisition of word meanings. Vocabulary, rather than grammar, was chosen for study because it is reasonable to assume that measurable acquisition of lexical items can occur as the result of completing a single task. It is less likely that learners will acquire grammatical structures in the course of a single task.[2]

MODIFIED INPUT AND COMPREHENSION

Two of the studies investigated the relative effects of simplified and inter-actionally modified input on the comprehension of directives containing new lexical items. In Ellis et al. (1994), two groups of Japanese high school students ($N = 79$ and 129) completed the kitchen task (see Figure 3.1) under three conditions: (1) baseline (i.e. the directives were based on the kind of language native speakers use when addressing each other); (2) premodified (i.e. the directives were simplified by the task designer in accordance with the kind of language native speakers use when addressing language learners; and (3) interactionally modified (i.e. the students had the opportunity to negotiate meaning when they did not understand a baseline directive). Examples of these three kinds of input have been provided above. The results were clear cut where the interactionally modified input was concerned. In both groups, the students comprehended the interactionally modified directives better (means = 9.91 out of 15 and 10.69 out of 16) than both the students who heard baseline directives (means = 2.32 and 1.2) and the students who heard the premodified directives (means = 4.0 and 6.79). The results were less clear cut in the case of premodified input. In one group, the students receiving the premodified input comprehended better than the students receiving the baseline input, but in the other group the difference was not statistically significant. This study, then, supports that part of the Interaction Hypothesis which claims that opportunities to modify input interactionally enhance comprehension. It lends somewhat less support for Krashen's claim that simplified input facilitates comprehension.

It is important to note, however, that no attempt was made to control the time taken to complete the tasks under the different conditions in the study. In fact, as might be expected, the tasks differed in time, with the learners receiving interactionally modified input enjoying a considerable advantage over the learners receiving both the premodified and baseline input. It is possible, therefore, that it was the additional processing time rather than the interactional modifications per se that was important for comprehension. In this respect, it is interesting to note that the two groups differed in the time they took to complete the task in the premodified input condition (20 minutes in the case of one group and 10 minutes in the other) and that the students with the longer time demonstrated a comprehension advantage over the students receiving baseline input. In other words, premodified input may work well for comprehension when it is accompanied with adequate processing time.

In the second study by Ellis and He (1999), the time taken to complete the task under the premodified and interactionally modified conditions was carefully controlled. All the students ($N = 50$) took the same amount of time. This was achieved by having the teacher repeat the premodified directions to fill up the same amount of time taken by the students receiving the interactionally modified input. In this study, the difference between the comprehension of the students listening to the two kinds of modified input (mean for premodified = 6.67 out of 10; mean for interactionally modified group = 7.13) was not statistically different. It would seem, therefore, that what is crucial for comprehension is not so much the *type* of modified input as the time available for learners to process it.

However, this conclusion should not be seen as dismissive of the need for interactionally modified input, for it is probably the case that in many real-life situations the only way in which L2 learners can obtain the time they need to process input for comprehension is when they can negotiate for meaning. As Loschky (1994: 313) has pointed out 'increased time is an inherent difference between negotiated and unnegotiated interaction'. Nevertheless, it does appear that premodified input can serve just as well as interactionally modified input provided that learners have sufficient time to process it. Repeating premodified directions can assist comprehension as effectively as providing opportunities for learners to negotiate.

It is also possible that certain kinds of learners may experience difficulty in negotiating input. Individual variation in the ability to negotiate for meaning is a potential intervening variable in these studies. In Ellis, Tanaka and Yamazaki, for example, relatively few of the classroom learners made any attempt to indicate problems in understanding (e.g. only 7 out of 42 in one group). Most of the learners preferred to remain silent. This may reflect Japanese students' dislike of initiating discourse in classroom contexts. Young children, in particular, may find it difficult to negotiate meaning because they generally fail to signal when they have not understood a message (see Patterson and Kister, 1981). Such was the finding of Ellis and Heimbach (1997) in a study which investigated the effects of giving young children aged 5 to 6 years ($N = 10$) the opportunity to negotiate for meaning. The task in this study involved asking the children to locate a picture depicting a bug or a bird and then place it in the correct position on a board. Different versions of the same task were performed, with the same children performing in pairs and then in groups, with their teacher giving the descriptions of the bugs and birds in both settings. In the pair setting, only three children made any attempt to negotiate, even though none of them knew the names of the bugs and birds. In the group setting, there was considerably more negotiation, but four of the children still declined to say anything. This difference was reflected in the comprehension levels (a mean of 28% for the pairs and 68% for the groups). In the pair work setting, the extent to which individual children engaged in negotiation was significantly correlated with comprehension ($r = 0.819$; $p < 0.01$). However, in the group work setting, the relationship was not statistically significant ($r = -0.142$), presumably because those children who did not negotiate were able to benefit from the interactional work of those children who did. This study, then, suggests that meaning negotiation is less important for children than for adolescent learners (see also Scarcella and Higa, 1981) but also that when children do negotiate it helps their comprehension.

Another issue of importance in considering the effect of meaning negotiation on comprehension concerns whether those learners who actively participate in signalling a problem in understanding benefit more from the ensuing modified input than those learners who do not, but are able to 'eavesdrop'. We have already seen that Ellis and Heimbach found that children who interacted did not comprehend any better than children who remained silent in the group work setting. Ellis and colleagues also found no relationship between the number of times individual students interacted with the teacher and their comprehension scores. These results, then, support Pica's (1992) finding that there was no difference in comprehension levels among negotiators and observers in a study that experimentally manipulated the two conditions. However, Mackey (1995) reports a study showing that learners who actively engaged in meaning negotiation advanced further in the acquisition of question forms than learners who observed interaction without participating. Clearly, further research is needed to identify the relative contributions of participation in and observation of meaning negotiation with different learning targets and in different settings.

To sum up, there is clear evidence that providing learners with the opportunity to negotiate meaning aids comprehension. However, interactionally modified input may only work better for comprehension than premodified input when it affords learners more time to process the input. Premodified input can prove as effective as interactionally modified input when learners have the same amount of time to process it. Also, interactionally modified input may not be beneficial for some learners, such as young children who have not learned to signal non-understanding. Finally, it appears that learners may not have to negotiate to understand, but can benefit from the modified input obtained through the interactional work of other learners. In the following section, the effects of task performance on the *acquisition* of new words will be considered.

MODIFIED INPUT AND ACQUISITION

As all the studies only examined vocabulary acquisition, the results cannot address the relationship between modified input and grammar acquisition. Also, only one aspect of vocabulary acquisition – word meaning – was studied, and these studies did not address the role of modified input in the acquisition of other aspects of vocabulary such as collocation. Limiting the research to the acquisition of word meanings is justified, however, on a number of grounds. First, there have been very few studies that have explored the effects of different kinds of oral input on any aspect of L2 acquisition. Second, it is reasonable to suppose that exposure to input in the context of a single task will have some measurable effect on learners' knowledge of word meanings, whereas it would be less reasonable to expect it would do so on learners' knowledge of grammar or even of word collocation. Third, according to some theoretical accounts of L2 acquisition (see, for example, Ellis, 1996) acquisition commences with the kind of item learning that these studies investigated. It should also be noted that both the Input and the Interactional Hypotheses encompass all aspects of L2 acquisition, including vocabulary acquisition.

The methodology for investigating the effects of modified input on the acquisition of word meanings was the same in all the studies. The learners were pre-tested a week or so before they performed the task in order to identify a set of items drawn from a single semantic field (e.g. the kitchen) that they did not know. The pre-tests included distractor items to ensure that the learners would not be forewarned about the items that were to be targeted. The items found to be 'new' to the learners were then embedded in the directives that comprised the task.[3] After performing the task the learners were tested on their knowledge of the new items. In Ellis et al. (1994) and Ellis and He (1999) there was both an immediate and a delayed post-test. In Ellis and Heimbach (1997), one post-test was administered seven days after the task. The nature of the tests differed somewhat from study to study. Ellis, Tanaka and Yamazaki used a translation test and a picture-matching test (i.e. the learners were given a written list of the target items and asked to match each item with a picture). Ellis and Heimbach used a picture-labelling test (i.e. the learners were asked to name the bugs/birds shown in a series of flash cards) and a picture-matching test (i.e. they were given the name of a bug/bird orally and asked to choose the matching picture from a set of six pictures). He and Ellis used a picture-matching test (i.e. as in Ellis, Tanaka and Yamazaki) and a picture-labelling test (i.e. the learners were asked to label pictures without a list of the target items).

Two of the studies found that giving learners the opportunity to signal non-understanding resulted in their acquiring more new words than exposing them to baseline or premodified input. Ellis, Tanaka and Yamazaki found that Japanese high school students receiving interactionally modified input (e.g. mean for Tokyo group = 5.55 out of 19 items) outscored both the learners receiving baseline (e.g. mean = 2.02) and premodified input (e.g. mean = 4.02) on the immediate post-test.[4] On the follow-up test, however, the advantage noted for interactionally modified input over the premodified input was no longer apparent in the Tokyo group, possibly because the learners had made conscious efforts to learn the target words between the post-test and follow-up test. Ellis, Tanaka and Yamazaki also found that premodified input led to more words being acquired and retained than the baseline input. All these differences were statistically significant. This study only investigated receptive vocabulary knowledge. Ellis and Heimbach, however, investigated both receptive and productive knowledge. They found that, in the case of young children given the opportunity to signal non-understanding, a reasonable level of receptive vocabulary was achieved (a mean of 28.3% in the pair work task and 25% in the group work task) but very little productive vocabulary (6.7% and 0% respectively). As in Ellis, Tanaka and Yamazaki, there was no relationship between the frequency with which individual learners signalled non-understanding and their receptive vocabulary learning in either the pair or group work condition. Finally, Ellis and He found that, in general, adult learners receiving interactionally modified input scored higher in tests of both receptive and productive knowledge of the targeted words (e.g. means = 7.0 and 5.75 out of 10 respectively) than learners receiving premodified input (e.g. means = 6.17 and 5.6). However, in contrast to the other studies, the differences were not statistically significant in this study.

One way of comparing the relative efficiency of premodified and interactionally modified input for vocabulary acquisition is by examining the number of words acquired per minute of exposure. Ellis (1995) undertook such an analysis using the data for one of the studies reported in Ellis et al. (1994). Table 3.2 gives the mean vocabulary acquisition scores for the premodified and interactionally modified groups of learners. It shows that whereas the mean acquisition scores for the interactionally modified group were higher than those for the premodified group the opposite was true for the mean words per minute scores. In other words, although the premodified group acquired fewer words overall, they acquired them more rapidly, suggesting that if they had had the same amount of time as the interactionally modified group they might have acquired more words.

To sum up, the studies lend some support to the principal claim of the Input and Interaction Hypotheses, namely that premodified and interactionally modified input facilitate *acquisition*. Premodified input in the context of non-reciprocal task promotes vocabulary acquisition, particularly of receptive knowledge. Interactionally modified input results in more words being acquired. However, this advantage largely reflects the additional time learners obtain for processing the input when they are given the opportunity to signal non-comprehension rather than qualitative differences in the nature of the input itself. In Ellis and He, when the time taken to complete the tasks under the different conditions was the same, the differences between the premodified and interactionally modified input groups' acquisition scores were statistic-ally non-significant. In some cases, as shown in Table 3.2, learners acquire new words more rapidly from premodified than from interactionally modified input, the explanation for which will become clear later. Finally, any advant-age for interactionally modified input does not appear to be dependent on learners actively participating in the task; learners who just listened learned just as many new words as those who participated.

Table 3.2 Mean vocabulary acquisition scores for the premodified and interactionally modified groups (Ellis, 1995: 418)

	Post-test 1	Post-test 2	Follow-up test
Premodified Group (N = 27)			
Mean score	2.52	2.59	4.70
Mean w.p.m.	0.25	0.26	0.47
Interactionally Modified Group (N = 24)			
Mean score	6.00	4.75	7.08
Mean w.p.m.	0.13	0.11	0.16

COMPREHENSION AND LANGUAGE ACQUISITION

The studies also provide data for examining the extent to which there is a relationship between comprehension and language acquisition. This rela-tionship is central to both the Input and Interaction Hypotheses as both claim that acquisition occurs when learners are able to comprehend input. However, as we noted earlier, there are theoretical grounds for disputing such a relationship – namely, that the processes of comprehension and language acquisition are not isomorphic and that they only co-occur to the extent that learners engage in bottom-up processing and thus 'notice' input features that are not yet part of their interlanguage systems. It is possible, then, that the strength of the relationship between comprehension and acquisition will depend on the kind of processing learners engage in, which, in turn, may be influenced by the kind of input they are exposed to. Modified input, for example, may make it easier for learners to engage in bottom-up processing both because it makes certain linguistic features more salient and because it allows learners more time to process than unmodified input. The key ques-tions, therefore, are:

1. How closely are comprehension and acquisition scores related?
2. To what extent is the relationship between comprehension and acquisition scores dependent on the type of input?

These questions were addressed by statistically correlating comprehension and acquisition scores.

Ellis (1995) reports the Pearson Product Moment Correlation coefficients for one of the two groups investigated by Ellis, Tanaka and Yamazaki. These are shown in Table 3.3. Three points are worth making. The first is that the relationship between the comprehension of the directives and the acquisition of word meanings is not a strong one. Ellis and Heimbach (1997) also found the relationship between their child subjects' comprehension scores and word acquisition scores to be weak ($r = 0.459$ in the pair work task and 0.215 in the group work task). The second point about Table 3.3 is that the relationship is much stronger in the case of the picture-matching test (the follow-up test) than in the case of the translation tests (post-test 1 and post-test 2). In fact, the coefficient for the follow-up test is statistically significant ($p < 0.05$), although it still accounts for only a relatively small portion of the variance in the comprehension and vocabulary acquisition scores. The third point is that the coefficients are very similar for both the premodified and interactionally modified input; in other words, the strength of the relationship was not affected by the nature of the input.

Table 3.3 Simple correlations between comprehension and vocabulary acquisition (Ellis, 1995)

Comprehension	Post-test 1	Post-test 2	Follow-up test
Premodified input	0.33	0.40	0.59**
Interactionally modified	0.42	0.43	0.51*

$N = 18$; * $p < 0.05$; ** $p < 0.01$
Note: In this analysis the mean comprehension and acquisition scores for each directive were correlated. Hence the N size is 18, corresponding to the number of directions in each condition.

In general, then, these results support the view that comprehension and acquisition may not necessarily be closely related, a view that follows logically from the earlier claim that intake functioning as intake for comprehension and acquisition need to be distinguished (see p. 55). There were occasions in these studies where learners comprehended a directive containing a new word but failed to acquire the word, and also where they failed to comprehend a directive and yet acquired the new word. The former situation is not surprising for clearly there are many factors impinging on whether a comprehended word is stored in long-term memory (e.g. whether it is, in fact, 'noticed', and, if so, whether it is deemed valuable enough to store). The latter situation is more puzzling. One possibility is that the learners sometimes understood a new item but still failed to understand the directive as a whole. As I pointed out in Ellis (1995), this raises the important question as to what is meant by 'comprehensible input', in particular the unit of discourse (word, utterance, text) to which this notion should be applied.

There is a fairly obvious reason why comprehension was found to be more strongly related to acquisition when this was measured by a picture-matching test than by the translation tests. The picture-matching test used the same materials as the treatment task. In effect, then, the picture-matching task constituted a very similar situational context to that in which the words were first encountered and thus may have triggered memory. It should be noted that the word acquisition scores for the picture-matching test were much higher than for the translation tests even though it was completed several weeks later.

There is no evidence in these studies that the kind of modified input affects the strength of the relationship between comprehension and acquisition. Thus, although, the comprehension and acquisition scores of the learners receiving the interactionally modified input were higher than those of the learners receiving premodified input, this was not reflected in a stronger relationship between comprehension and acquisition. This again suggests that the advantages conferred by the interactionally modified input in the original study (Ellis, Tanaka and Yamazaki) are to be explained in terms of time rather than the inherent properties of this type of input.

QUALITATIVE ASPECTS OF MODIFIED INPUT AND ACQUISITION

So far we have focused very generally on the relative effects of baseline, premodified and interactionally modified input on vocabulary acquisition. However, potentially of greater theoretical and practical importance, is what features of modified input are important. It is this question that I addressed in Ellis (1995). It is useful to consider two sets of input properties – those inherent in the specific linguistic items/features and those that derive from the linguistic contexts in which the items/features were encountered. Both sets of features are potentially manipulable in the design of reciprocal tasks.

Two item-inherent properties were examined: *word length* and *prototypicality*. The choice of the first was motivated by evidence suggesting that longer words are generally more difficult to comprehend and learn than shorter words. (See, for example, Harrison's (1980) discussion of word length in relation to readability and Meara's (1980) observation about the effect of word length on Chinese learners' acquisition of English vocabulary.) In Ellis (1995) word length was measured in terms of number of syllables. The choice of prototypicality as the second property was informed by Rosch's (1975) research, which has shown that native speaker's have intuitions regarding which words in a semantic field (such as 'birds') are more basic (i.e. more 'bird-like') than others. It seemed possible that learners would be more likely to remember the more prototypical items. To provide a measure of the prototypicality of the lexical items, I asked 20 native speakers of American English to rate the 'kitchenness' of each target item in the kitchen task on a five-point scale and then averaged the scores for each word.

Word length scores were weakly and non-significantly related to acquisition scores for both premodified and interactionally modified input (e.g. $r = 0.03$ and $r = -0.25$ in the immediate post-test). Where the words in this study were concerned, therefore, length was not a factor. In contrast, prototypicality was. Learners were much more likely to remember 'basic' kitchen terms such as *stove, plate* and *sink* than less basic terms such as *lid* and *shelf*. Interestingly, the effect for prototypicality was stronger for premodified ($r = 0.64$ for the follow-up test) input than for interactionally modified input (i.e. $r = 0.49$) suggesting that one of the effects of interaction might be to modify the inherent learnability of words (i.e. negotiating the meaning on non-prototypical items helps learners to learn them). The effects of prototypicality on vocabulary acquisition warrant further study.

A number of linguistic context factors were investigated. The discussion here will be restricted to those found to be significantly related to vocabulary acquisition. The factors found to be most important were (1) frequency, (2) range and (3) length of directive. Frequency refers to the number of times a particular targeted item occurred in all the directives addressed to the learners. Range refers to the number of different directives in which a target item appeared. Length of directive was calculated by counting the number of words said by the teacher in performing each directive; in the case of the premodified input this was determined in advance, whereas in the interactionally modified input it depended on the amount of negotiation that occurred.

As might be expected, learners were more likely to remember those words that occurred more frequently. However, range proved a more important factor overall than frequency and constituted the single most important factor for the learners receiving the interactionally modified input. Together frequency and range accounted for half of the variance in vocabulary acquisition scores in both sets of learners. This result bears out the general finding of vocabulary acquisition studies (see Nation, 1990). The most interesting result, however, involved length of directive. In the case of premodified input, length increased the likelihood a word would be acquired (e.g. in the case of the follow-up test $r = 0.59$; $p < 0.05$), but in the interactionally modified input, the effect was reversed; the longer the directive, the least likely the learners were to remember the target word ($r = -0.47$; $p < 0.05$). The two protocols of interactionally modified input below illustrate this phenomenon. In the case of 'stove' the directive is short, providing succinct and relevant definitional information, whereas in the case of 'lid' it is lengthy and contains definitional information that the learners might have found difficult to process. This is reflected in the acquisitional scores for these two words. Thus, whereas elaborative simplification may help acquisition, over-elaborated input, of the kind that can arise through meaning negotiation, may have a deleterious effect – see also Chaudron (1982) and Ehrlich et al. (1989).

(4) 'stove'
  STUDENT: What is a stove?
  TEACHER: Stove is a hot place for cooking.

Acquisition scores: Post-test 1, 83%; post-test 2, 46%; picture-matching test, 96%

(5)   'lid'

> STUDENT: What is a lid?
>
> TEACHER: Lid? A lid is round. It's round like a circle, and you put it on top of a pan and it's like a hat for a pan and it keeps the food inside. You understand?
>
> STUDENT: One more time.
>
> TEACHER: OK. There's a lid. OK? And take the lid and hang it over the sink. On the left side of the frying pan.
>
> STUDENT: What is a lid?
>
> TEACHER: Lid? A lid is round, it's a circle, round, and you put it on top of a pan. It's like a hat, it's like a hat for a pan, for cooking.

Acquisition scores: Post-test, 10%; post-test, 20%; picture-matching test, 13%.

These results again cast doubts on the kinds of claims that have been made for interactionally modified input. Earlier we saw that when time is carefully controlled, interactionally modified input may prove less efficient in promoting acquisition than premodified input (see Table 3.2). One of the reasons should now be clear. Meaning negotiation takes up time and, on occasions, can result in input that overloads the processing capacities of learners and thus impedes rather than facilitates acquisition. In contrast, premodified input is economical with time and, providing learners are given sufficient clues to the meanings of new words, can promote acquisition more efficiently. Learners, it seems, need input that is elaborated (the length of the premodified directives was *positively* and significantly related to acquisition scores) but not over-elaborated (the length of the interactionally modified directives was *negatively* and significantly related to acquisition scores). This is not to say that negotiation does not work; it does, but clearly it is the *quality* not the *amount* that matters. This casts some doubt on the large number of studies investigating tasks that have been based on counts of the kinds of topic-incorporation features associated with meaning negotiation (e.g. comprehension checks; requests for clarification; requests for confirmation). Tasks that induce lots of negotiation work are not necessarily the ones that work best for acquisition.

There is, of course, much more work that needs to be done to investigate the types of modified input properties that are important for acquisition. The amount of input data analysed in Ellis (1995) was relatively small. Also relatively few properties were studied. Nor, of course, can it be assumed that the input properties found to be important in one task for one group of learners will prove significant in other tasks and for other groups of learners.

MODIFIED OUTPUT AND COMPREHENSION/ACQUISITION

So far we have focused on studies that have made use of non-reciprocal tasks involving premodified and interactionally modified input. A theoretically important question, however, is whether, as Krashen (1994) has claimed, acquisition is entirely input-driven, or whether learner output also plays a role, as Swain (1995) has argued. The study reported in Ellis and He (1999) addresses this issue, allowing for a direct comparison of the relative effects of modified input and modified output on both comprehension and acquisition.

In this study, the non-reciprocal task used in the earlier studies (and also in two of the conditions examined by Ellis and He) was redesigned to afford opportunities for learners to produce the target items in directives. Learners were given a matrix picture of an apartment and a set of small pictures depicting pieces of furniture. The teacher read out the words labelling the small pictures and the subjects wrote them down next to each picture. The teacher then gave an example of how to make up a directive about using the words and asked the learners to write directives about where to place the pieces of furniture in the apartment, one directive for each word.[5] The learners worked in pairs, giving their directions orally and negotiating meaning whenever they did not understand. The interaction afforded opportunities for the learners to modify their own output. The resulting task, although still primarily non-reciprocal in so far as it required only a one-way flow of information (i.e. from the student performing the directives), clearly corresponds more closely to the kinds of tasks discussed in the task-based research literature in that it required the learners to engage in speaking as well as listening.

The study, therefore, allowed comparisons to be made between the groups of adult learners receiving premodified and interactionally modified input on the one hand and a group which was required to speak the directives. As in the previous studies, the comparisons involved both comprehension and vocabulary acquisition. The results were quite conclusive. Giving the learners the opportunity to produce and negotiate the directives in pairs resulted in significantly higher levels of comprehension than exposing them to premodified directives or giving them the opportunity to negotiate the teacher's baseline directives (i.e. a mean of 8.13 out of a total of 10 as opposed to means of 6.67 and 7.13). Also, the speaking task produced higher vocabulary acquisition scores on the receptive and productive vocabulary tests administered immediately after the task was completed, and on all subsequent tests (see Table 3.4). In short, the speaking task proved more effective than the listening tasks with regard to both comprehension and vocabulary acquisition. It should be noted that all the tasks in the He and Ellis study took the same length of time.

Table 3.4   Mean vocabulary acquisition scores for the premodified, interactionally modified and modified output groups in He and Ellis (1999)

Group	Vocabulary post-tests ($N = 10$)				
	1	2	3	4	5
Premodified	6.2	5.6	6.3	6.2	6.7
Interactionally modified	7.0	5.8	7.6	6.4	7.3
Modified output	8.2	7.6	9.0	8.2	8.6

Post-tests 1, 3 and 5 = recognition tests; post-tests 2 and 4 = production tests

A simple explanation of these results is that giving learners the chance to produce new words (in both writing and speech) helped them to process them more deeply, whether for comprehension or for acquisition, than simply hearing them. This is very plausible. It should be noted, however, that the speaking task involved not just production but production in the context of interaction. One possibility, then, is that the interactions that occurred when the learners where interacting in pairs were qualitatively different from those that occurred when the students interacted with the teacher in the interactionally modified input condition.[6] This seems to have been the case. To illustrate the differences, consider protocols (6) and (7) below.

(6)   T: Here is a rocker. Please put the rocker next to the sofa in the living room.
       S: What is the rocker?
       T: A rocker is a chair that can be rocked back and forth.
       S: One more time.
       T: A rocker is a chair which can be rocked back and forth.
       S: Please repeat.
       T: A rocker is a chair that can rocked back and forth.

(7)   S1: Please put the rocker on the living room.
       S2: What is rocker?
       S1: Rocker is like chair. You can sit and move. Look at the picture. You know now?
       S2: Yes. Put rocker where?
       S1: In the living room. There are three rooms in your big picture. Put rocker in the room in the middle of the picture.
       S2: OK.

The interactionally modified group's comprehension score for this directive was 75% while the production group's was 93%.[7] Similar differences were evident in the various vocabulary tests. It is not difficult to see why the production group outscored the interactionally modified group. Protocol (7) is qualitatively different from (6) in a number of respects. First, the definitional information provided by S1 is couched in vocabulary ('chair', 'sit and move') that is likely to be familiar to S2. In contrast, the definition supplied by the teacher in (6) uses a low-frequency item ('rock') that the students may not have known. Second, the learners in (7) tackle the task systematically by breaking it into two parts; they begin by locating the correct picture of the rocking chair, dealing with the meaning of the unknown lexical item in the process, and then they work out where this piece of furniture is to be placed in the matrix picture of the apartment. S1 scaffolds the task for S2 by encouraging her to relate the definitional information he supplies to the picture and he then checks whether she has successfully accomplished this ('You know now?'). This kind of scaffolding does not occur in (6). In short, (7) demonstrates how the two learners collaborate effectively to achieve their goal. Of course, in such exchanges one learner's output is another learner's input. Thus, we cannot be sure whether it was opportunity to modify output or to access high-quality input (or, of course, both) that was beneficial. All we can say on the basis of this study is that giving learners the opportunity to produce and negotiate the directives created conditions especially favourable to comprehension and vocabulary acquisition.

IMPLICATIONS FOR LANGUAGE TEACHING

The studies reviewed in the previous sections have shown that it is possible to use non-reciprocal tasks as a tool for teaching specific linguistic items by embedding them in the text of the task. Because these tasks require a primary focus on message rather than code (i.e. the learners have to understand and act on a series of directives) they provide a pedagogic means for integrating what White (1988) refers to as the Type A and Type B traditions in language teaching. The tasks allow the teacher to focus on linguistic content and thus to attempt to intervene directly in the process of learning (Type A) while at the same time creating conditions that will foster the natural processes of language acquisition (Type B). In other words, the tasks foster the *incidental acquisition* of teacher-nominated items, with the students given the opportunity to acquire specific items while engaging in communicative activity. This is achieved by 'hiding' the linguistic focus of the tasks from the learners.[8] Nevertheless, the tasks do promote 'noticing' of the targeted items, as these must be processed in order to complete the task. The noticing takes place 'under real operating conditions' (Johnson, 1988) – that is, the students are required to attend to form while grappling with the process of making sense of what they hear. It is, of course, not impossible to devise reciprocal tasks that make the production of specific linguistic features essential, thus integrating Type A and Type B syllabuses, but as Loschky and Bley-Vroman (1993) and Pica (1996) have both pointed out, this requires considerable ingenuity as learners are adroit at avoiding the use of features they find problematic.

The main purpose of the various studies was to discover the particular conditions relating to the design of non-reciprocal tasks that promote acquisition of lexical items. The following are some of the conditions that the studies indicate may be important:

1. *Simplified input*

   Giving students the opportunity to listen to simplified input promotes both comprehension and language acquisition. It constitutes a time-effective way of ensuring that learners obtain the kind of input they need. Simplified text appears to work best for acquisition when it contains sufficient redundancy to aid processing, when the targeted items embedded within it occur frequently, and when they appear in a range of contexts.

2. *Interactionally modified input*

   Giving students the opportunity to signal their non-understanding of input can also prove effective for both comprehension and acquisition. However, there are a number of important provisos. Young children may not be able to benefit from such an opportunity because they have not yet developed the necessary interactional skills. There is a danger of interactionally modified input becoming over-elaborated with consequent negative effects for learners' comprehension and acquisition. A lot depends on the quality of the meaning negotiation (e.g. with how a teacher handles a problem when it arises). Teachers need to be skilled at 'pitching' the input at the right level for their students.

3. *Modified output*
Allowing learners the opportunity to clarify their own output has a qualitative effect on the interaction that facilitates both comprehension and language acquisition. Asking students to perform non-reciprocal tasks in pairs, then, can be seen as methodologically sound.[9]

4. *Comprehension*
While comprehending input is obviously important for completing a task successfully, it does not guarantee acquisition of the targeted items. Acquisition can occur even if the input has not been fully comprehended. It does not follow, therefore, where acquisition is concerned, that a task has to be carried out in such a way that students achieve full comprehension.

The studies involved child, adolescent and adult learners of English as a foreign/second language. However, the groups investigated, as in most other L2 classroom studies of this kind, have been relatively small (between 10 and 43). The studies have involved just one type of non-reciprocal task where students listen to or speak directives and demonstrate their understanding by locating objects on some kind of visual display. Given the enormous diversity in instructional settings, in types of learners and the kinds of tasks now available, it is obviously necessary to 'apply with caution' (Hatch, 1978). The conditions outlined above, therefore, should be treated as 'provisional specifications' (Stenhouse, 1975); they require further research of an 'insider' kind (Widdowson, 1990).

CONCLUSION

The studies reviewed in this chapter were carried out with the dual purpose of testing various hypotheses drawn from theories of L2 acquisition and also investigating the potential pedagogical uses of a particular kind of task (non-reciprocal tasks). As such, they reflect much of the task-based research that has taken place to date. As Pica (1997) has pointed out, the use of communicative tasks constitutes 'a growing area of compatibility between the fields of L2 teaching and research' (p. 61). Non-reciprocal tasks warrant careful study because they provide a context for investigating the Input, Interaction and Modified Output Hypotheses which have assumed such importance in mainstream SLA, and because they constitute a powerful device for integrating interventionist and non-interventionist teaching. They serve as an effective way of directing learners' attention to the linguistic code while communicating for meaning. In this respect, they are of great potential value to researchers and teachers.

There is, however, a general limitation of task-based research that is reflected in the studies we have examined. The theoretical framework which informed the studies was drawn from a computational model of L2 acquisition. This assumes that acquisition occurs when learners have the opportunity to process input and output. In this framework, tasks constitute a pyscholinguistic context for studying acquisition by providing or eliciting samples of input and output.

However, tasks are in actuality devices for creating social contexts as the 'activity' that arises from them can vary in accordance with the culturally and socially constituted goals of the participants (Coughlan and Duff, 1994). For example, in the study by Ellis and He (1999), the teacher and the students appear to have interpreted the task differently. The teacher saw it as a kind of 'test' designed to measure how well the students could understand the directions and learn the new words, whereas the students treated it more as a collaborative problem-solving activity. This suggests the need to examine tasks from a socio-cultural perspective[10] by investigating how task participants come to perform a task in the way they do and how this impacts on acquisition. Such a perspective may also have the advantage of corresponding more closely to how teachers and students, as social agents, orientate to tasks. Future research, then, also needs to consider how opportunities for processing language arise out of the choices that the task participants make as social agents; it ideally requires attention to both the psycholinguistic and social contexts that are created when different learners perform different tasks under different conditions.

NOTES

1. Long (1996) has revised and expanded the Interaction Hypothesis. Whereas earlier versions, as summarised here, refer only to comprehensible input, the later version also recognises that interaction can contribute to language acquisition by providing negative feedback and opportunities for learners to modify their output.

2. Of course much depends on what is meant by the term 'acquire' a grammatical structure. It is quite possible that learners will 'notice' a new grammatical feature while performing a task and perhaps also store this feature in long-term memory. It is much less likely, however, that they will 'acquire' it in the sense of being able to use it accurately in their own subsequent productions. Tasks involving structured input can provide a basis for investigating the 'noticing' of grammatical features (see, for example, Alanen, 1995).

3. In some of the studies, not all the targeted items were 'new' to the learners (i.e. some of the learners already knew some of the items). This was because it proved impossible to identify sufficient items that were entirely new to all the learners. However, at least 80% of the items were unknown by all learners in each study.

4. In one of the groups studied by Ellis et al. (1994), no scores were available for the learners receiving baseline input. However, the learners in this group who received interactionally modified input outscored those receiving premodified input.

5. It should be noted that, although the learners were instructed to use the words they were given to write their directives, they were nevertheless primarily focused on meaning rather than form in this task. Their task was to prepare, say and negotiate directives about where to place the pieces of furniture. The interactions that took place were quite clearly message oriented, as protocol (7) on p. 68 illustrates.

6. The study by Ellis and He does not make it possible to decide between these two explanations of the beneficial effects of the output condition as the learners had both the opportunity to produce the directives orally and negotiate them when they did not understand. It should be noted, however, that this confounding of variables (output and interaction) is inevitable when the output occurs in the context of conversation.

7. The premodified groups' comprehension and vocabulary acquisition scores were very close to those of the interactionally modified group.

8. Of course, it is always possible that the learners will become aware of the linguistic focus in which case they are more likely to engage in *intentional acquisition*. In such a case, it might be argued that the 'activity' that results from the 'task' is more like that which might be expected from a 'practice exercise'. In the studies reported in this chapter, the teachers did not feel that this happened (i.e. the learners did not attempt to deliberately memorize the target items while they were performing the tasks).

9. The use of pair and group work in task-based teaching is, of course, well established. However, its value has been disputed – for example, by Prabhu (1987). There is, in fact, very little research in the field of language teaching that has directly addressed the relative advantages of performing the same task in lockstep and pair-work conditions.

10. Brooks and Donato (1994) report a study of tasks from a socio-cultural perspective. They conclude that 'encoding–decoding perspectives, prevalent in much second language research on learner-to-learner speech activity, are inappropriate for capturing and understanding what . . . learners are attempting to accomplish during their face-to-face activity' (p. 262).

REFERENCES

Alanen, R. (1995) Input enhancement and rule presentation in second language acquisition. In R. Schmidt (ed.) *Attention and Awareness in Foreign Language Learning*. Honolulu: University of Hawai'i Press.

Anderson, A. and Lynch, T. (1988) *Listening*. Oxford: Oxford University Press.

Brooks, F. and Donato, R. (1994) Vygotskian approaches to understanding foreign language learner discourse during communicative tasks. *Hispania*, 77: 262–74.

Chaudron, C. (1982) Vocabulary elaboration in teachers' speech to L2 learners. *Studies in Second Language Acquisition*, 4: 170–80.

Coughlan, P. and Duff, P. (1994) Same task, different activities: Analysis of SLA from an activity theory perspective. In J. Lantolf and G. Appel (eds).

Crookes, G. and Gass, S. (eds) (1993) *Tasks and Language Learning: Integrating Theory and Practice*. Clevedon: Multilingual Matters.

Ehrlich, S., Avery, P. and Yorio, C. (1989) Discourse structure and the negotiation of comprehensible input. *Studies in Second Language Acquisition,* 11: 397–414.

Ellis, N. (1996) Sequencing in SLA: Phonological memory, chunking and points of order. *Studies in Second Language Acquisition,* 18: 91–126.

Ellis, R. (1995) Modified input and the acquisition of word meanings. *Applied Linguistics,* 16: 409–41.

Ellis, R. and He, X. (1999) The roles of modified input and output in the incidental acquisition of word meanings. *Studies in Second Language Acquisition,* 21.

Ellis, R. and Heimbach, R. (1997) Bugs and birds: Children's acquisition of second language vocabulary through interaction. *System,* 25: 247–59.

Ellis, R., Tanaka, Y. and Yamazaki, A. (1994) Classroom interaction, comprehension and the acquisition of word meanings. *Language Learning,* 44: 449–91.

Faerch, C. and Kasper, G. (1986) The role of comprehension in second language acquisition. *Applied Linguistics,* 7: 257–74.

Gass, S. and Madden, C. (eds) (1985) *Input in Second Language Acquisition.* Rowley, MA: Newbury House.

Hatch, E. (1978) Apply with caution. *Studies in Second Language Acquisition,* 2: 123–43.

Harrison, C. (1980) *Readability in the Classroom.* Cambridge: Cambridge University Press.

Henzl, V. (1979) Foreigner talk in the classroom. *International Review of Applied Linguistics,* 17: 159–65.

Johnson, K. (1988) Mistake correction. *English Language Teaching Journal,* 42: 89–96.

Klippel, F. (1984) *Keep Talking.* Cambridge: Cambridge University Press.

Krashen, S. (1981) *Second Language Acquisition and Second Language Learning.* Oxford: Pergamon.

Krashen, S. (1985) *The Input Hypothesis.* London: Longman.

Krashen, S. (1994) The input hypothesis and its rivals. In N. Ellis (ed.) *Implicit and Explicit Learning of Languages.* London: Academic Press.

Lantolf, J. and Appel, G. (eds) (1994) *Vygotskian Approaches to Second Language Research.* Norwood, NJ: Ablex.

Long, M. (1983) Native speaker/non-native speaker conversation and the negotiation of comprehensible input. *Applied Linguistics,* 4: 126–41.

Long, M. (1996) The role of the linguistic environment in second language acquisition. In W. Ritchie and T. Bhatia (eds) *Handbook of Language Acquisition,* Vol. 2: Second Language Acquisition. New York: Academic Press.

Loschky, L. (1994) Comprehensible input and second language acquisition: What is the relationship? *Studies in Second Language Acquisition,* 16: 303–23.

Loschky, L. and Bley-Vroman, R. (1993) Grammar and task-based methodology. In G. Crookes and S. Gass (eds).

Mackey, A. (1995) *Stepping up the pace: Input, interaction and interlanguage development. An empirical study of questions in ESL.* Unpublished doctoral thesis, University of Sydney, Australia.

Meara, P. (1980) Vocabulary acquisition: A neglected aspect of language learning. *Language Teaching and Linguistics: Abstracts,* 13: 221–46.

Nation, P. (1990) *Teaching and Learning Vocabulary.* New York: Newbury House/Harper Row.

Nunan, D. (1989) *Designing Tasks for the Communicative Classroom.* Cambridge: Cambridge University Press.

Patterson, C. and Kister, M. (1981) The development of listener skills for referential communication. In W. Dickson (ed.) *Children's Oral Communication Skills.* New York: Academic Press.

Pica, T. (1992) The textual outcomes of native speaker–non-native speaker negotiation: What do they reveal about second language learning. In C. Kramsch and S. McConnell-Ginet (eds) *Text and Context: Cross-disciplinary Perspectives on Language Study*. Lexington: D.C. Heath & Co.

Pica, T. (1996) The essential role of negotiation in the communicative classroom. *JALT Journal*, 78: 241–68.

Pica, T. (1997) Second language teaching and research relationships: A North American view. *Language Teaching Research*, 1: 48–72.

Pica, T., Kanagy, R. and Falodun, J. (1993) Choosing and using communication tasks for second language instruction. In G. Crookes and S. Gass (eds).

Pica, T., Young, R. and Doughty, C. (1987) The impact of interaction on comprehension. *TESOL Quarterly*, 21: 737–58.

Prabhu, N.S. (1987) *Second Language Pedagogy*. Oxford: Oxford University Press.

Rosch, E. (1975) Cognitive representations of semantic categories. *Journal of Experimental Psychology: General*, 104: 192–233.

Robinson, P. (1995) Attention, memory, and the 'noticing' hypothesis. *Language Learning*, 45: 283–331.

Scarcella, R. and Higa, C. (1981) Input, negotiation and age differences in second language acquisition. *Language Learning*, 31: 409–38.

Schmidt, R. (1990) The role of consciousness in second language learning. *Applied Linguistics*, 11: 129–58.

Schmidt, R. (1994) Deconstructing consciousness in search of useful definitions for applied linguistics. *AILA Review*, 11: 11–26.

Schmidt, R. and Frota, S. (1986) Developing basic conversational ability in a second language: A case-study of an adult learner. In R. Day (ed.) *Talking to Learn* (pp. 229–326). Rowley, Mass.: Newberry House.

Sharwood Smith, M. (1986) Comprehension vs. acquisition: two ways of processing input. *Applied Linguistics*, 7: 239–56.

Skehan, P. (1996) A framework for the implementation of task-based instruction. *Applied Linguistics*, 17: 38–62.

Skehan, P. (1998) *A Cognitive Approach to Language Learning*. Oxford: Oxford University Press.

Stenhouse, L. (1975) *An Introduction to Curriculum Research and Development*. London: Heinemann.

Swain, M. (1985) Communicative competence: some roles of comprehensible input and comprehensible output in its development. In S. Gass and C. Madden (eds), pp. 235–52.

Swain, M. (1995) Three functions of output in second language learning. In G. Cook and B. Seidlhofer (eds). For H.G. Widdowson: *Principles and Practice in Applied Linguistics*. Oxford: Oxford University Press, pp. 125–44.

VanPatten, B. (1989) Can learners attend to form and content while processing input? *Hispania*, 72: 409–17.

Varonis, E. and Gass, S. (1985) Non-native/non-native conversations: A model for negotiation of meaning. *Applied Linguistics*, 6: 71–90.

White, L. (1987) Against comprehensible input: The input hypothesis and the development of second language competence. *Applied Linguistics*, 8: 95–110.

White, R. (1988) *The ELT Curriculum*. Oxford: Blackwell.

Widdowson, H. (1978) *Teaching Language as Communication*. Oxford: Oxford University Press.

Widdowson, H. (1990) *Aspects of Language Teaching*. Oxford: Oxford University Press.

Chapter 4

Rules and routines: A consideration of their role in the task-based language production of native and non-native speakers

Pauline Foster

INTRODUCTION

Until comparatively recently, 'idiomatic' was something of a rag-bag category into which language teachers were apt to consign anything too awkward to be accounted for by the rules of syntax. 'Idiomatic' would explain, for example, why we have *main roads* but cannot say *this road is main*, why our houses can be *spick and span* but not just *spick*, why we can say *you idiot* but not *me idiot* or *you stupid*. These oddities were regarded as on the fringe of language, amusing but not nearly as important as the syntactic rules which regulate the largest part of language use. Second language teachers might use up a few lighted-hearted classroom minutes giving learners a colourful idiomatic phrase of the day, especially of the fixed or metaphorical phrase variety (*he let the cat out of the bag, come to think of it, you're telling me!*) but the main focus of the lesson should be on productive and law-abiding syntax. Although the notion that language is largely generated by a system of rules is still central to much second language acquisition research, there has been a shift of emphasis in some linguistic quarters (though not in most classrooms) away from the centrality of grammatical knowledge in language use and towards taking the rag-bag of 'idiomatic' usage far more seriously. There is now a body of research in linguistics which studies the extent to which words operate in fully or partially fixed combinations as opposed to within a productive system of syntactic rules (see Weinert, 1995, for an excellent review, also Howarth, 1998). The use of fully or partially fixed combinations of words has been suggested as a processing strategy in both first and second language use which permits fluent and fast language production (Raupach, 1984; Pawley and Syder, 1983). It has been further suggested that this is also a learning strategy adopted by both first and second language learners whereby regularly encountered combinations of words are committed unanalysed to memory and then analysed for productive grammatical regularities (Ellis, 1996).

This chapter will look briefly at why knowledge of grammar has hitherto been regarded as the most important feature of the production of language, before considering in more detail why a knowledge of idiomatic word sequences can more properly account for a large part of normal language use. The second half of this chapter reports on a study into native and non-native oral language production in a task-based context. The study was designed to investigate the extent to which the native and non-native speakers exploited fully or partially made sequences of words during an interactive task, and whether giving planning time before the task began would affect the degree to which such language was called upon. The chapter concludes by discussing how an understanding of the role of memorised language in second language acquisition could be exploited in the task-based classroom.

RULES AND ROUTINES IN LANGUAGE PRODUCTION

Chomsky (1957) draws a famous distinction between *competence* (the native speaker's knowledge of his language) and *performance* (the native speaker's actual use of language in concrete situations). Having *competence* means having knowledge of the set of rules which enables speakers to tell which combinations of words are grammatical and which are not, and gives them the potential to generate an infinitely large number of well-formed utterances. According to Chomsky, this knowledge arises from an innate language faculty, endowed with the principles of a 'Universal Grammar' which underlies all human language. Chomsky is unapologetically more interested in this than in *performance*, which he sees as complicated by such factors as false starts, slips of the tongue and deviations from grammatical rules brought about by the burden of organising a stream of thought within the limitations of memory. In investigating linguistic *competence*, Chomsky prefers to invent sentences for analysis rather than use ones taken from life, with the result that his examples, though grammatical, are often remote from anything likely to turn up in conversation.[1]

Though hugely influential, and responsible for inspiring a lot of work into the nature of Universal Grammar and the 'deep' structures of syntax that might reveal it, Chomsky had his critics from early on. His lack of interest in real linguistic data made many people uneasy, especially when Conversational Analysis (e.g. Sacks et al., 1974) and Speech Act Theory (Searle, 1976) were both showing how language was as much restricted by social convention as it was governed by rules. In the field of second language teaching, the advent of Notional and Functional language syllabuses in the 1970s (e.g. Wilkins, 1976), together with Communicative Language Teaching, put a much greater emphasis on contextual appropriateness, recognising that certain situations required the use of conventionalised language and that to avoid embarrassment or misunderstanding a learner needed to know what these were. The faultlessly grammatical can be rude, odd, or comical.

Becker (1975) was one of the first to observe that, although native speakers might possess grammatical and lexical knowledge that enables them to produce a potentially infinite number of novel well-formed utterances, in practice they do nothing of the kind, preferring to cobble together memorised groups of words that everyone has heard before. He called this bank of memorised sequences a 'phrasal lexicon'.

> We start with the information that we wish to convey and the attitude towards that information that we wish to express or evoke, and we haul out of our phrasal lexicon some patterns that can provide the major elements of this expression. . . . Then the problem is to stitch these phrases together into something roughly grammatical, to fill in the blanks with the particulars of the case at hand, to modify the phrases if need be, and if all else fails to generate phrases from scratch to smooth over the transitions or fill in any remaining conceptual holes.   (p. 28)

Essentially the same observation has been made many times since (see, among others, Pawley and Syder, 1983; Widdowson, 1989; Willis, 1990; Sinclair, 1991; Nattinger and Decarrico, 1992; Lewis, 1993). The fluency and familiarity of native-like language can be explained by the fact that it is generally *not* composed of novel combinations of words but uses a lot of prefabricated sequences shared by everyone in the speech community.

Although there seems to be a general consensus as to the reality of these prefabricated sequences, they are difficult to define concisely. They take many forms and have many names (Becker, 1975; Weinert, 1995). There are fixed phrases such as *'be that as it may'*, *'see you later'*, *'when all is said and done'*; sayings such as *'there's no time like the present'*, *'dead men don't tell lies'*; metaphors such as *'ignorant as dirt'*, *'proud as a peacock'*; collocations such as *'flatly refuse'*, *'catch a cold'*, *'submit an application'*; phrasal verbs such as *'take after'*, *'get along with'*, *'look forward to'* and, perhaps least obvious but nevertheless widespread, partially preconstructed sentence stems such as *'to bring something to the attention of someone'*, *'to be sorry to keep someone waiting'*. The common feature shared by all is that they comprise or contain elements produced as wholes. Pawley and Syder note that conversational speech is characterised by fluent, grammatical clauses of four to ten words delivered at a faster than normal rate of articulation, and claim this as further evidence that the stream of speech is constructed of fully or partially memorised chunks that are single choices, not individual words brought together for the occasion.[2]

At the simplest level, we can see this in the frequency with which individual words form compounds with their neighbours. In a language such as English, the merging of two or more words into a single choice can be seen clearly in the way they are written down. *Needlework, suitcase, houseboat* are three obvious examples; *cupboard, understand, eavesdrop* are perhaps less so because their meaning is no longer the sum of their parts. Others, such as *inglenook* and *wainscot*, are among many that have outlived the words that gave rise to them. Etymological research shows us that some we might never suspect to be compounds are just that: *lady*, for example, is all that is left of the combination of two Anglo-Saxon words *hlaf* (loaf) and *dige* (knead). If we were able to investigate even further back into the origins of our words we might find that many more are unsuspected mergers of older and now vanished words.[3]

The spelling of compounded words – a process with which the spoken language is mercifully unconcerned – can be unpredictable. There is no firm rule on when to merge, keep separate, or hyphenate. Thus we have (according to the Webster's New Collegiate Dictionary) *wineglass* but *wine cellar*, *fingernail* but *finger bowl*, *halfback*, but *half brother* and *half-mast*. Ignoring the niceties of orthography, it is clear that words which commonly occur together in order to denote something are behaving as if they were single choices, and dictionaries are confirming as much by giving compounds such as *finger bowl* and *half brother* their own entries. For the spoken language, of course, there is no more gap between *wine* and *cellar* than there is in the middle of *wineglass*. In both cases the words have been in each other's company so long that they have effectively fused.

Spelling also reveals the fusion of grammatical words that occur together in a fixed sequence. We have *another, although, albeit, therefore, thereby, nonetheless, nevertheless, whatsoever, however, inasmuch*, and many others. In these cases, people have become so accustomed to them as seamless units that they do not perceive them as anything else, and it can be a surprise to see one written out as separate or hyphenated items, as sometimes occurs in older texts. *To-day* and *to-morrow* are still the preferred spellings of some older people, while many younger ones assume (with some justification) that *alright* is all right. Whereas these lexical sequences are produced as invariable chunks, others are open to some degree of analysis and substitution of elements. Consider, for example, the following sequences which appear to act as discourse organisers, indicating the general nature of what is about to be expressed.

> I was (just) wondering if . . .
> Yes, but the point/fact is . . .
> you'll never guess/believe . . .
> what really gets/bugs/kills me is . . .
> that's all right/OK for some people but . . .

Perhaps less obvious, but still powerful, are the bonds between words that work at greater distances than immediate proximity, as in the case of partially preconstructed phrases, sometimes called sentence stems. In these, a ready-made framework is provided into which the speakers have to fit only the particulars of the precise meaning to be expressed.

> who the hell do you think you are?
> who the devil does she think she is?
> who the blazes do they think I am?

> She's not the sort of person who would go around murdering people.
> Am I the sort of person who would go around stealing milk bottles?
> He's exactly the sort of person who would go around looking for trouble.

The development of computer software that can carry out lexicographical analyses of large databases of language has enabled researchers to collect hard evidence of the remarkable pervasiveness of fully and partially preconstructed elements in both the spoken and written language. The COBUILD project was one of the first extensive lexicographical analyses of the English language. Its director, Sinclair (1991), was led to conclude that language use was guided in the main by 'an idiom principle', and was best described as streams of collocational patterns that flow into each other. On the evidence of computer analysis we are not really creative when we compose language, preferring to use words in the same sequences and combinations as everybody else. *Knuckles* are *rapped*, *slates* are *wiped clean*, *tables* are *turned*, and some people wouldn't know a metaphor if it came up and bit them.

This does not mean that we are doomed to speak in clichés (though some people do more than others). Clearly we all have knowledge of grammar and use it to fit together familiar sequences of words, as well as to construct entirely novel ones. From the perspective of psychology, Ellis (1996) offers a process model of language learning, based on our often underestimated capacity to detect and remember patterns, which elegantly accounts for both our creative knowledge of language rules and our store of ready-to-use word sequences. Ellis argues that both first and second language learning is essentially the acquisition and analysis of memorised sequences. A learner acquires sequences of sounds in order to learn words, and sequences of words, in order to learn phrases. In both cases acquisition follows repeated exposure to examples. The more often certain sounds are heard in the same sequence the more likely is that sequence to be transferred to long-term memory. The more often words are encountered in particular patterns, the more likely are those patterns to be stored in long-term memory.[4] The learner acquires a database of words and their relationship to the other words that regularly occur with them. In the case of the first language learner, there is an automatic and implicit analysis of these relationships that results in the abstraction of grammatical regularities, but this does not override the memory store. We don't select the rule-based *this road is main* over the routine *this is a main road*. In this view, it is not necessary to explain first language acquisition, as Chomsky does, by reference to an innate set of linguistic principles. Grammatical knowledge is the outcome of language use, and not the other way round.[5]

Consequently, we are able to process language in two ways: the syntactic rules abstracted from memorised exemplars are used for the comprehension and/or production of novel or complex structures, while for the comprehension and/or production of routine and familiar structures we use more our instant access to a memory store of fixed or partially formed phrases. The time available and our familiarity with the subject matter are important determinants. The less time we have to prepare what we are going to say and decode what we have just heard (and in normally fluent conversations we have little), the more we exploit memory. The more familiar we are with the subject matter, the more likely it is that our memory will contain relevant ready-to-use language and the faster we are able to process it. The opposite case is equally true. Anyone who has tried to follow complex instructions for an unfamiliar task (such as tuning a remote control to a new television), will know that a slow and repeated word-by-word analysis of the language is often necessary, even if none of the words themselves are unknown. Ellis (1996: 116) puts it succinctly: 'linguistic analysis is as deep as necessary and as shallow as possible.'

This observation accords well with the model of the brain as a limited-capacity information processor (Anderson, 1982; McLaughlin, 1987). Paying attention to both the form and meaning of language represents a considerable cognitive burden. If we had to process all words by reference to the rules of grammar, we might have insufficient capacity to attend to the content of their message, especially when the forms are complex and the message is unfamiliar. We might often have to pause for thought, or even to stop everything we are doing, in order to carry on a conversation. Our reliance on ready-to-use 'chunks' of one kind or another is a useful processing strategy, enabling normal speech to be produced at seamless speed. This is well illustrated in the language of radio sports commentators. These people have the taxing job of describing events at the same time as they are happening, and without lapsing into silence. They seem to accomplish this by using a high proportion of language that is fully or partially prefabricated. In this way they reduce the cognitive burden of composing novel utterances in fast real time, and they reduce the cognitive burden of the listeners who have to decode them in fast real time. The examples below should be familiar to anyone who listens to football, cricket, tennis or baseball on the radio. Predictable shared routines make life easier for all.

> 'Manchester United, defending the goal away to our left, . . .'
> 'Warne now, from the pavilion end, comes in and bowls to Stewart, who . . .'
> 'Sampras, serving to the right hand court, is good, backhand return from Henman . . .'
> 'And here's the pitch. Swing and a miss, strike three!'

CHUNKS OF LANGUAGE AND SECOND LANGUAGE ACQUISITION

How far this chunking model fits second language acquisition is an interesting question. First language learners are small children with thousands of hours on the task of interacting with native speakers and building a memory store of word sequences. They abstract grammatical regularities from it without intention, or awareness that this is what they are doing (Locke, 1996). Second language learners are not in the same situation. Their exposure to the target language may be considerably restricted, and their ability to build a store of memorised sequences accordingly reduced. They may anyway, as adults, have a worse memory for patterns than young children appear to do.[6] Unlike first language learners, second language learners are likely to have some degree of explicit knowledge of grammar, either through their own conscious analysis, or through classroom teaching. This, coupled with a restricted bank of memorised language, may mean that they are more apt to use rules when composing language, or to overuse the stock of sequences they have memorised.

Casting some light on the way non-native speakers ressemble or differ from native speakers in their use of memory in processing language might explain some of the difficulties second language learners face, and how these might possibly be addressed in the classroom. To do this it is necessary to analyse corpora of native and non-native language for evidence of fully or partially prefabricated sequences – a process which is far from straightforward. In the first place it is necessary to define what you are looking for. As we have noted, there are various terms (some overlapping) for the different ways words link up together: lexical phrases, phrasal lexemes, chunks, sentence stems, multi-word items, formulaic phrases, etc. The research reported below is concerned with the whole range of these, and for the sake of simplicity the term *'lexicalised'* is used to describe any combination of words which are stored in memory as a fully or partially formed sequence, as opposed to words that are brought together on a particular occasion.

The next task is that of identification. Computers can work with huge databases of language quickly, but they cannot distinguish language which is lexicalised from language which is not, except for any fixed phrases and collocations which occur repeatedly. Unfortunately, the majority do not occur repeatedly even in huge corpora. Moon (in preparation), reporting on an analysis of a 118 million word database of English, finds that whereas phrasal lexemes (her word for the whole range of fixed and semi-fixed word sequences) were very common, most individual examples occurred less than once every million words. Even a corpus as large as The Bank of English at the University of Birmingham, now nearly three hundred million words, fails to show even a single example of many phrases that would be considered a normal part of any native speaker's repertoire. This indicates that the memory store of lexicalised sequences is (a) vast, (b) retentive and (c) made up in great part by items which are infrequently called upon. It also means that in a relatively small corpus most lexicalised sequences are very unlikely to occur more than once, and therefore a computer analysis which uses frequency as a criterion for identifying lexicalised language is not going to be helpful.

An alternative technique of identifying lexicalised language in a given corpus is to exploit a native speaker's intuition because, unlike a computer analysis, this can recognise even rarely used lexicalised sequences.[7] However, native speakers, especially those who are not accustomed to a conscious analysis of language, can be inconsistent in their judgements. (Willis (2000) reports uneven results.) One way to avoid this problem is to use native speakers who are already well versed in applied linguistics, whose intuition is shaped by professional experience, and who therefore have a good understanding of what is required of them. This ought to give greater reliability of judgement.

There is, of course, a further problem with analysing data from non-native speakers for lexicalised language. Native speaker intuition cannot necessarily penetrate all the way into the phrasal lexicon of individual learners. Non-native speakers are likely to have memorised sequences which are peculiar to themselves and unrecognisable to others unless flagged by frequent repetition.

The problem of identifying these may be insuperable, but may be addressed to some degree by using native speakers with extensive English language teaching experience who are thus familiar with non-native varieties of English and can make an informed judgement as to whether and where lexicalised sequences occur.

Finally, as even applied linguists with extensive English language teaching experience can be unreliable, it is important to collect information from several, to collate it, and to accept as lexicalised only those word sequences which the majority have identified. In this way, dubious or borderline examples can be eliminated and rare but clear examples are not missed. This is the approach adopted in the study reported here.

The corpus used for analysis was taken from that gathered initially for two research studies – Foster and Skehan (1996), and Foster (2000) – which investigated the effects of planning time on the language produced by native and non-native speakers doing classroom language tasks. For both studies the overall research question was the same: If people have a chance to think about what they are going to say before they have to say it, will their language be more fluent, more syntactically complex and (for non-native speakers) more grammatically accurate? To answer this, both studies compared language produced without any planning time with language that had been planned beforehand to some degree.

Foster and Skehan (1996) looked at the performance of 32 intermediate level adult learners of English. They were recorded as they transacted three classroom tasks, each time working with the same partner. The three tasks were: a *personal information* exchange in which the participants had to describe to a partner the route to their home from the college; a *narrative* in which the same pairs of participants had to invent a storyline for a set of loosely related pictures; and a *discussion* in which the same pairs again had to agree on a suitable prison term for a list of people convicted of various crimes. Foster (2000), using exactly the same three tasks, looked at the performance of 32 native speakers of English of approximately the same age and educational attainment as the non-native speakers. In both studies, half of the participants had to carry out these speaking tasks with no time at all to think about what to say. The tasks were explained, and then started at once. The other half of the participants received the same explanation of the tasks, but were then given 10 minutes of individual planning time before they had to begin. For the Foster and Skehan (1996) study only, there was a subdivision in the planning condition. Half of the planning condition participants were given guidance on how to go about planning what to say. They each received a written list of suggestions that they should consider carefully what vocabulary would be useful to them in the task, what grammatical structures would best express their ideas, and how they would reply if their partner challenged what they said. The other participants in the planning condition were given no guidance at all and were left alone to prepare for the task in whatever way they chose. The combination of the speaker-type and planning conditions in these two studies is shown in Figure 4.1.

Native speakers Foster (2000)	Non-native speakers Foster and Skehan (1996)
16 participants with unguided planning time	8 participants with unguided planning time
	8 participants with guided planning time
16 participants with no planning time	16 participants with no planning time

Figure 4.1　Number and type of speakers in the corpus

It was felt that to have asked volunteer informants to analyse the transcripts of all three tasks (almost 60,000 words) would have been extremely onerous. Therefore, as a preliminary study into the use of lexicalised language by these groups of speakers, only the data from the discussion task were analysed. The resulting corpus is thus only about 20,000 words (still a huge reading task), but has the unusual virtue of being recorded from speakers of approximately the same age and educational attainment, all discussing the same topic under identical conditions. Most large corpora used for lexical analysis suffer somewhat from being made up of data from disparate sources. To some extent, what this corpus lacks in size it makes up for in uniformity.

The seven native speaker informants who analysed the transcripts were all university teachers of applied linguistics with many years experience in teaching English as a foreign language. All were given a complete set of the transcripts of the decision task from Foster and Skehan (1996) and Foster (2000), shuffled so that native speaker and non-native speaker, planned and unplanned conditions were randomly mixed. The informants were given the same instructions to read through the transcripts and, without consulting anyone else, to mark any language which they felt had not been constructed word by word, but had been produced as a fixed 'chunk', or as part of a sentence 'stem' to which some morphological adjustments or lexical additions had been required. This information was then collated onto a master document by bracketing each phrase every time it was identified by an informant as lexicalised. The result was a set of transcripts marked like this:

> (((((((it doesn't matter))))))) (((((what the circumstances))))), (((((she didn't have the right to))))) (((((take his life))))). If she was that er emotionally (((((((you know))))))) er distressed, then she should have- (((((((I don't know))))))) (got out of the situation). (((((It's difficult to say))))) when you are not (((((in the situation))))) but ((((((at the end of the day)))))) she did (((((take another human life))))). (((((((There you go.)))))))

Only those phrases which were bracketed by five or more of the informants were used in the analysis.

According to the written comments of all seven informants, theirs was not an easy task. Lapses of concentration with reading meant missing even obvious examples of prefabricated language, so progress was slow and exhausting. All seven reported difficulty in knowing where exactly to mark boundaries of some lexical chunks and stems as one could overlap or even envelop another. Nevertheless, after a certain amount of self-imposed revision, each reported feeling reasonably confident with their coding. Figure 4.2 shows how the lexicalised language identified by each of the seven informants was distributed across the four conditions.

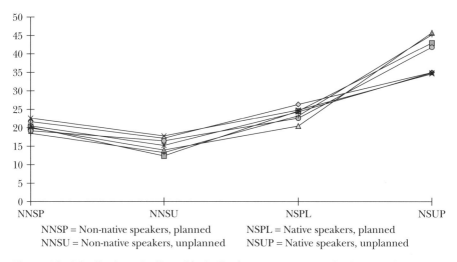

NNSP = Non-native speakers, planned   NSPL = Native speakers, planned
NNSU = Non-native speakers, unplanned   NSUP = Native speakers, unplanned

Figure 4.2 Distribution of tallies of lexicalised sequences across the four conditions (expressed as % of each informant's total)

As can be seen, all seven informants found the most lexicalised language in the native speaker unplanned condition, and all seven found the least in the non-native speaker unplanned condition. In fact, the graph shows considerable consistency in its curve at all points and indicates that the seven informants, working independently, were producing similar results. Thus, for each of the four conditions (native and non-native, planned and unplanned) the number of lexicalised chunks which had been bracketed at least five times was counted. This meant that the results would report on only those words which five, six or all seven of the informants had intuitively judged to be lexicalised in some way. Also calculated for the four conditions was the number of words appearing inside brackets as a percentage of the total number of words produced by the speakers in that condition. Compound words (e.g. *breadknife*) were counted as single items if so spelled in Webster's Dictionary. Others (e.g. *life sentence*) were counted as two. The analysis included both the fixed words in a lexicalised sequence as well as any required by the context to be added within it, i.e. *set him free* and *set her free* both count as three words. This was not an entirely satisfactory way to proceed because informants sometimes disagreed as to where exactly the sequence boundaries were (*it's a question of* vs *it's a question of asking* . . .). In these cases, the majority decision was accepted. There is a further difficulty, however. If lexicalised sequences are used and stored as wholes, it is not straightforward to justify counting the individual words into which they can be analysed. But in the absence of a better way to calculate the proportion of lexicalised language in the data, this preliminary analysis was undertaken, with reservations. The results are shown in Table 4.1.

Table 4.1 Amount of lexicalised language identified in the corpus

	Total number of words produced	Number of identified lexicalised sequences	Number of words inside lexicalised sequences	Words inside lexicalised sequences as % of total words
NNS unplanned	4089	261	690	16.87%
NNS planned	5577	349	961	17.23%
NS unplanned	5584	621	1803	32.29%
NS planned	4544	342	1140	25.08%

NS = Native speaker   NNS = Non-native speaker

The data are all from the first five minutes of the task, presented as simple totals and percentages. The results show that, whatever the planning condition, the native speakers' language was composed of a much higher proportion of identified lexicalised sequences. The planning condition had a different effect on the language of the native and non-native speakers. With the advantage of planning, the non-native speakers produced a lot more language in these five minutes (5577 words compared to 4089 words), whereas the native speakers with planning produced less (4544 words compared to 5584 words). However, for the non-native speakers the percentage of these words occurring as part of lexicalised sequences is practically unchanged by the planning condition (16.87% compared to 17.23%), while for the native speakers the planning condition causes the proportion of lexicalised language to reduce considerably from about one-third to one-quarter (32.29% to 25.08%). Taken together, these results suggest that native speakers are less verbose when they plan what they are going to say, and produce language which is less reliant on lexicalised sequences. For non-native speakers, the results suggest that planning enables them to speak more, but without affecting the level of identified lexicalised sequences in their language which is anyway rather low.

A finer-grained analysis of the data noted those sequences which appeared often, i.e. seven or more times,[8] those which appeared between two and six times, and those which appeared only once. The results are shown in Table 4.2 (overleaf).

This analysis reveals that the non-native speakers used some lexicalised sequences often. Of the 261 lexicalised sequences identified in the non-native, unplanned condition, a remarkable 42.5% is accounted for by just four recurring sequences.

Table 4.2 Frequency and variety of lexicalised sequences identified in the data

Speaker	Number of lexical sequences identified	Lexical sequences found only once			Lexical sequences found 2–6 times			Lexical sequences found 7+ times		
		No. of types	No. of tokens	% of total	No. of types	No. of tokens	% of total	No. of types	No. of tokens	% of total
NNS unplanned	261	65	65	24.9	29	85	32.6	4	111	42.5
NNS planned	349	56	56	16.0	37	100	28.7	10	193	55.3
NS unplanned	621	198	198	31.9	77	222	35.7	11	201	32.4
NS planned	342	190	190	55.6	33	81	23.7	4	71	20.8

I think (70 times),
I don't know (23 times)
how long (11 times)
all right (7 times)

With the planning condition, the non-native speakers show a similar depend-
ence on a slightly larger number of lexicalised sequences. Fifty-five per cent
of their 349 identified lexicalised sequences were accounted for by ten frequently recurring phrases, the majority of which appear to function as fillers
or discourse organisers.

I think (87 times)
you know (33 times)
I don't know (17 times)
I don't think (9 times)
I know (used to signal agreement, 9 times)
for me (used to begin an utterance, 9 times)
I mean (8 times)
what do you think (7 times)
a lot of (7 times)
real life sentence (7 times)

Interestingly, something similar is happening in the two native speaker conditions. In the no-planning condition, 621 lexical sequences were identified
of which 32.4% were accounted for by just 11 oft-recurring phrases. Some of
these were the same as those relied upon by the non-native speakers, but
most were not:

I think (51 times)
I mean (34 times)
I don't think (20 times)
you know (19 times)
sort of (16 times)
I don't know (15 times)
a life sentence (12 times)
I suppose (9 times)
set him/her free (9 times)
yeah, but (to begin an utterance, 9 times)
or something (7 times)

In the native speaker planning condition, only 342 lexical sequences were identified, and of these 20.8% were accounted for by four recurring sequences.
Again the majority of these oft-used phrases are fillers and organisers:

I think (35 times)
you know (19 times)
I mean (9 times)
I don't know (8 times)

In the unplanned non-native condition, 24.9% of identified lexical sequences
occured only once. In the planned non-native condition this figure is only
16.0%, indicating much less variety in their selection of lexicalised sequences.

There is an opposite trend in the native speaker conditions. Without planning, 31.9% of the identified lexicalised sequences occur only once. With planning this figure is much higher at 55.6%, suggesting a more varied selection of lexicalised sequences.

We may sum up these observations by saying that, whatever the planning condition, there was much more lexicalised language identified in the native speaker data than was identified in the non-native speaker data. Planning time not only reduced the proportion of lexicalised language in the native speaker data, it also reduced the repeated use of a small number of sequences while increasing the variety of the rest. For the non-native speakers, on the other hand, though planning time increased the amount of language they produced it did not reduce their repeated use of a small number of sequences which accounted for around half of all the lexicalised language identified in their data. Moreover, and in contrast to the native speaker results, planning time seems to have produced a less varied range of lexicalised language in the non-native speaker data, possibly because non-native speakers have a smaller pool of lexicalised sequences to draw upon and the more language they produce, the greater the chances are that sequences will be repeated. However, this finding, as with all the non-native speaker findings, could be because the seven informants who coded the data were not able to recognise language that was un-native-like, but nevertheless lexicalised. This is a point we must return to below.

It is interesting to compare these results with the findings of the syntactic analysis of the same data in Foster and Skehan (1996) and Foster (2000). In both studies identical measures were used to code the first five minutes of the data. Syntactic complexity was expressed as the average number of clauses per c-unit[9] and syntactic accuracy as the average percentage of clauses that did not contain an error. Fluency was also measured. This was expressed in two ways: firstly, as the average number of pauses of one second or longer in the first five minutes of the task and, secondly, as the average total amount of silence represented by these pauses. The mean totals for the discussion task only are given in Table 4.3.[10]

Table 4.3 Mean accuracy, complexity and fluency scores for the discussion task

	Non-native speakers (Foster and Skehan, 1996)			Native speakers (Foster, 2000)	
	Unplanned	Unguided planning	Guided planning	Unplanned	Unguided planning
Accuracy	63%*	73%*	71%*	n/a	n/a
Complexity	1.23**	1.35**	1.52**	1.36**	1.62**
No. of pauses	37**	17**	17**	28**	14**
Total of pauses	91 secs*	26 secs*	29 secs**	41 secs**	20 secs**

* = $p < 0.01$; ** = $p < 0.001$ for ANOVA (Foster and Skehan, 1996) and t-tests (Foster, 2000).

The Foster and Skehan (1996) study on non-native speakers found that the participants in the discussion task who had ten minutes' planning time were able to produce language that was more fluent, more accurate and more complex than that of the comparison group who had no planning time. Apart from accuracy, which was not calculated, exactly the same effects can be shown for the native speakers doing the discussion task in Foster (2000): without planning time the native speakers were more complex and fluent in their language than their non-native counterparts, but given planning time they too were able to increase the syntactic complexity and reduce the dysfluency of their language. The effects of guided planning on the non-native speakers revealed an interesting trade-off between accuracy and complexity. With unguided planning the participants were able to increase the mean syntactic complexity of their language from 1.23 clauses per *c*-unit to 1.35 clauses per *c*-unit. With the extra help of guided planning, this increased greatly to a mean of 1.52 clauses per *c*-unit. However, the parallel gain in accuracy, from 63% to 73%, which the unguided planning had achieved did not hold up under the guided planning condition, and instead fell back 71% – a small but statistically significant difference. Foster and Skehan (1996) conclude that the guided planners were attempting ambitious language over which they had poor control, even with the extra attention afforded by planning time.

If we take the results of the syntactic and lexical analyses together, it is possible to discern a different tactic operating in the native and non-native speakers. Both groups had to form opinions about appropriate punishments for a list of offenders, a task considered by the researchers to be cognitively fairly demanding. Under the pressure of having to produce language on this tricky subject without time to plan its content, the native speakers used a higher proportion of lexicalised language (much of which was not propositional but functioned as discourse organisers and fillers), a narrower range of lexicalised sequences, a moderate level of syntactic complexity and some degree of pausing. When planning time eases this pressure, we see a corresponding fall in the proportion of lexicalised language, from one in three words to one in four. The lexicalised phrases they did use were considerably more varied and there was much less need for time-filling phrases such as '*I don't know*', '*I mean*', '*or something*', '*sort of*' as well as less need to pause while speaking. In addition to these differences, the planners were also using language that was much more syntactically complex. Taken together, these observations suggest that planning time enabled the native speaker planners to use a more fluent, open-choice, rule-based style of language than their non-planning fellow native speakers.

For the non-native speakers, however, planning had no impact on the level of lexicalised language, which remained much lower than that detected in the native speaker data. A reliance on lexicalised language is perhaps not a time-gaining strategy for non-native speakers. For non-native speakers the greatest time-gaining strategy seems to be the most obvious, and that is: pausing. In the unplanned condition, they paused often (a mean of 37 times) and at length (a mean total of 91 seconds out of the five minutes). When planning time was available, pausing was dramatically reduced (to a mean of 17 times and a mean total of 28 seconds) while syntactic complexity and accuracy increased. This suggests the non-native speakers were using a rule-based approach to language production which requires either pausing or, better, planning time to execute. With the help of guided planning, we see ambition in rule-based production outstripping ability to maintain accuracy.

IMPLICATIONS FOR TEACHING

A tentative conclusion from studying these data is that the non-native speakers were constructing a great proportion of their language from rules rather than from lexicalised routines, with or without the benefit of planning time. One might speculate that classroom teaching which valued accuracy more than fluency would encourage this rule-based strategy with the unfortunate result that the learners are helped to be grammatical at the cost of being slow and odd. However, as we noted above, it is possible that the non-native speakers in this study were using idiosyncratic memorised sequences that no one else could detect. If it is the case that language learners are building their own memory bank of fixed or partially fixed sequences that may not be native-like, then there is a concomitant danger that successfully and regularly used examples will become too deeply entrenched in memory to be dislodged easily by further reflection. Inappropriate but useful sequences are, in a sense, undetectable signs that the learners are creating their own idioms, and these could form one source of fossilised language.

To help to prevent learners from committing inappropriate word sequences to memory, and/or to encourage them to build a more native-like memory store, it may be useful for teachers to enable learners to reflect upon their own language use and to compare it to native-speaker norms. This does not mean devoting part of the class time to an 'idiom of the day'. In the past there has perhaps been too much of an assumption that teaching idiomatic language means phrase-book type parroting, and no one wants to learn by heart, and out of context, phrases which he or she might never use appropriately. It would be far better to give learners the chance to see what language choices native speakers make in specific contexts. A task-based classroom could be an ideal place for this. Learners who have done or who are about to do a language task could listen to a tape or read a transcript of native speakers doing exactly the same task (cf. COBUILD course, Willis and Willis, 1988). Individual learners could thereby be prompted into reanalysing some part of their own interlanguage sequences or adding some new native speaker ones which they notice as useful. Additionally, teachers could choose to draw the explicit attention of the whole class to some native speakers' choices.

It was, for example, clear from the data used in this discussion task study that the non-native speakers were fond of a variety of expressions centred around the verb 'to agree'. It appeared many times and in many forms, some grammatical and some not:

> I agree with you
> I don't agree with you
> I am agree with you
> I am not agree with you
> I am agree.
> Are you agree with me?

In the native speaker data, the verb *agree* occurs rarely and in a rather different way. (*So, we're pretty much agreed on this one, I agree with that.*) For the native speakers, expressing agreement was usually done by using the phrases *that's right* or *that's true*; expressing disagreement was usually done rather obliquely by beginning an utterance with *then again*, or *yeah but*. The non-native speaker who overuses the grammatical *I agree with you* and *I don't agree with you* needs to expand his or her repertoire to become more native-like. The learner who constantly uses the ungrammatical *I am not agree with you* and *are you agree with me?* needs to reanalyse this verb as well as perhaps replace it in a discussion-type context with a more native-like selection.

CONCLUSION

I have argued in this chapter that words do not often, or even usually, work on their own. They work in close association with other words with which, over time, they form close collocational links, even to the point of occasionally blending with them into single words or fixed multi-word phrases. In our daily lives, we are fluent and native-like in our speech because we can exploit the many thousands of lexicalised sequences in our memory rather than having always to exercise our grammatical knowledge to create entirely novel ones. The native speaker data analysed here suggests that easing the language-processing burden by allowing planning time decreased the proportion and increased the range of lexicalised language needed to maintain real-time language production. This simultaneously permitted the native speakers to increase the complexity and fluency of their speech. The analysis of the non-native speaker data showed that planning time increased syntactic complexity and accuracy but did not affect the rather low levels of identified lexicalised sequences, possibly because the speakers were processing language more through rules than through routines. I have further suggested that the low levels of identified lexicalised language in the non-native speaker data were due to the fact that, if present, it was un-native-like, idiosyncratic and therefore undetectable. I have proposed that language teachers could exploit native speakers' examples in the classroom by helping learners to compare these to their own language choices during tasks. Building a memory store of lexicalised sequences that are subjected to analysis and reanalysis may be one way for learners to become more fluent, more accurate *and* more target-like.

ACKNOWLEDGEMENTS

I would like to thank Alan Tonkyn, Michael Foster, Kevin Germaine, Benny Teasdale, Alex Teasdale, Jane Willis, Dave Willis and Peter Skehan for providing native speaker intuition and invaluable help in this research.

NOTES

1. One of these, '*Sincerity may frighten the boy*', which is anatomised in minutest detail in both *Aspects of the Theory of Syntax* (1965) and *Syntactic Structures* (1957), is a particular case in point.
2. A Chomskyan might argue that the use of such chunks is simply a *performance* feature, a necessary strategy for the realisation of *competence* under the time-pressure of speaking. But these chunks of language are also evidenced in written data, where there is no such excuse. Moreover, the fact that all members of a speech community appear to share the same language chunks means that they are not one-off solutions to particular performance demands but are themselves an important part of any native speaker's knowledge.
3. A large majority of English place-names were originally two or more words. For example, Yaxley in Cambridgeshire is a compound of Old English *geac* (cuckoo) + *leah* (clearing in a wood).
4. There is good evidence that the ability to remember and repeat sequences of sounds (phonological short-term memory) is an accurate indicator of language learning aptitude (Bley-Vroman and Chaudron, 1994).
5. In a recent study by Myles et al. (1999) learners of French who were shown to have the best memories for formulaic language were also shown to be able to use elements of these formulae creatively as they progressed in the L2.
6. The tenacity of young children's memory for word sequences is demonstrated every time an unsuspecting adult makes even a minor change when reading aloud a favourite bedtime story.
7. I don't think I have ever used the expression 'well, you could have knocked me down with a feather' and I cannot recall the last time I heard it or read it, but I have no trouble recognising it at once as part of the normal British English idiom.
8. This is necessarily an arbitrary choice, as it is not possible to define what constitutes 'often' in this particular context. However, it was felt that it is reasonable to consider a sequence which occurs at least seven times in a 4000–5000 word sample as appearing 'often'.
9. A *c*-unit is an utterance consisting of either an independent simple clause, or sub-clausal unit, together with any subordinate clause(s) associated with either. See Foster et al. (2000) for a full discussion of measuring spoken language and a detailed definition of a unit to measure speech.
10. In the case of the Foster and Skehan (1996) data, the figures are from a one-way ANOVA. In the case of the Foster (2000) data, which is comparing only two groups, the figures are from a *t*-test. For these analyses of accuracy, fluency and complexity, individual speaker scores were measured and a mean obtained. This is different from the scores reported for the lexical analysis, where lexicalised sequences were measured for the group corpora as a whole.

REFERENCES

Anderson, J.R. (1982) Acquisition of cognitive skill. *Psychological Review*, 89: 369–406.
Becker, J.D. (1975) *The phrasal lexicon*. Report no.3081. Advanced Research Projects. Agency of the Department of Defense.
Bley-Vroman, R. and Chaudron, C. (1994) Elicited imitation as a measure of second-language competence. In E. Tarone, S.M. Gass and A.D. Cohen (eds) *Research Methodology in Second-Language Acquisition*. Hillsdale, NJ: Earlbaum.
Chomsky, N. (1957) *Syntactic Structures*. The Hague: Mouton.
Chomsky, N. (1965) *Aspects of the Theory of Syntax*. Cambridge, MA: MIT Press.
Ellis, N. (1996) Sequencing in SLA: Phonological memory, chunking, and points of order. *Studies in Second Language Acquisition*, 18: 91–126.
Foster, P. (2000) *Attending to message and medium: The effects of planning time on the task-based language performance of native and non-native speakers*. Unpublished Doctoral Thesis, King's College, London.
Foster, P. and Skehan, P. (1996) The influence of planning on performance in task-based learning. *Studies in Second Language Acquisition*, 18 (3): 299–324.
Foster, P., Tonkyn, A. and Wigglesworth, G. (2000) Measuring spoken language: A unit for all reasons. *Applied Linguistics*.
Howarth, P. (1998) Phraseology and second language proficiency. *Applied Linguistics*, 19 (1): 24–44.
Lewis, M. (1993) *The Lexical Approach*. Language Teaching Publications.
Locke, J. (1996) Why do infants begin to talk? *Journal of Child Language*, 23 (2): 251–68.
McLaughlin, B. (1987) *Theories of Second Language Acquisition*. London: Edward Arnold.
Moon, G. (in preparation). Frequencies and forms of phrasal lexemes in English.
Nattinger, J. and De Carrico, J. (1992) *Lexical Phrases and Language Teaching*. Oxford: Oxford University Press.
Pawley, A. and Syder, F. (1983) Two puzzles for linguistic theory: native-like selection and native-like fluency. In J. Richards and R. Schmidt (eds) *Language and Communication*. London: Longman.
Raupach, M. (1984) Formulae in second language speech production. In H. Dechert, D. Mohle and M. Raupach (eds) *Second Language Productions*. Tubingen: Gunter Narr.
Sacks, H., Schegloff, E. and Jefferson, G. (1974) A simplest systematics for the organisation of turn-taking in conversation. *Language*, 50 (4): 696–734.
Searle, J.R. (1976) A classification of illocutionary acts. *Language in Society*, 5: 1–23.
Sinclair, J. (1991) *Corpus, Concordance, Collocation*. Oxford: Oxford University Press.
Weinert, R. (1995) The role of formulaic language in second language acquisition: A review. *Applied Linguistics*, 16 (2): 181–205.
Widdowson, H. (1989) Knowledge of language and ability for use. *Applied Linguistics*, 10: 128–37.
Wilkins, D. (1976) *The Notional Syllabus*. Oxford: Oxford University Press.
Willis, D. (1990) *The Lexical Syllabus: A New Approach to Language Teaching*. London: Collins.
Willis, J. (2000) Lexical chunks: Identifying frequent phrases, classifying and teaching them. Paper presented at the *Association for Language Awareness 2000 Conference*, University of Leicester.
Willis, J. and Willis, D. (1988) *Collins COBUILD English Course: Book 1*. London: Collins.

Part II

STUDIES OF TASKS IN LANGUAGE CLASSROOMS

The three chapters in this part are all based on real learners, going about their business in class as normal, but nonetheless functioning as the subjects for research which is completed in naturalistic circumstances. In this respect the chapters contrast with those in Part I where, in each case, a research study was designed and carried out under focused investigative circumstances. In the studies in Chapters 5, 6 and 7, learners were operating within existing classrooms, and the creativity of the researchers is what enabled ongoing activities to be turned into research projects. Problems of generalisation to educational circumstances are thereby evaded, although, of course, this does not mean that the chapters in this part relate equally well to all other pedagogic circumstances, irrespective of proficiency level, gender, educational conditions, and so on.

Despite the acceptance of naturalistic environments, the chapters do manage to report on contrasts between different task types. In Chapter 5, Swain and Lapkin contrast performances on jigsaw and dictogloss tasks, two very common tasks within contemporary communicative language teaching. The authors propose that dictogloss tasks are more likely to generate a conscious focus on language. Samuda, in Chapter 6, contrasts what she terms knowledge-constructing and knowledge-activating tasks. The former, on which her study is focused, are tasks which are more likely to push learners to identify gaps in their interlanguage systems and to do something to fill these gaps. The latter concern tasks which make more salient existing – but possibly not well-controlled – language, placing the focus more on how an active repertoire of available language can be made more accessible. In Chapter 7, Lynch and Maclean study the performance of students across a series of question–answer interactions around the same poster presentation. They identify ways in which participants' use of language and focus of attention changes through the series of interactions.

Methodologically, there is a clear contrast between this set of chapters and those in Part I. There is some use of quantitative data analysis here, but this is largely at the descriptive level (although Swain and Lapkin do report significant results for some of the task comparisons that they use). In contrast, there is considerable reliance in these chapters on transcript data of task performance, and on the careful analysis of such data to locate examples of active engagement of form (in the context of meaning). Each of the chapters identifies issues of central concern, such as learner expressions of modality, before interrogating the conversation transcripts for relevant evidence. The focus is not as much on conversational analysis and its associated techniques as on the use of such data as a window to give access to language processes and interlanguage change. The authors rely on what have been termed critical episodes (Samuda and Rounds, 1993) to reveal the focus of attention for learners working on tasks. They attempt to show, with such evidence, how learners are focusing on language (cf. Chapters 5 and 6) or how their language changes over time (Chapter 7). This is difficult, since decision criteria similar to those for quantitative research do not apply (the cost of this kind of methodology), but each of the chapters is able to bring out how systematic data collection and research questions enable a productive data focus, and reasonably precise future replication of the studies.

Regarding specific research questions, the chapters are interesting in their similarities and differences. All are concerned with a micro level of analysis, in which researchers examine transcript data to reveal how ongoing language-processing decisions are made, and how acquisitional changes can be triggered. A pervasive feature in the chapters is how learners can be induced, through supported output, first to notice gaps in their interlanguage, and then to do something about such gaps. In this regard, they each build upon recent conceptualisations of interlanguage development (e.g. Schmidt, 1990; Swain, 1995), which have argued for the centrality of noticing as a precursor to language change, and 'pushed output' as the method that can (among other things) predispose learners to notice.

The chapters, however, are not simply concerned with the conceptualisations themselves: they also attempt to show how classroom conditions can be manipulated to make such desirable consequences more likely to occur. Swain and Lapkin explore this through the influence of task design, and the support provided to one another by interlocutors in collaborative negotiation. Samuda shows how task design can be exploited to make form–function mappings more transparent. She also shows how the teacher can play a very supportive role in making such mappings clearer to the student, by working with meanings encoded by the student which can then be elaborated, in terms of form, by the teacher, all during ongoing task completion and at a point when learners are likely to be particularly receptive to change.

Lynch and Maclean also explore the contributions that interlocutors can make during collaborative discourse, showing how some students (but not all) are able to exploit the cues given to them by a higher-proficiency interlocutor, and incorporate more complex language in their own discourse. But Lynch and Maclean are also able to show how, in a cycle of task repetition (and see Bygate in this volume), some learners are progressively more able to monitor their own performance (i.e. noticing their own output as potential input) and thereby improve. They also show how beneficial practice effects can occur during the repeated task completions that are required in the 'poster carousel' pedagogic task cycle that they have designed.

The three chapters in this part of the volume represent an exciting development in task-based research. They complement the more quantitative studies reported in Part I, and show how the insights from contemporary theorising about language learning processes (noticing, awareness, learners' identification of gaps in the interlanguage sysytems) can be translated into research studies which are deeply embedded in classroom realities. It is likely that this type of research will grow considerably in influence in future years.

REFERENCES

Samuda, G. and Rounds, P. (1993) Critical episodes: Reference points for analysing tasks in action. In G. Crookes and S. Gass (eds) *Tasks in a Pedagogical Context: Integrating Theory and Practice.* Clevedon, Avon: Multilingual Matters.

Schmidt, D. (1990) The role of consciousness in second language learning. *Applied Linguistics*, 11: 17–46.

Swain, M. (1995) Three functions of output in second language learning. In G. Cook and B. Seidlhofer (eds) *Principle and Practice in Applied Linguistics.* Oxford: Oxford University Press.

Chapter 5

Focus on form through collaborative dialogue: Exploring task effects

Merrill Swain and Sharon Lapkin

INTRODUCTION

In our recent research[1] we have been using tasks as a stimulus for generating talk among students (Swain and Lapkin, 1998). We have been interested in discovering whether, through output (the activities of talking and/or writing), learners notice gaps in their linguistic knowledge, triggering an analysis of input or of existing internal resources to fill those gaps (Swain and Lapkin, 1995); whether learners' output serves as a hypothesis of how to convey their intended meaning (Swain, 1995); and whether learners use language to reflect on their own (or their interlocutors') language use – that is, whether learners externalise their hypotheses about form and meaning, exposing those hypotheses to scrutiny and discussion (Swain, 1998; 2000). Our research has involved a search for tasks that will generate this sort of student talk with the goal of demonstrating its relationship to second language learning. The tasks we have used to generate such talk engage students in linguistic problem solving, are done collaboratively, and involve the production of a spoken and written text.

Studies such as those of Donato (1994), LaPierre (1994; see also Swain, 1998), Swain and Lapkin (1998) and Tse (1996) suggest that the talk which surfaces when students collaborate in solving linguistic problems encountered in communicative task performance represents second language learning in progress. In these studies, later language use has been traced back to dialogue occurring as the students worked collaboratively to express their intended meaning and carry out the task at hand. In these dialogic exchanges related to their ongoing language use, noticing, hypothesis formulation, and hypothesis testing have been observed to have taken place. These studies have relied on pedagogical tasks to serve as the stimulus to collaborative dialogue (Swain, 1997a).

One of the main rationales offered in the literature for using communicative tasks in language teaching is that second language acquisition is enhanced through the negotiation of meaning: '. . . language learning is assisted through the social interaction of learners and their interlocutors, particularly when they negotiate toward mutual comprehension of each other's message meaning'

(Pica et al., 1993: 11). According to Pica and colleagues, a jigsaw task – one in which each participant has some, but not all, the information needed to complete the task – is the type of task where opportunities for meaning negotiation are most likely to be generated.

With few exceptions (e.g. Fotos, 1994; Lyster, 1994; Swain, 1997b), definitions of communicative tasks emphasise the importance of a focus on meaning. Nunan (1989), for example, offers the following definition of a communicative task: 'A piece of classroom work which involves learners in comprehending, manipulating, producing or interacting in the target language while their attention is principally focused on meaning rather than form' (p. 10). An alternative view,[2] however, is that a task can still be considered communicative even if learners focus quite explicitly on form (Breen and Candlin, 1980; Swain, 1997b). This explicit focus on form comes about as learners attempt to express their intended meaning as accurately and as coherently as they are able (Swain and Lapkin, 1995). Experimentation with several different types of classroom activity (Kowal, 1997; Kowal and Swain, 1997; Swain, 1998) suggested that, when completed collaboratively, they led to a focus on form as students engaged in constructing the meaning required by the task. We chose one of these task types (dictogloss, described below) to use in the current study, anticipating that it would elicit from our students a greater focus on form than would a jigsaw task which, as suggested above, provides greater opportunities for meaning negotiation.

In this chapter we report on a study in which two communicative tasks, similar in content[3] but different in format, were used with adolescent learners of French. Our goal was to examine the data for instances of second language learning during task performance, anticipating differences due to the format (dictogloss vs jigsaw) of the task. Specifically, we anticipated that there would be less focus on form by students doing the jigsaw task, a typical meaning negotiation task, than by students doing the dictogloss task and that, therefore, the dictogloss task would provide more opportunities for language learning. This prediction was based on our earlier research using the dictogloss (e.g. Kowal and Swain, 1997). We also anticipated that because, with the dictogloss, a native speaker model text was provided, students' production would be more accurate. What we did not anticipate was that providing a text would focus the range of student performance in a variety of ways.

THE STUDY

Background

One purpose in conducting this study was pedagogical, since our interests focus on French immersion students, who, even after some eight years of comprehensible input, remain non-native-like in their spoken and written French (e.g. Harley and Swain, 1984; Swain, 1985). Although the instructional focus in immersion is primarily experiential or content oriented, there is some formal teaching of grammar. It has been observed that grammar teaching often takes the form of presenting and practising isolated rules and paradigms, and manipulating form rather than relating form to function (Allen et al., 1990). In terms of the three goals of second language learning that Skehan (1996) discusses – i.e. fluency, complexity and accuracy – it can be argued that immersion students attain fluency early in the programme and linguistic complexity continues to develop to meet the cognitive demands of their academic curriculum. Linguistic accuracy remains a goal to be actively worked on. The need to address the teaching of grammar in immersion curricula is well established, but there is little consensus concerning the most effective ways of doing so (but see Lyster, 1995; Swain, 1996).

For these reasons, our recent research has been aimed at considering pedagogical ways to encourage immersion students to focus on the accuracy of their spoken and written French while still maintaining the philosophy of immersion education – that second language learning be embedded in a contextually rich, content-based curriculum. We therefore considered tasks that would lead these students to focus on form without losing sight of the meaning they are trying to convey. Thus, as noted above, we have begun to explore the implications of different task types, in this case with a common content, for encouraging a focus on form.

In the present study, we asked students to carry out two contrasting tasks. Class J did jigsaw tasks; Class D did dictogloss tasks. In both cases, the tasks were preceded by a short lesson on French pronominal verbs as an input enhancement activity. Our hypothesis was that students doing the dictogloss tasks would focus more on form than the students doing the jigsaw tasks. Furthermore, other differences in students' dialogues and written texts would become apparent due to the differences in the nature of the two tasks, in spite of the similarity of content.

TASKS

As indicated above, we collected data using two contrasting tasks – a jigsaw task and a dictogloss (Wajnryb, 1990). The jigsaw task we used involved pairs of students working to construct a story based on a series of eight pictures (Appendix 5.1) in a two-way information gap activity. One student in each pair held pictures numbered 1, 3, 5 and 7 and the other, those numbered 2, 4, 6 and 8. The students were required to construct the story told by the pictures by looking only at the cards each held. Typically the students worked through the cards sequentially, alternately telling each other what their pictures contained. Then they wrote the story. As noted above, this type of task is thought to maximally foster negotiation of meaning.

The dictogloss task we used involved students listening to a passage read twice at normal speed. Each student took notes on its content, then worked with his or her partner to reconstruct the passage in writing based on the two sets of notes. Since the dictogloss provides content in the form of a native speaker text, we thought this task would cause students to focus their attention on the accurate use of linguistic form to a greater extent than the jigsaw activity.

To make the two tasks as comparable as possible in terms of content we proceeded as follows. We showed the series of eight pictures to three adult native speakers of French and asked them to narrate the story they saw unfolding. Combining their transcribed narratives gave us the text we used for the dictogloss (Appendix 5.2). The dictogloss text contains seven pronominal verbs (see note 4 on page 111), and the story told by the jigsaw pictures creates a similar number of contexts for pronominal verbs.

Participants

We worked with two grade 8 mixed-ability French immersion classes from the same school. Class D had 30 students and Class J had 35 students. The students were from a lower middle to middle class socio-economic background. The two classes were described by their teachers and the researcher who collected the classroom data as interchangeable. Also, the average pretest scores of the classes did not differ statistically. (The pretest is described below.) These two classes of grade 8 anglophone students had been in a French immersion programme since kindergarten. Until grade 3, all instruction was in French; thereafter, English language arts was introduced, and from about grade 5 onwards, approximately 50% of instruction was in French and 50% in English. During the French portion of the instructional day, selected academic subjects were taught in French along with French language arts.

Time-frame and activities

Data collection took place over a five-week period. In the first week, we administered a pre-test (described below). In the second week, we conducted a session to familiarise the students with the type of task they would be doing. To do this, we focused on the agreement of adjectives (which vary in number and gender) in French. A member of the research team taught a short mini-lesson on adjective agreement and led the class in either a jigsaw (Class J) or dictogloss (Class D) activity that foreshadowed the data-gathering session which took place the following week.

In the third week, we focused on a grammatical point – the pronominal verb.[4] A pre-recorded mini-lesson on French pronominal verbs (5 minutes) was shown on video. The video also showed two students working together on the relevant task (J or D), which served as a model for what the students were to do immediately following the viewing of the videotape when the new stimulus (jigsaw task or dictogloss passage) was introduced. The instructions were provided to the students for both tasks in French. An English translation of these instructions can be found in Appendix 5.3. The conversation of each pair of students was tape-recorded as they did their task.

During the fourth week, we transcribed the tapes. Based on the content of the dialogues of the student pairs, additional test items were developed and added to the pre-test items, producing a 'tailor-made' post-test for each class for administration in the fifth week of the study. Because the transcriptions and new item development were done under considerable time pressure, and because the identification of language-related episodes (LREs) in the conversations of these second language speakers turned out to be a complex and time-consuming task, only the most obvious and clear examples were incorporated into items for the post-tests. (Example 5 below is an LRE arising in the dialogue of one pair of students in Class J which formed the basis of the class-specific post-test item shown in Appendix 5.4, item type B.)

Pre- and post-tests

We conducted a pilot study with the set of pictures shown in Appendix 5.1 with a different class of grade 8 immersion students than the two used in the current study. Based on the transcribed, tape-recorded interactions of the students in the pilot classroom, and on the assumption that the content of some of these interactions would be similar between the pilot students and the main study students, a pre-test was constructed for use in the main study (see Swain and Lapkin, 1998). The three item types are illustrated in Appendix 5.4.

In item type A, because the student dyads often questioned the gender of nouns, a choice of masculine or feminine articles is provided to accompany each noun listed. Learners check the masculine or feminine article, or indicate that they do not know (*je ne sais pas*).

Item type B provides a 'certainty scale' where test takers make a judgement about the grammaticality of each sentence with respect to a picture, indicating that each sentence is definitely wrong (*certainement incorrect*), probably wrong (*probablement incorrect*), probably correct (*probablement correct*) or definitely correct (*certainement correct*). Students also have a 'don't know' option.

Item type C has a picture stimulus followed by multiple-choice answers. Students select the correct lexical item from among a set of four. Many of the distractors included were based on the dialogues of students in the pilot data.

The post-test contained all pre-test items in addition to the new tailor-made, class-specific items referred to above.

Scoring procedures for written narrative

The written narratives produced by each pair of students were scored by two experienced immersion teachers using five-point rating scales to evaluate content, organisation, vocabulary, morphology and syntax. (See Appendix 5.5 for the descriptors developed for the end points of the five scales and Appendix 5.6 for two writing samples, one from Class J and one from Class D, each with an overall average rating of 4 out of 5.) The two sets of ratings for each writing sample were averaged to produce the scores shown in the relevant section below (see Table 5.3).[5] One of the researchers also counted idea units[6] to see whether the two tasks yielded substantially different content.

Language-related episodes

The initial transcripts were checked carefully for accuracy. Then we analysed them for language-related episodes. A language-related episode (LRE) is defined as any part of a dialogue where students talk about language they are producing, question their language use, or other- or self-correct their language production (Swain and Lapkin, 1995). LREs thus entail discussion of meaning and form, but may emphasise one of these more than another. In our analyses we distinguish 'lexis-based' and 'form-based' LREs. Lexis-based LREs involve searching for French vocabulary and/or choosing among competing French vocabulary items. Form-based LREs involve focusing on spelling or on an aspect of French morphology, syntax or discourse. Both types of LREs usually occur in the context of writing out the story rather than in the initial telling of it. Conferencing achieved consensus among the research team members in identifying and classifying LREs.

RESULTS

Task differences identified through analyses of LREs

As noted above, we hypothesised that the jigsaw task would produce more emphasis on meaning (more lexis-based LREs), while the emphasis in the dictogloss would be on form (i.e. Class D would produce more form-based LREs on average than Class J). Before turning to the quantitative results, we present some examples illustrating how task differences are reflected in the dialogues of the pairs of students. At least three salient differences between the tasks emerged from the qualitative analyses of LREs.

The first difference relates to the nature of the task stimulus: Class J received a visual stimulus, whereas Class D's stimulus was auditory. The eight pictures in Appendix 5.1 were very colourful, and this, along with the fact that in the training activity (second week of the study) adjective agreement was taught using colour adjectives (*rouge, brune* in Example 1 below), had an impact on what the pairs negotiated. The influence of the visual (Class J) and auditory (Class D) nature of the two tasks is evident in Examples 1 and 2 respectively.

Example 1

(Class J, Pair 2)
A: Réveille-matin.
     (Alarm clock.)
B: Et il y a un réveille-matin rouge . . . sur une table brune, et le réveille-matin . . . dit six heures et c'est tout.
     (And there is a red alarm clock . . . on a brown table, and the alarm clock says 6 o'clock and that's all.)[7]

Example 2

(Class D, Pair 9)
A: But what's that thing that woke him up that, they said something mickanick, but I have no idea what that is.
B: 'Mickanick?'
A: Yeah, that's what it sounded like.

Example 2 involves an attempt to mimic a sequence of sounds heard in the dictogloss, the word *mécanique* (see Appendix 5.2 for the context).

A second important difference is that one task provides a linguistic model while the other does not. The dictogloss exposes students to a relatively sophisticated native speaker (or writer) text. No such model is available to Class J. Consider Example 3.

Example 3

(Class D, Pair 7)
B: Une plume sort du réveil . . .
     (A feather comes out of the alarm clock . . .)
A: Et chatouille.
     (And tickles.)
B: Et LUI chatouille les pieds.
     (And tickles her feet.)

The possessive adjective (**her** feet) is represented in French in the indirect pronoun preceding the verb (**lui** *chatouille les pieds*). These students use the structure correctly in their written narrative, and are the only pair in either group to achieve complete accuracy in this particularly difficult structure.

A third difference between the two tasks relates to the cognitive demands they entail. The most obvious difference observed in the data is that the jigsaw task, with its numbered pictures, does not require students to expend effort to sequence their stories. In fact, it is interesting to note that 6 of 12 pairs of students in Class J actually numbered the sentences in their written texts rather than writing their stories as paragraphs. All Class D pairs wrote their narrative in paragraph form. Unlike Class J, Class D has to rely on notes taken while listening to the story read aloud. These students do concern themselves with the discourse requirement to sequence events in the story, as shown in Example 4.

Example 4

(Class D, Pair 11)
B: Isn't it ET se peigne les cheveux [**and combs his hair**], because it's the last one?
A: Non. Peigne ses cheveux et prépare pour son chemin.
     [**No, combs his hair and prepares for the road.**]
B: Right.

Student B emphasises the 'and' (*et*) in the first utterance here because he intends it to introduce the last in a series of actions taken by the character in the story before leaving for school. Student A points out that 'combing his hair' is not the final activity; rather there is still the activity of 'preparing' for school. (The relevant part of the translated dictogloss text shown in Appendix 5.2 reads 'She brushes her teeth, combs her hair and gets dressed to go to school'.) This LRE is clearly concerned with temporal sequencing.

Task differences: language-related episodes

Table 5.1 shows the average number of LREs that students in Classes D and J generated, the average number of lexis-based and form-based LREs generated, and the average percent of LREs generated that were lexis-based or form-based. As Table 5.1 shows, no significant differences emerge between the pairs of students doing the dictogloss task and the pairs of students doing the jigsaw task. These results do not support our initial hypothesis that there would be more form-based LREs in the dictogloss task relative to the jigsaw task.

An interesting feature of the data that appear in Table 5.1 is that the standard deviations of Class D are, in general, considerably smaller than those of Class J. We conducted Levene's test for equality of variances, a statistical test which allows one to determine if there are statistical differences between groups in the spread of their scores. The results show that the range in the total number of LREs was smaller for Class D than Class J ($p < 0.05$, one-tailed test). This suggests that the dictogloss task constrains student responses to a greater degree than the jigsaw task. This makes sense given that students were provided with a specific linguistic text in the dictogloss task.

Table 5.1 Language-related episodes (LREs)

	Class J			Class D			
	N	$\bar{X}$	**S.D.**	*N*	$\bar{X}$	**S.D.**	**Sig.***
Count of total episodes	12	8.8	8.0	14	9.2	4.2	ns
Count of lexis-based LREs	12	4.0	3.7	14	3.7	2.3	ns
Count of form-based LREs	12	4.8	4.5	14	5.5	2.9	ns
Percent lexis-based LREs	12	41%	21%	14	40%	19%	ns
Percent form-based LREs	12	59%	21%	14	60%	19%	ns

* Two-tailed *t*-test.

Task differences: time taken to do task

Table 5.2 shows the average amount of time the students took to do the task and the average amount of time students remained on task. These did not differ significantly between the classes.

Table 5.2 Time taken to do a task

	Class J			Class D			
	N	$\bar{X}$	S.D.	N	$\bar{X}$	S.D.	Sig.*
Total interactive time (minutes)	13	12.6	7.5	14	13.0	3.7	ns
Total time on task (minutes)	13	10.2	6.9	14	10.2	3.3	ns

* Two-tailed *t*-test.

The Levene test for homogeneity of variances shows the differences in variances for time on task to be highly significant ($p < 0.000$, one-tailed test), indicating a much smaller range for Class D relative to Class J. This might have been expected given the more open-ended nature of the jigsaw task.

Task differences: quality of written narratives

The narratives that the students wrote as part of the task were rated. Table 5.3 shows the average ratings given for each of content, organisation, vocabulary, syntax, and number of idea units. Once again, no statistically significant differences were observed between the stories written by the students in Classes D and J. The Levene test for homogeneity of variances was used to compare the variances for each variable rated. Although the range of scores was smaller for each variable in Class D relative to Class J (with the exception of number of idea units generated), a statistically significant difference was found only in range of vocabulary use ($p < 0.05$, one-tailed test). Again, this suggests that the language input provided to students focuses and constrains their language production.

Because the pronominal verb was the focus of the mini-lesson, we counted instances of pronominal verb use (correct and incorrect) in the written narratives of Class J and Class D. To control for length of the stories, we first

Table 5.3 Average ratings of written stories

	Class J			Class D			
	N	$\bar{X}$	S.D.	N	$\bar{X}$	S.D.	Sig.
Content*	12	2.9	1.2	14	2.4	0.8	ns
Organisation*	12	3.1	1.1	14	2.9	0.9	ns
Vocabulary*	12	3.1	1.1	14	2.9	0.7	ns
Morphology*	12	2.9	1.0	14	2.8	1.0	ns
Syntax*	12	2.8	1.2	14	2.7	0.9	ns
Idea units (max. = 21)	12	12.5	2.9	14	12.7	3.7	ns

* For each dimension, a five-point scale is used with '1' representing very poor performance, and '5' representing excellent performance. Only the end points of the scales have descriptors (see Appendix 5.5).

counted all main verbs and then calculated the ratio of pronominal verbs to total verbs. The proportions were similar for the two classes: 52.3% for Class J and 45.5% for Class D ($p > 0.3$, two-tailed t-test). However, of the pronominal verbs used by Class J, only 59.4% (SD = 32) were correct. Many of the errors were overgeneralised instances of the pronominal form (e.g. using *se sortir*, a non-existent verb in French, where the context required *sortir*). In contrast, 88.9% (SD = 20) of the pronominal verbs used by Class D were correct. The difference between these percentages was statistically significant ($p < 0.0001$, one-tailed t-test), underlining the importance of the dictogloss in providing grammatically accurate input for second language production.

Task differences: test outcomes

Direct comparisons of Class J and Class D post-test scores are possible only with the 'core items', that is, those items that were in both the pre- and post-tests. This is because, for the 'full' post-test, each class was administered a different version, one that incorporated items based on the particular LREs generated by students in each class. These latter post-test items have been used to trace occurrences of language learning in the dialogues of pairs of students (see Swain and Lapkin, 1998; and below).

We compared the average core post-test scores of Class J and Class D using a two-tailed test, and found no significant differences. We further compared the average core pre- and post-test scores for each class, and found no statistically significant differences, indicating that neither class made any measurable gain. However, we observed numerous occurrences of language learning in which students, as they wrote out their stories, encountered a linguistic problem and worked towards solving it (as seen in their LREs). We provide two illustrative examples below.

Example 5 illustrates one of the possible effects of the mini-lesson, namely overgeneralisation in the use of the pronominal form of the verb. This LRE occurs in the dialogue of a student pair from Class J.

Example 5

(Class J, Pair 4)
B: Yvonne va à l'école.
      (Yvonne goes to school.)
A: Se part à l'école.
      (Yvonne leaves [uses non-existent pronominal form] for school.)
B: Oui. Elle . . . se marche
      (She walks [uses non-existent pronominal form])
A: Se part, parce que . . .
      (Leaves [uses non-existent pronominal form], because)
A: Est-ce que c'est part ou se part?
      (Is it leaves or leaves [in the non-existent pronominal form])
B: Part.
      (Leaves.)

A: Part? Just part?
(Leaves? Just leaves?)
B: Ya.
A: Ok. Yvonne part à l'école, um . . .
(Yvonne leaves for school)

The French verb *partir* does not exist in the pronominal form; but clearly these students are hesitating, perhaps overgeneralising as a result of the mini-lesson they had just seen on the video. In any event, they agree on the correct form, and, on post-test item B shown in Appendix 5.4, they correctly identify *partir* as a non-pronominal verb and reject *se partir*, a non-verb in French. They also write the verb correctly in their story. For Example 5, unfortunately there is no pre-test item. We may infer, however, that learning has occurred from the post-test response to the relevant tailor-made item, and from the written text produced by the pair of students.

In Example 6, students from Class D negotiate the gender of the lexical item *la cloche*.

Example 6

(Class D, Pair 11)
B: Puis, le cloche[8] *a sonné.*
(Then the bell rang [=the alarm clock rang].)
A: LA cloche?
(The bell [emphasis on feminine form of article].)
B: La cloche, le cloche, je pense c'est LA.
[Alternating masculine and feminine forms of article.]
A: Oui.
(Yes.)
B: La cloche a sonné.
(The bell rang.)

Student A questions the gender of *cloche* in line 2 of the example, but her rising intonation signals uncertainty. B then tries out both the feminine and masculine alternatives, and settles on the correct feminine form (*la*). For this LRE (Example 6), there are both pre-test and post-test data (see item type A, Appendix 5.4): one student got the pre-test item wrong and the other got it right. On the post-test, both students marked *la* as the correct choice. The gender is also written correctly in their story.

Examples 5 and 6, one from each class, illustrate language learning in progress. Both task types, therefore, are shown to engender learning.

Discussion

The two tasks used in this study generated fewer differences than we had expected. The most salient difference is that the dictogloss task imposed a set of constraints that were not imposed by the jigsaw task. The dictogloss task appears to have constrained the range of students' time on task, the range in the total number of language-related episodes produced, and the range of student performance in their written narratives, in particular with respect to vocabulary use. This smaller range of behaviour observed among pairs of students in the dictogloss class suggests that the use of the dictogloss task may focus students' attention, thus constraining students' output somewhat more than the jigsaw task, which is more open-ended linguistically.[9]

Other task-related differences included:

1. *Accuracy*: The jigsaw students produced proportionately fewer correct pronominal verbs than the dictogloss students in their written narratives.
2. *Discourse structure*: Many jigsaw pairs of students numbered the sentences in their narratives, whereas dictogloss students wrote in paragraphs. Furthermore, jigsaw students did not need to attend to logical and temporal sequencing, whereas the transcripts of the dictogloss students' discourse show evidence of such attention.
3. *Nature of the language-related episodes*: On the one hand, jigsaw students were influenced by the visual aspects of the stimulus material, referring often to the colour of objects in their pictures. On the other hand, dictogloss students' attention to the spoken text influenced students' attempts at producing vocabulary and complex linguistic structures.

Contrary to our expectations, task differences were not reflected in the degree of attention students paid to language form. In particular, in carrying out either task, students focused equally on form as they collaboratively constructed and wrote out their stories. On reflection, we believe there are two reasons for this similarity.

One reason is that the mini-lesson given prior to actually doing the task served, as we had expected, to focus students' attention on language form. This is particularly clear in the stories of the jigsaw students who, even one week after having had a mini-lesson on adjective formation, made considerable use of colour adjectives in describing their brightly coloured pictures.

The second reason is that the tasks had in common the necessity to produce written language. As the students wrote, they questioned each other about how to write their story, focusing their joint attention on form. The activity of writing collaboratively led students to discuss their own language use as they encountered problems. They brought to conscious attention gaps in their own knowledge and worked out possible solutions through hypothesis formation and testing, relying on their joint linguistic resources.

The similarity in the types of LREs generated by the students may, in part, account for the reason that no quantitative differences in their written stories or their core post-test scores were observed. Furthermore, no improvement from pre-test to post-test scores was observed. We believe the reasons for this are three-fold. First, relatively few of the LREs were captured in the core test items, so the language learning we had hoped to test with the pre-test/post-test design could not be revealed in those items. Secondly, students only spent on average 10 minutes on a task, a very brief period indeed to lead to quantitative differences on a test. Thirdly, the students' interlanguage, although non-native-like, was relatively stable.[10] Both of the tasks, however, seem to have had the effect of focusing students' attention on their own language use with the effect, in some cases, of providing occasions for language learning to take place.

Our results do not imply that one task is better than another for pedagogical purposes. The value of the tasks depends upon the instructional goals of the teacher. Both tasks generated a similar and substantial proportion of form-focused language-related episodes. Within the context of French immersion programmes, this is a welcome finding. Additionally, the dictogloss enhanced accuracy in the production of pronominal verbs and led students to notice and reproduce complex syntactic structures. The jigsaw task led to a greater range of vocabulary use and language-related episodes, suggesting that perhaps its open-ended nature might inspire greater linguistic creativity. It may be that with greater variation in language performance there is a corresponding reduction in accuracy.

Although our original purpose in conducting this study was to relate language-related episodes to second language learning, the study plays its part in extending our understanding of how attentional processes can be channelled within second language instruction.

ACKNOWLEDGEMENTS

We wish to thank Joan Howard and Doug Hart for their invaluable help in data collection and analysis respectively, and Alister Cumming, Nancy Halsall, Birgit Harley, Sylvia Spielman and Miles Turnbull for insightful comments on an earlier draft of this chapter.

NOTES

1. This research was made possible by a grant (No. 410-93-0050) to Merrill Swain and Sharon Lapkin from the Social Sciences and Humanities Research Council of Canada.
2. See also the introduction to this volume for a discussion of different definitions of task.
3. To our knowledge, other task comparisons in the literature have not controlled for content across task types.
4. Pronominal verbs in French can be grouped into four semantic categories (Connors and Ouellette, 1996). The pronominal verbs in the dictogloss text (Appendix 5.2) fall into the reflexive category (e.g. *se laver*, to get washed or to wash oneself). In the reflexive reading of a pronominal verb, the pronoun 'represents a Patient co-referential with the Subject Agent argument' (p. 216).
5. The two sets of ratings differed by more than one point in only 4% of cases.
6. Idea units were determined as follows. Three adult native speakers did our jigsaw task (their texts were used to develop the dictogloss passage). The transcribed version of the longest jigsaw oral narrative was broken into information 'chunks'

or idea units which constituted the key pieces of information needed to convey the story told by the series of eight pictures. There were 21 of these key pieces of information: sun rises, 6 a.m., alarm rings, Martine sleeping soundly, feet on pillow, head at foot of bed, does not want to get up, with big toe (or foot), shuts off alarm, falls asleep again, at 6:02, the perfect alarm clock, designed to prevent sleep, extends mechanical hand with feather, tickles her foot, wakes her up, finally (OR given no choice), she gets up, gets ready, for school, puts on her back pack (OR arrives in good time). A point was given for each idea unit, regardless of the accuracy of its expression.

7. All the examples in this chapter, with the exception of Example 1, constitute an LRE.
8. The correct lexical item for 'alarm clock' is *le réveil* or *le réveille-matin*. *La cloche* is best translated as 'bell'.
9. Bygate (1988) found that a guessing game task produced far lower standard deviations than a picture differences task on the incidence of a set of features.
10. Bygate (personal communication, 1998) suggests 'Another possibility is that language that was learnt in the context of task formats either was only partially learnt at the point (the learning process having been engaged but not resolved); or else the learnt material was available within the context of the task, but wasn't available for access in test contexts.'

REFERENCES

Allen, P., Swain, M., Harley, B. and Cummins, J. (1990) Aspects of classroom treatment: Towards a more comprehensive view of second language education. In B. Harley, P. Allen, J. Cummins and M. Swain (eds) *The Development of Second Language Proficiency* (pp. 57–81). Cambridge: Cambridge University Press.

Breen, M.P. and Candlin, C.A. (1980) The essentials of a communicative curriculum in language teaching. *Applied Linguistics*, 1: 89–112.

Bygate, M. (1988) *Linguistic and strategic features of the language of learners in oral communication exercises.* Unpublished doctoral dissertation, University of London Institute of Education.

Connors, K. and Ouellette, B. (1996) Describing the meanings of French pronominal-verbal constructions for students of French–English translation. *Language Sciences*, 18: 213–26.

Donato, R. (1994) Collective scaffolding in second language learning. In J. Lantolf and G. Appel (eds) *Vygotskian Approaches to Second Language Research* (pp. 33–56). Norwood, NJ: Ablex.

Fotos, S. (1994) Integrating grammar instruction and communicative language use through grammar consciousness-raising tasks. *TESOL Quarterly*, 28: 323–51.

Harley, B. and Swain, M. (1984) The interlanguage of immersion students and its implications for second language teaching. In A. Davies, C. Criper and A.P.R. Howatt (eds) *Interlanguage* (pp. 291–311). Edinburgh: Edinburgh University Press.

Kowal, M. (1997) *French immersion students' language growth in French: Perceptions, patterns and programmings.* EdD thesis, Ontario Institute for Studies in Education: University of Toronto.

Kowal, M. and Swain, M. (1997) From semantic to syntactic processing: How can we promote metalinguistic awareness in the French immersion classroom? In R.K. Johnson and M. Swain (eds) *Immersion Education: International Perspectives* (pp. 284–309). Cambridge: Cambridge University Press.

LaPierre, D. (1994) *Language output in a cooperative learning setting: Determining its effects on second language learning.* MA thesis, Ontario Institute for Studies in Education: University of Toronto.

Lyster, R. (1994) La négociation de la forme: stratégie analytique en classe d'immersion. *Canadian Modern Language Review,* 50: 446–65.

Lyster, R. (1995) *Instructional Strategies in French Immersion: An Annotated Bibliography.* Canada: Canadian Association of Immersion Teachers.

Nunan, D. (1989) *Designing Tasks for the Communicative Classroom.* Cambridge: Cambridge University Press.

Pica, T., Kanagy, R. and Falodun, J. (1993) Choosing and using communication tasks for second language instruction. In G. Crookes and S. Gass (eds) *Tasks and Language Learning: Integrating Theory and Practice* (pp. 9–34). Clevedon, Avon: Multilingual Matters.

Skehan, P. (1996) A framework for the implementation of task-based instruction. *Applied Linguistics,* 17: 38–62.

Swain, M. (1985) Communicative competence: Some roles of comprehensible input and comprehensible output in its development. In S. Gass and C. Madden (eds) *Input in Second Language Acquisition* (pp. 235–53). Rowley, Mass.: Newbury House.

Swain, M. (1995) Three functions of output in second language learning. In G. Cook and B. Seidlhofer (eds) *Principle and Practice in Applied Linguistics: Studies in Honour of H.G. Widdowson* (pp. 125–44). Oxford: Oxford University Press.

Swain, M. (1996) Integrating language and content in immersion classrooms: Research perspectives. *Canadian Modern Language Review,* 52: 529–48.

Swain, M. (1997a) Collaborative dialogue: Its contribution to second language learning. *Revista Canaria de Estudios Ingleses,* 34: 115–32.

Swain, M. (1997b) The output hypothesis, focus on form, and second language learning. In V. Berry, R. Adamson and W.T. Littlewood (eds) *Applying Linguistics* (pp. 1–21). English Language Centre: University of Hong Kong.

Swain, M. (1998) Focus on form through conscious reflection. In C. Doughty and J. Williams (eds) *Focus on Form in Classroom Second Language Acquisition* (pp. 64–81). Cambridge: Cambridge University Press.

Swain, M. (2000) The output hypothesis and beyond: Mediating acquisition through collaborative dialogue. In J.P. Lantolf (ed.) *Sociocultural Theory and Second Language Learning* (pp. 97–114). Oxford: Oxford University Press.

Swain, M. and Lapkin, S. (1995) Problems in output and the cognitive processes they generate: A step towards second language learning. *Applied Linguistics,* 16: 371–91.

Swain, M. and Lapkin, S. (1998) Interaction and second language learning: Two adolescent French immersion students working together. *Modern Language Journal,* 83: 320–37.

Tse, B.T.W. (1996) *Student output, teacher feedback and collaborative learning: a study of adolescent students in a Chinese heritage language classroom.* MA thesis, Ontario Institute for Studies in Education: University of Toronto.

Wajnryb, R. (1990) *Grammar Dictation.* Oxford: Oxford University Press.

APPENDIX 5.1: PICTURES USED IN THE JIGSAW TASK

APPENDIX 5.2: DICTOGLOSS

Le réveil-matin de Martine

Il est six heures du matin and le soleil se lève. Martine dort tranquillement dans son lit. Elle fait de beaux rêves, la tête au pied du lit and les pieds sur l'oreiller. Quand le réveil sonne, Martine ne veut pas se lever. Elle sort son pied and avec le gros orteil, elle ferme le réveil. Elle se rendort tout de suite. Mais elle a le réveil qu'il faut pour ne pas être en retard. A six heures et deux minutes, une main mécanique tenant une petite plume sort du réveil et lui chatouille le pied. C'est efficace. Finalement Martine se lève. Elle se brosse les dents, se peigne les cheveux and s'habille pour prendre le chemin de l'école. Encore une journée bien commencée.

Translation of dictogloss task

It's 6 am and the sun is rising. Martine is sound asleep in her bed. She's having sweet dreams, her head at the foot of the bed and her feet on the pillow. When the alarm clock rings, Martine doesn't want to get up. She sticks her foot out, and with her big toe, she shuts off the alarm. She falls asleep again immediately. But she has the kind of alarm clock you need to prevent being late. At 6:02, a mechanical hand holding a small feather comes out of the alarm clock. It tickles her foot. To good effect! Finally Martine gets up. She brushes her teeth, combs her hair and gets dressed to go to school. Another great start to the day!

APPENDIX 5.3

Instructions for the dictogloss, translated into English

Now you are going to work in groups of two and you will reconstruct a story together that I'll read to you. While I read, take some notes – words or phrases to help you remember the story. Try to write the story exactly as I tell it, and then write it in excellent French. Try to use the exact words from the story as much as possible, but use other words if you forget the original words. Discuss among yourselves the grammatical decisions you take, and think above all, about the reflexive verbs that we have just looked at.

Instructions for the jigsaw task, translated into English

Now you are going to work in pairs to follow up on the lesson you just saw. This has two parts: first, you'll reconstruct the story together, based on the pictures you have. Then, you'll write the story out that you have created together.

Each of you will receive four numbered pictures. One of you will receive pictures 1, 3, 5, and 7; and the other, pictures 2, 4, 6, and 8. Without looking at each other's pictures, try to tell the story. Once you have done this, I want you to write out the story together. Remember that you are not just describing the pictures but telling the story that the pictures suggest. Also, because we have just reviewed reflexive verbs, see if you can use them in your story. After writing your story, re-read it to make sure everything is correct.

APPENDIX 5.4

IV.   <u>Examples of Test Item Types</u>

A.   Pour chaque mot français ci-dessous, choisissez la forme correcte de l'article indéfini (*un, une*) et cochez la case appropriée. Si vous ne savez pas, cochez la case *Je ne sais pas* à droite.

un	une	mot	Je ne sais pas
		couverture	
		gant	
		chandail	
		cloche	

B.   Pour chaque phrase ci-dessous, indiquez si la phrase est correcte ou incorrecte selon l'image. Indiquez jusqu'à quel point vous êtes certain de votre réponse en cochant la case appropriée.

Dans chaque groupe il y a au moins une phrase correcte, mais il est aussi possible d'avoir plusieurs phrases qui sont correctes dans chaque groupe.

	Certaine-ment correct	Probable-ment correct	Probable-ment incorrect	Certaine-ment incorrect	Je ne sais pas
1. Les garçons partent pour l'école.					
2. Les garçons se partent pour l'école.					

C.   Choisissez <u>la meilleure réponse</u> dans chaque groupe. Cochez la case appropriée à droite de la phrase.

1. Voilà mon horloge.   [ ]

2. Voilà mon réveille-matin.   [ ]

3. Voilà mon rêve-matin.   [ ]

4. Voilà ma cloche.   [ ]

APPENDIX 5.5

Written narratives: descriptors used for the end points of the five scales

Content

1 It's difficult to know what the paragraph is about; no story is told.
5 A 'complete' story is told; narrative is interesting and holds one's attention.

Organisation

1 Ideas are stated in haphazard order; or insufficient information is provided to assess organisation.
5 Information is clearly stated and sequenced; use of paragraph as appropriate for a narrative; presence of a title.

Vocabulary

1 Vocabulary generally impoverished; some reliance on English; overuse of some 'high coverage' terms.
5 Sophisticated vocabulary; precision in word choice; use of appropriate register.

Morphology

1 Many errors in gender; agreement errors (noun–adj.; person agreement in the verb; spelling of verb inflections, etc.).
5 High degree of accuracy in use of person, number, and gender agreement.

Syntax

1 Sounds more like English than French; many errors involving tense, articles, clitics; faulty word order, etc.
5 Quite idiomatic use of French; generally gets the structure of verbs and their complements correct; presence of one or two sophisticated syntactic structures.

APPENDIX 5.6

Two written narratives (exactly as written by the students)

Class D, Pair 5

Le Reveille-Matin de Martine

C'était 6 heures du matin et le soleil se lève. Martine dort tranquillement, elle fait de beau rêves. Sa tête sur le haut, ses pieds sur l'oreillé. Son reveille-matin sonne, mais Martine ne voulait pas se lever. Son pied sort des couvertures et avec son grand orteille elle ferme le reveille-matin, et elle s'endort. À 6 heures et deux minutes un main mechanique est sorti et avec un plume a chatouiller les pieds de Martine. C'est éficace.

Martine se lève et elle se brosse les dents, se peigne les cheveux et s'habille pur prendre le chemin à l'école.

La Fin

Class J, Pair 4

1. Le soleil jaune se lève, c'est le matin.
2. Yvonne s'endort dans son lit avec une couverture bleue.
3. C'est 6:00 et la cloche sonne fortement. Ring! Yvonne se lève ses pieds sur l'autre côté du lit.
4. Elle pousse le bouton sur son cloche rouge avec son orteille rose pour arrêter le sonnement.
5. Yvonne s'endort encore.
6. La cloche voit que Yvonne s'est endormi pendant 2 minutes, alors il sort sont main mécanique qui porte un gant jaune, et le chatouille avec une plume noire comme les cheuveux d'Yvonne.
7. Yvonne va au lavatoire et se regarde dans le miroir pendant qu'elle se peigne les cheveux et se brosse les dents. L'eau s'écoule basin.
8. Yvonne part à l'école avec une nouveau chandaille rose et un napsack bleu.

Chapter 6

Guiding relationships between form and meaning during task performance: The role of the teacher

Virginia Samuda

INTRODUCTION

Tasks do not take place in a vacuum; nevertheless, until recently, much of the task-based learning and teaching (TBLT) literature has had a tendency to treat them as if they did. Few studies have been set in intact classes (Foster, 1998), and even then, have not always had as their central concern the broader pedagogical context in which tasks occur (Samuda and Rounds, 1993; Bygate et al., 1998). This is not to deny the value of studying 'tasks in isolation': the insights gained from such studies, where task has been viewed primarily as an arena for the examination of unscripted language performance, rather than as a unit of classroom activity operating within a broader pedagogical framework, have contributed to current understanding of the potential for tasks to shape aspects of L2 development (for example, Gass and Varonis, 1994; Robinson, 1995; Foster and Skehan, 1996; Bygate, 1999; among others). However, this understanding must also depend on how tasks are implemented across a range of pedagogic contexts.

When tasks are studied in isolation, the kinds of issue that might affect subsequent pedagogic choices risk getting blurred. In particular, there is a danger that the role of task as a factor affecting overall language development gets emphasised over factors such as individual difference, context of instruction, group dynamics, the interaction of task work with other modes of instruction, and so on. It is against this background that the role of the teacher as a mediating factor in task-based language development remains virtually unexamined. If, however, one of the enduring challenges in the implementation of TBLT lies in the tension between engaging naturalistic learning processes on the one hand and systematically managing pedagogic processes on the other (Skehan, 1996), then the contribution of the teacher warrants closer scrutiny. To what extent, for example, is it possible to identify discoursal and interactional features of teacher performance that might be said to constitute elements of 'task-based' teaching? And in what ways may these distinguish the role of the teacher in TBLT from the role of the teacher in more transmission-oriented approaches?

Within a standard pedagogic framework such as the Presentation, Practice and Production sequence, the teacher operates as provider of bite-sized input, supplier of feedback and engineer of controlled progressions of classroom activity, prompting metaphors that include 'controller', 'organiser', 'assessor', 'prompter' and 'tutor' (Harmer, 1991). In order to highlight the different types of demand placed on the teacher in TBLT, Willis (1996) draws on a contrasting set of metaphors: 'adviser', 'chairperson', 'monitor', 'language guide', 'facilitator'. However, if there is a case to be made for a task-based pedagogy, we need to understand how these metaphors may be operationalised *vis-à-vis* instructional features for which psycholinguistic underpinnings have been claimed – for example, positive evidence, form focusing, negative feedback and production practice (Doughty and Williams, 1998; Ellis, 1998).

Given this, central to the role of the teacher in TBLT must be ways of working *with* tasks to guide learners towards the types of language processing believed to support L2 development. This implies a relationship between task and teacher that is essentially complementary, in which a role for the task is to create opportunities for the formulation and negotiation of meanings, and a role for the teacher is to 'lead from behind' (Gibbons, 1998) the task to complement and support what the task has set in motion.

This chapter explores the notion of 'leading from behind' as an aspect of the teacher's role in TBLT. Drawing on classroom transcripts, it focuses on the interplay among features of task design (in channelling attentional resources) and features of instructional strategy (in guiding form/meaning mappings) as a task unfolds.

Given the complementary relationship between task and teacher to be explored here, I begin by foregrounding issues in task design that have the potential to affect the ways that teachers implement tasks. These relate to: (1) the general pedagogic purpose of a task; (2) the management of attentional focus across a task; and (3) the framing of task input data. In order to contextualise the discussion of the data that follows, I relate these issues to specific aspects of the task design employed in this study.

ISSUES IN TASK DESIGN

Tasks and pedagogic purpose

Although the degree of prominence that tasks occupy in an overall programme of instruction may vary, the standard pedagogic purpose most associated with task work is the provision of oral communication practice, through which language-processing capacities may be developed in contexts of language use. This use of tasks has long been recognised as a central feature of communicative language teaching, and as such is widely addressed in teacher education, and in the development of instructional materials; so much so that, for many teachers primed to deal with tasks for activating language and stretching fluency, TBLT has become synonymous (albeit misguidedly) with unscripted oral activity.

It is also this aspect of task use that explicitly or implicitly underlies much of the research literature, where emphasis has been on the role of tasks in shaping language development by mobilising, stretching and refining current inter language (IL) resources. In consequence, most studies have focused more on the impact of tasks on emerging or partially internalised rules than on what Skehan (1998) terms 'introducing new language to the IL system'.[1] Thus, although the introduction of 'new' language data remains a major function of language teaching (and hence a major preoccupation with language teachers), very little is known about the roles that tasks may actually play in this process, and even less about the ways that teachers might contribute.

From a pedagogic perspective, therefore, making explicit a broad distinction between the use of tasks primarily to activate, stretch and refine current IL resources and processing capacities (*language-activating/fluency-stretching tasks*) and the use of tasks primarily to enable new form–meaning connections to be made (*knowledge-constructing tasks*) may illuminate more precisely issues of task design and teacher role.[2] For language-activating/fluency-stretching tasks, for example, task design features might seek to maximise opportunities for negotiation of meaning around topics with a potential to engage (see Gass and Varonis, 1985; Doughty and Pica, 1986; Yule, 1997, among others), with the teacher's role encompassing pre-task preparation, post-task debriefing, and monitoring of task performance. Knowledge-constructing tasks, however, might be expected to place different demands on task design and teacher role, particularly in the ways that attentional resources are managed, and opportunities for the types of noticing and form focusing believed to enhance L2 development (Doughty and Williams, 1998) are created. It is the use of knowledge-constructing tasks and its impact on task design and teacher role that this chapter addresses.

Task design and the management of attentional focus

It may seem paradoxical to be addressing task design at some length in a chapter on the teacher's role. However, in order to examine how this role may be shaped in different ways at different stages of task completion, an understanding of the overall design of a given task may be necessary. The task design employed in this study was built around three basic components: *input data, operations on data, outcomes* as a sequence of interlocking stages, in which output from one created input for the next. This basic task framework underpins a meaning → form → meaning progression, that seeks to manage shifts in attentional focus as the task unfolds.

Built into this model are opportunities for focusing attention on novel form/meaning connections. Although it is agreed that not all aspects of form require focus, it is becoming clear that some do (Harley, 1993), and various pre- and post-task proposals for the timing of form-focusing activity in TBLT have been made (Long and Crookes, 1993; Willis, 1996; Skehan, 1998). While pre- and post-task approaches have the advantage of leaving task performance intact, they both pose pedagogic challenges. A post-task approach, for example, brings with it the risk that certain aspects of certain forms may escape focus altogether if not in some way highlighted in task input, or nudged in task performance. It is also possible that the implementational demands involved could limit applicability to a fairly narrow range of instructional contexts (Doughty and Williams, 1998). On the other hand, a pre-task approach that directs attention to language features before learners experience the need to use them implies a progression from form to meaning which not only risks dislocating language form from language use. From a teacher's perspective, in both approaches, the challenge would lie in guiding attention from meaning to form or from form to meaning in ways that enable learners to see their connection.

The approach explored here therefore seeks to build a focus on form–meaning relationships into the task itself. In this, the task initially highlights an area of meaning in order to create a semantic 'space' which learners' current IL resources may be able to fill only partially. As task demands are designed to push learners to fill this space with some precision, the task activates 'a need to mean' (Samuda et al., 1996), through which learners may recognise holes in their current IL repertoires while engaged in the process of making meaning (Swain, 1998). Since it is at this point that the IL system may be most permeable and open to change (Tarone and Liu, 1995), it is at this point that a language focus[3] may be introduced. The siting of the language focus to coincide with learners' recognition of its role in supporting meanings that are in the process of being expressed contrasts with the timing of pre- and post-task foci discussed above, and relates to a view of language in which form is viewed as a resource for meaning (Halliday, 1985; Hasan and Perrett, 1994).

The overall task design is illustrated in Figure 6.1, with the dotted lines representing potential siting of the language focus.

The use of tasks to target specific language features is controversial (Long and Robinson, 1998) and open to charges of 'structure trapping' (Skehan, 1998). Nevertheless, it is becoming clear that by targeting specific discourse genres, some tasks (for example, story reconstruction and prioritising tasks) have the potential to elicit different constellations of language features (Bygate, 1999). Building on this, the approach discussed here does not aim to target specific instances of form, but starts instead with specific areas of meaning,

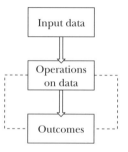

Figure 6.1   Basic elements of a pedagogic task

hence the meaning → form → meaning progression central to its design and to its implementation.

The framing of task input data

Task design based around meaning → form → meaning progressions needs to find ways of intially highlighting the targeted semantic area, and then guiding attention to meaning–form relationships. Given this, what kinds of enhancement techniques might the input data require in order to maximise noticeability? Since we cannot assume that all linguistic features require bringing to attention in the same way (Hulstijn, 1995), or that they can be, answers to this question must depend on the nature of the form–meaning relationships in question.

Although it is far from clear what comprises rule complexity, distinctions can be drawn between form–meaning relationships that can be made relatively transparent from immediate context and those that cannot. The latter category includes 'semantically complex' items that may be relatively straightforward at the level of form, but whose rules for use are based on wider semantic and discoursal cues (Westney, 1994). Given this, initial task design options may depend on the degree of 'transparency' of the targeted form–meaning relationships. For relatively transparent relationships, the task input may be 'seeded' with language features relating to the semantic area targeted by the task, and possibly enhanced (typologically or pictorially, for example) to increase salience and maximise opportunities for noticing. The operations that learners are required to perform on this input can be manipulated to reduce redundancy and highlight form–meaning relationships (VanPatten, 1996; Samuda et al., 1996). However, although these steps may create sufficient salience for relatively transparent relationships that are being encountered for the first time, or for those that it is possible to 'pictorialise' (as in some of the tasks discussed in VanPatten, 1996), they may be less effective where more opaque semantically complex items are concerned.[4]

However, if the learning challenge for semantically complex features is situated not in the form *per se*, but in rules of use rooted in discoursal and semantic choices (Larsen-Freeman, 1991), then perhaps it is those discoursal and semantic choices that should be enhanced in the input. Given that, under pressure of task performance, learners may process primarily for meaning before processing primarily for form (VanPatten, 1996), it may be the semantic, rather than the linguistic, environment that requires initial enhancement in order to attract attention to semantically complex features. In this, the role of the task input data would not be to highlight tokens of preselected items, but to illuminate areas of meaning as a type of semantic priming prior to the introduction of 'new' language data.

Hence we might draw a distinction between task input that has been *semantically* enhanced, and task input data that have been *linguistically* enhanced. This widens the scope of what is conventionally understood by the term 'input enhancement', and its implications are discussed further below.

To summarise, the task design explored here initially seeks to create a semantic space; as learners orient themselves within this space, they may be pushed by operations carried out on the task input data to notice holes (Swain, 1998) in their current IL resources. In the potential learning space thus formed, opportunities may be created for new form–meaning mappings to be made. The nature of the highlighted form–meaning relationships may also affect initial design options, and determine whether it is more appropriate for the task input data to be linguistically seeded or semantically enhanced.[5]

In what ways, then, may a teacher work with such a task design to complement its essential meaning $\rightarrow$ form $\rightarrow$ meaning progression and guide attention 'from behind' as the task unfolds? In the remainder of this chapter, these issues are developed in relation to one teacher's implementation of a 'semantically complex' task with an intact class of high-beginning/low-intermediate adult ESL students.

BACKGROUND AND CONTEXT OF DATA COLLECTION

The classroom transcripts on which this discussion is based form part of a larger dataset of learner performance on the same tasks at different levels of proficiency, with different teachers. The original concern had not been the teacher, but as I began to document a number of classes, one teacher stood out for her apparent ability to work in tandem with task and learners. It is this teacher's management of one task type that forms the basis of the discussion in the next section.

Setting and participants

Audio and video recordings and samples of student writing were collected over a semester in an intact class in a pre-academic intensive ESL programme located on the campus of a North American university. The proficiency level of the class, the lowest in a five-level programme, was determined by institutional placement procedures as high beginning/low intermediate. The lessons that were observed and recorded were identified in the institutional schedule as 'Grammar/Communication'. Although required to 'cover' a syllabus of grammatical features, the teacher was allowed considerable latitude in how she chose to implement it. The Grammar/Communication lessons occupied 10 hours of approximately 25 hours of instruction a week.

The class comprised nine students, predominantly Japanese and Korean, with an average age of 22. Reasons for studying English in the USA ranged from long-term goals of a US college education to short-term stays of four to nine months to improve language skills and enhance future job or educational opportunities. At the start of the data collection, they had been in the USA for an average of six weeks. All placed oral fluency and grammatical accuracy as their highest learning priorities.

The teacher

The teacher had had approximately eight years' experience with similar student populations, and was well versed in communicative approaches. In the classes observed, she made extensive use of oral communication tasks and games to activate language and stretch fluency: to introduce 'new' language features, she drew, where possible, on specially designed knowledge-constructing tasks of the kinds discussed above. These were supplemented with a range of tasks, communicative activities and various exercise types from published and in-house resources. A North American form-based textbook was used primarily for learner reference and homework assignments.

Over the semester, I spent one morning a week in her classroom. During this time, she selected content according to the requirements of the institutional syllabus, and on the basis of these selections, we planned and taught lessons collaboratively. In the light of this shared experience, we had extensive discussions about learning/teaching issues, which coloured the tasks we used and the ways we implemented them. As a result of my involvement, the teacher and the students were familiar with my presence as observer and co-teacher. By the same token, prior to data collection, I was able to develop tasks around topics of interest to the students, based on the design principles described above.

The form–meaning relationships in focus

The tasks were developed around areas of meaning relating to the institutional syllabus and were chosen by the teacher. The basis of selection lay in her perception of the particular pedagogic challenges afforded learners at that level of proficiency.

The task to be discussed here was based around epistemic modality, which, deriving from 'the area of meaning that lies between yes and no' (Halliday, 1985), might be considered a semantically complex challenge from a pedagogic perspective. The teacher's syllabus prescribed a limited range of linguistic exponents for realising possibility and probability: the modal auxiliaries *must, might, may* and *could*, but, although the rules of form for these may be relatively straightforward, the socio-semantic options underpinning the choice of one form over another are more complex, and less easily illuminated.

As the task input data were semantically enhanced, but not linguistically seeded, the task design in itself did not prescribe the use of these particular forms. However, when the task was piloted with three native speaker (NS) and two highly proficient non-native speaker (NNS) groups, it was found that although the target modal auxiliaries did not occur in the input data, they were present (in varying degrees) in the output of all pilot groups, suggesting that the task design created sufficient semantic salience to elicit the target features in unscripted performance. As might be expected, expressions of possibility and probability in the pilot data were not restricted to modal auxiliaries; across the pilot groups, nine further types of possibility/probability formulation occurred.[6]

Pre-testing

A pre-test was administered to determine pre-existing levels of familiarity with the target features. This consisted of a discrete point multiple-choice test, in a format familiar to the students, and a gapped text, in which choice of form was based on embedded contextual and discoursal cues. Pre-test scores (mean = 3.73, maximum score = 26) suggest that the task would be potentially 'knowledge constructing'.

The task

Given the relative opacity of the targeted form–meaning relationships, the input data were not seeded with the target features, but were designed to attract initial attention to *probability* and *possibility* as areas of meaning. The input data comprised the task instructions (rubric), a bag of objects (allegedly the contents of a person's pockets), and a chart. The task rubric instructed participants to work in small groups to speculate on the identity of the person, and come to consensus in order to present and justify their conclusions, firstly as an informal oral presentation to the rest of the class and finally as a poster.[7] The overall task sequence is summarised in Figure 6.2.

Operations on the input data comprised several substeps set in motion by the chart, on which groups recorded initial hypotheses about the person's

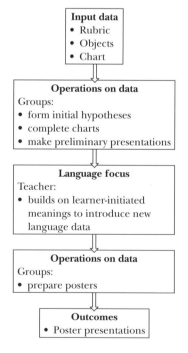

Figure 6.2   Task design: things in pockets

identity under categories such as age, gender, occupation, etc. The chart also required groups to register the degree of probability/possibility of each initial hypothesis. An extract is illustrated in Figure 6.3.

HOW CERTAIN ARE YOU?			
	Less than 50% Certain (It's possible)	90% Certain (It's probable)	100% Certain (It's certain)
Name			
Sex			
Age			
Marital Status			

Figure 6.3 Extract from task chart: things in pockets

TASK AND TEACHER IN TANDEM

This section focuses on the task in action, and follows the task, teacher and learners as the task unfolds. In this, it seeks to identify features of the teacher's implementation, from which categories of analysis might be derived and applied to subsequent studies of task design and implementation. To this end, discussion of task performance is divided into three macro phases: Pre-language Focus, Language Focus and Post-language Focus. The discussion of the first and last of these phases draws on the performance of one of the small groups (3 female Japanese speakers; 1 female French speaker); the Language Focus phase includes the teacher with the whole class.

Pre-focus

During the Pre-focus phase, 124 expressions of *probability* and *possibility* occurred in the group's output, across 22% of total turns in this phase of the task. It is important to keep in mind that none of the target modal auxiliaries was included in the task input data and that none was present in the group's output. This suggests that, under pressure of task demand (coming to consensus across an opinion gap), the learners had available to them other resources for expressing *probability* and *possibility* and thus conveying basic task meaning. These resources divide into two categories:

- language 'mined' from task input data (for example 'certain'; possible'; '90%');
- language mobilised from current IL repertoire.

This is illustrated in the extract below. Underlining represents language 'mined' from task input data; embolding represents language mobilised from current IL resources:

A: Is this hobby or job? **Maybe** it's hobby but
N: **Maybe**
A: **Maybe** it's job
C: Both
A: Both
C: It's <u>possible</u>
N: <u>Possible</u> or <u>90%?</u>
Y: <u>90%</u> I think

As we can see, the learners seem to mine and exploit task input data as a communication strategy that enables greater precision of expression than that allowed by language mobilized from current IL resources. The breakdown for these categories of language resource in this phase of the task is summarised in Table 6.1.[8]

Table 6.1   Expressions of probability and possibility: pre-focus

Mined		Mobilised	
(It's) possible:	13	Maybe	66
(It's) probable:	7	(I'm) sure:	14
90%:	6	(I'm) not sure	11
Certain:	5		
50%:	2		
Sub-total:	33	Sub-total:	91
		Total: 124	

Thus, these learners appear to be able to draw on mined language as prefabricated lexical chunks, that operate on their own or vertically, in combination with current IL resources, to scaffold meaning and fill IL gaps. Under pressure of task demand, this may well work to free up attention for the formulation of propositional content, and in this serve a function similar to that claimed for satellite units in oral discourse (Bygate, 1988). Given that the first stage of this task was built around unplanned, unscripted oral activity, this is not surprising (although this particular use of task language may have implications for task design, as discussed below). However, it is also possible that unanalysed task language mined in this way will simply operate as a highly lexicalised task shorthand, through which IL restructuring may be effectively bypassed, unless output is 'pushed' in ways suggested by Swain (1998, and elsewhere). This aspect of teacher role is discussed next.

Language focus

During the pre-focus phase of the task, the teacher adopted the 'standby' role standard to the management of group work in communicative language teaching. No interventions or error corrections were made. As the learners came together as a whole group to make their informal and preliminary presentations, the teacher joined them, gradually introducing first an implicit and then an explicit focus on language.

Implicit focus

In the implicit language focus, the teacher adopted a co-communicator role, solely responding to the message of learner utterances, and not to form. She did not recast or reformulate ill-formed utterances and requested clarification or expansion only to confirm intended meaning. However, in this, she initiated a gradual shift from meaning towards form, by deploying two manoeuvres: (1) mining task input data to scaffold learner meanings, and (2) conversationally interweaving these meanings with new form. These are illustrated in the following extract, in which one group is presenting its findings to a sceptical audience (since each group had received a different set of objects, the presentation operated partly as an information gap, across which learners were pushed to justify conclusions and hone meaning). Underlining represents mined language in the teacher's contributions; the arrow indicates interweaving of new form; S1 and S2 indicate students from a different group.

1	S1:	Habits?
2	Y:	Well first he smokes
3	C:	But we think uh 50% we think just 50%
4	N:	Yes just maybe. We're not sure
5	T:	Oh yeah? Only <u>50%</u>? Why's that?
6	S2:	Yes, give proof (laughter)
7	N:	Because here (showing matchbox). A matchbox
8	T:	Hmmm, but you're <u>not certain</u> if he smokes, huh? (looking at matchbox)
9	A:	Look (opens matchbox). Many matches so maybe he just keep for friend, not for him (laughter)
10 →	T:	Mmmm I- I guess <u>it's possible</u> he might smoke. It's hard to tell just from this
11	A:	Yeah, not sure
12	S2:	You have more proof?

On one level, the teacher appears to adopt a quasi co-participant role here. In this, responsibility for driving the interaction forward is shared across participants (turns 1, 6 and 12), but it is also marked through her use of mined language, a strategy already adopted by the learners. Thus, in following their lead, the teacher aligns herself with the group, as if to converge to their pre-established conversational norms.

However, and more importantly, by mining the language of the task input (and hence effectively, many of the learners' own contributions), the teacher is not simply aligning herself as co-participant. She is also priming the meaning space delineated by task and learners (turns 5, 8 and 10), prior to the introduction of form that could expand resources for filling that space (turn 10). Hence, this strategic use of mined language appears to serve as a proactive move, with the teacher 'leading from behind' to illuminate what is yet to come.

Once the meaning space has been highlighted, the teacher interweaves the form conversationally, without teacherly intonation, without metacomment on its presence in the input, and without deflecting task flow (turn 10). The introduction of the new form does not come as a response to an unsuccessful learner attempt, nor does it recast a previous learner utterance. Rather, it is the result of a series of proactive moves, partly built on lexical chunks mined from task input data, that cumulatively 'precast' the introduction of new form. Thus, formulaic chunks mined from input data are here exploited by the teacher as an instructional strategy to highlight novel form–meaning relationships.

Proactive moves such as these may play an important part in the implementation of knowledge-constructing tasks in that they enable the teacher to work from behind in illuminating form–meaning connections and in the provision of positive evidence. In contrast, much of the current literature on instructional strategies within a communicative framework concentrates on reactive moves, deployed after an unsuccessful learner attempt at form. Such moves aim to prompt attention to emerging or partially internalised forms in the developing system without unduly deflecting the message being conveyed, and as such convey negative evidence which may or may not be noticed (Lyster, 1998). Examples include the corrective recasts and other forms of responsive FonF reported by Doughty and Varela (1998) or the teacher 'nudging' reported by Lynch (1997). Proactive 'precasts' (as illustrated above), on the other hand, may function as advance organisers for the introduction of new form and, as such, serve as pivot points in task implementation, whereby gradual shifts in emphasis from semantic to syntactic processing may be initiated.

Given this, it could be argued that *precasts* (based on a systematic mining of pre-established meaning), in conjunction with *conversational interweaves*, constitute two instructional strategies that operate at the interface between attention to meaning and attention to form, and as such illuminate one facet of the teacher's role in task implementation (although further work is clearly necessary to identify other types of task-driven move).

During this stage of the task, the teacher deployed 22 interweaves, averaging three precasts per interweave. Of these, not one was taken up by the learners. Although absence of uptake does not necessarily imply absence of noticing, it might be argued that this is not surprising, given that the intense focus on meaning is likely to have left little spare capacity for processing for form (VanPatten, 1996) and that the target features may not have been sufficiently salient to be noticed in the input (Schmidt, 1990). Also, given that their current resources appeared adequate to the immediate task in hand, and that there was no need to hone meaning with more precision or to structure it more accurately, the learners were not 'pushed' to notice holes in their current IL systems and thereby notice the gap between current performance and target form (Swain, 1998). However, as confirmed in a post-lesson debriefing, the teacher's goal here was not to push immediate production of the new forms, but to offer a 'first pass' at them, without requirement of learner uptake. Hence, from the teacher's perspective, the shift from semantic to syntactic processing was deliberately gradual.

Explicit language focus

In the absence of any overt response to the 'new' form, the teacher moved to a more explicit language focus. This was marked by a number of false starts, as seen below, in which the teacher's attempt at a preliminary step towards form (turn 1) gets consistently derailed by learners' continuing preoccupation with meaning (turns 2–4). At turn 5, the attempted shift, framed as a suggestion to briefly 'look at how the language works' is finally and explicitly made. (Underlining represents mined language; arrows indicate lines containing the target features.)

1   T: So lots of interesting ideas here. Paula, letters, uh schedule, opera, a busy man
2   C: Japanese classes
3   T: Yeah right, I forgot he's learning Japanese too (laughter)
4   N: And golf
5   T: Oh yes very busy (laughter). Hmmm let's – why don't we look at how the language works here? Just for a minute uhh (looking at objects). Let's see now. Did you have anything here you thought was 'probable'? Like 90%?
6   Y: Businessman
7   T: Businessman? 90%? OK. So you're 90% certain he's a businessman, right? Here's another way to say this. You think it's 90% certain, so you think he
    → must be a businessman. He must be a businessman (writes it on board). So this (point to must be on board) is showing how CERTAIN how SURE you are. Not 100%, but almost 100%. 90%.
8   →A: So 100% is 'be' or 'must'?

In this extract, the teacher's use of mined language is much less subtle than in the implicit focus, and has the effect of focusing attention narrowly on the form–meaning relationships in question. In this, she verifies intended meaning, offers the form as one way of encoding it, and provides a brief meta-comment (turn 7).

However, it is not only the teacher who exploits mined language to focus on form; it also enables A to frame her question poised between meaning and form at turn 8. Thus, mined language appears now to function as a kind of shared currency that enables teacher and learners to work together at the boundaries of form and meaning. It is on this that the teacher draws in order to respond to A's question:

9   T: 100? 100%? Then you can say he IS a businessman (writes on board) When you when you're NOT 100% certain, you can use must. OK? Not he is a businessman, but he must be a businessman. So 'be' here (pointing to must be on board) is from this verb (pointing to is). Let's uh what other things do you have for 'probably'?

In her response, the teacher continues to follow A's lead, and further exploits mined language to bind meaning and form and to elicit further examples from the same semantic category to support her explanation:

10   C: Travel a lot
11   T: OK so if it's <u>90%</u>, you can say he must travel a lot (writes on board) so we use uh we use must with the verb (pointing)
12   N: No 's'?
13   T: Right, no 's'
14   A: Simple verb
15   T: Yeah, you use the simple verb here because must is a modal verb. It doesn't change. No 's' on must and no 's' on the simple verb (pointing to <u>travel</u> on board). So anything else for <u>'probable'</u>?

At turn 12, more elaborated form focusing is initiated by the learners, beginning with N's question at turn 12 and A's metacomment at turn 14. The learners' active involvement in explicit focus on form suggests that a learning space has been primed by the task design, although it could also suggest a 'hunger' for form that task performance has denied thus far. However, whatever the motivation, their active engagement with form at this stage of the task directly follows an active engagement with meaning, and is thus in line with the meaning → form → meaning progression of the overall task design and of the teacher's implementation.

Framed as a confirmation in which the teacher unpacks A's metacomment, turn 15 is one of the few teacher turns that is exclusively focused on form unhinged from meaning. In this, she builds on the declarative knowledge that learners bring with them as a resource in sorting out form without making it a requirement of the task. Again, she returns to meaning by eliciting a further example from the same semantic category. The response comes below:

16   Y: Chess?
17   T: So what about chess?
18 →N: Umm (looking at chart) he must like chess?
19 →T: Yeah right he must like chess he's got this chess thing in his pocket (writes on board) So is that it for <u>'probable'</u>? Or did you have anything else?
20   Y: Married

Turn 18 marks the first emergence of the target forms in learner speech, and is the result of a direct teacher prompt. The teacher responds at the level of meaning, not form. Her 'Yeah right' and repetition of N's utterance is confirmatory, not evaluative; in this, it is not simply the linguistic choice that is being confirmed, but more particularly the basis on which judgement about meaning has been made.

In responding to ill-formed utterances, however, the teacher provided negative feedback only on the items under focus. In this, she responded to problems relating to form (73% of responsive moves) and to problems relating to meaning (27% of responsive moves). Although this might suggest that contrary to expectation, the learners experienced greater difficulty with form than with meaning, it is also possible that the extensive use of proactive moves had highlighted meaning somewhat effectively.

In her provision of corrective feedback, the teacher appeared to respond to form and meaning in different ways. In responding to form, 60% of her moves comprised repetition of the ill-formed part of the utterance with rising intonation, followed by repetition of the correct utterance as topic continuation, after it had been supplied by a learner. For example:

1   S2: She must she must has many, many, MANY boyfriends
2   T: (laughing) She must has?
3   S2: Must yes uh must have
4   A: Have
5   T: Yeah she must have LOTS of boyfriends – look at all these phone numbers (laughter)

When responding to problems with meaning, 82% of her responses drew on language mined from the task input to signal the required focus of repair:

1   S4: We think just 50% so we think she must live in California
2   T: Mmm hang on a minute how <u>certain</u> are you?
3   S4: 50 (looks at chart) yes 50
4   T: <u>50%</u>? So you're not VERY <u>certain</u>, but you think it's <u>possible</u>?
5   S4: Not very not very just 50 ahhh she might
6   T: Yeah she might live in California. With must, the grammar is good, but the meaning changes
7   S4:   Ahh she might live in California yes

All but one of the corrective responses were taken up, in contrast to the previous lack of uptake of the implicit interweaves (see Lyster, 1998, and Spada, 1997, for discussion of the effectiveness of explicit over implicit approaches to directing attention to form). Although the teacher maintained a tight focus on form in this phase of the task, she appeared to treat it as a 'time out' from task operations, but not from the bigger picture of the task as whole. The implicit language focus gave free rein to meaning, but only when meaning had been extensively rehearsed was the teacher ready to bind meaning to form more explicitly. In this, her continued exploitation of language mined from task input data was one way of maintaining overall topic continuity and guiding attention to the role of form as a resource for meaning driven by task demands.

Post-focus

As groups collaborated on the poster preparation, the teacher resumed the 'standby' role of the pre-focus phase. There was a considerable pressure for time during this phase of task completion,[9] which may have had an effect on group performance and on final output in that no further amendments were made to the original task categories and the final captions were short, and relatively unelaborated. The choice of caption writing as part of the task outcome was a deliberate attempt to hone output and to reduce redundancy, and so narrow the focus of attention on the expression of possibility and probability.

The group continued to mine task input data in the post-focus phase of the task: 24% of total expressions of possibility and probability deployed, compared with 27% pre-focus. Comparison of the categories mined pre- and post-focus shows a small decrease in the use of *possible*, no post-focus occurrences of *certain* and *50%*, and an increase in the uses of *probable* and *90%*. This is summarised in Table 6.2.

Table 6.2   Pre- and post-focus oral output: mined expressions of possibility and probability

Mined	Pre-focus: % of *total* expressions of probability and possibility	Post-focus: % of *total* expressions of probability and possibility
Total mined	**27**	**24**
Breakdown of categories		
(It's) possible	10.5	7.3
(It's) probable	5.6	9.7
90%	4.8	7.3
Certain	4.0	0
50%	1.6	0

There was a small increase in the use of non-mined language post-focus: 76% compared with 73% pre-focus. Of this, *maybe* continued to be the most widely used means of expressing possibility and probability, but its use decreased post-focus: 36.5% compared with 53.2% pre-focus. Two non-mined categories (*sure* and *not sure*) were not used at all post-focus, while the target modal auxiliaries (*must, might, may, could*) all occurred, although to varying degree, as shown in Table 6.3.

Table 6.3   Pre- and post-focus oral output: non-mined expressions of probability and possibility

Non-mined	Pre-focus: % of *total* expressions of probability and possibility	Post-focus: % of *total* expressions of probability and possibility
Total non-mined	**73**	**76**
Breakdown of categories		
Maybe	53.2	36.5
(I'm) sure	11.3	0
(I'm) not sure	8.9	0
Must	0	17.0
May	0	12.1
Might	0	7.3
Could	0	2.4

Mined language, then, continued to play a part in supporting intended meaning at this stage of task completion. The decrease in the use of *maybe* as the principal means of expressing possibility and probability and the emergence of the modal auxiliaries suggest some possible initial expansion of learners' repertoires in this semantic domain (although this is discussed further below). However, when this is viewed alongside the increase in the use of *probable* and *90%*, it would appear that the relationship between mined and non-mined expressions of possibility and probability is complex, and that mined language use does not necessarily decrease as new forms are incorporated. Instead, it would appear that mined language may be deployed to anchor new forms as they emerge in output, therein mirroring in part the ways in which it had been deployed in the teacher's precasts and interweaves. This may be seen in the following extract, where, in the final stage of task completion, the learners were pushed finally to 'declare' the strength of their speculations, and thus narrow choices between competing language forms. (N has taken responsibility for writing the captions.)

```
 1    Y:  He likes
 2    N:              Golf
 3    A:                      Tennis
 4    C:  Art
 5    N:  Mmm (looking at chart) art just probable and chess
 6    C:  So probable?
 7    A:  Probable
 8  →N:  (writing) He must like chess?
 9    A:  And art
10    C:  That's all?
11  →Y:              Yeah must is probable
```

Here, N, C and A make use of mined language to check intended meaning in turns 5–7; on the basis of this negotiation, N supplies the appropriate form in turn 8, which is confirmed in turn 11, as Y mines *probable* to frame her metacomment integrating meaning and form. Thus, it is not simply the case that these learners continued to mine task language, but rather that, in so doing, they appeared to extend its range of functions to serve current task demand. At the pre-focus stage, as we have seen previously, mined language appeared to function primarily as a communication strategy to enable greater precision in negotiating meaning to the extent necessary for that stage of task completion; post-focus, mined language was interwoven with the target features in the negotiation of meaning and the negotiation of form, and thus, pushed by task demand, potentially functioning as metatalk deployed in the process of making meaning (Swain, 1995).

In written output, out of 13 poster captions, seven contained the target features, with 100% accuracy. The six captions containing non-modal forms reflected absolute certainty about the propositions expressed, for which non-modal use was appropriate. Hence, the written output reflects both appropriate and accurate use of the target features.

However, it would be both naïve and misguided to suggest that occurrence of the forms in both spoken and written output under these conditions (where attention was on composing and drafting for public consumption) signals internalisation. It might be the case, however, that what this output does indicate is evidence of initial form–meaning mapping and, as such, evidence of intake that could be available for further processing (VanPatten, 1996). Given this, knowledge-constructing tasks like the one described here may function as initial building blocks that permit schematisation of novel form–meaning relationships. As such they should not be expected in themselves to cause specific features to enter learners' grammars, but may provide a critical (albeit preliminary) step towards IL change. Viewed from this perspective, a knowledge-constructing task may function as a contextual anchor for a cycle of subsequent tasks, the precise composition of which would be determined by learner need, but which might include various combinations of form-focused tasks with less structured language-activating/fluency-stretching tasks.

In the absence of a control group and experimental conditions, no claims can be made here about learning. A post-test (paralleling the pre-test) and administered 10 days later, yielded a mean score of 19.01 (maximum score 26), an increase of 15.28. How much of this gain can be attributed to the task and the teacher's implementation and how much to the follow-up work (structured and unstructured tasks, activities and exercises) is of course unknown.

IMPLICATIONS FOR TASK DESIGN AND TEACHER DEVELOPMENT

The step taken in this chapter is modest, and limited in the narrowness of its scope. The instructional strategies discussed here need to be rigorously investigated across a broader range of contexts in order to build a picture of how they might interact with other instructional strategies (for example, recasts, nudging, various types of pushing, *inter alia*) and how these may shape acquisition over time before claims for a task-based pedagogy can be made. However, although it is preliminary to talk of implications for task design and teacher development, some issues have emerged that warrant further mention.

First, a case may be made for a more rigorous appraisal of task design, both as a research agenda and in pedagogic practice. Relatively little attention has been paid to systematic details of task design in the literature, beyond the capacity of a given task to set a specific type of talk in motion or maximise potential for the negotiation of meaning. This chapter has sought to highlight the contribution of specific design features both to the management of attentional resources at different phases of task completion, and as a scaffolding device that may permit teachers to work at the developing edge of current IL repertoires. However, the design features discussed here relate only to one aspect of the framing of task input data, and it is clear that there is scope for much more to be accomplished.

This chapter has also sought to open discussion on the nature of the complementary relationship between task and teacher in the context of tasks in which semantically complex form–meaning mappings are to be made. In this, it has argued that an important role for the *task* may be to attract initial attention to designated areas of meaning, and through task operations, create a need to mean; an important role for the *teacher* may be to complement the task by guiding attention towards form–meaning relationships. In particular, it has suggested that task input data may play a significant, although hitherto overlooked, role as a resource to be 'mined' by learners and teachers in different ways and for different purposes during task performance. In the classroom under discussion, this facet of task design was drawn on by the learners: (1) as a communication strategy in unscripted oral performance; (2) as a means of framing questions to the teacher about form; and (3) as a resource in the negotiation of form and meaning. However, more importantly for the present focus on the role of the teacher in TBLT, it contributed to ways in which the teacher was able to 'lead from behind' to support learning processes across a task context. In particular, the teacher's systematic use of language mined from the task input data helped her: (1) to create alignment with learner groups; (2) to scaffold an implicit language focus through precasts and interweaves in the provision of positive evidence; (3) to introduce an explicit focus on new form–meaning relationships, while maintaining topic continuity; and (4) to frame negative feedback so that form and meaning may be integrated.

Nevertheless, this chapter raises more questions than it addresses. In particular, it is tempting to wonder whether the gradual meaning → form → meaning moves deployed by this teacher are, in the long run, worth the effort. To this end, descriptive studies are needed in order to identify further instructional moves that may be deployed in managing attentional resources across this progression within a task context, and on the basis of this, experimental studies designed to determine long-term acquisitional gain.

NOTES

1. Exceptions include the input-processing tasks developed in VanPatten (1996). 'Structure tasks', for example those reported in Loschky and Bley-Vroman (1993), operate on existing hypotheses rather than 'new' language data.
2. This distinction clearly oversimplifies the issue, given learners' capacities to recontextualise tasks to their own ends (Breen, 1989). It is also clear that, depending on the current state of a learner's IL grammar, the same task may be potentially knowledge constructing, potentially language activating or, most likely, a bit of both. Properly speaking then, this distinction is less a property of the task, and more a property of the learner. Nevertheless, from a teacher's perspective, the distinction would presumably have an effect on the way a task gets implemented.
3. The term 'language focus' is deliberately chosen over the more widely used 'focus on form' in order to reflect the integration of form and meaning central to this approach to task design.

4. However, the relationship between this aspect of task design and the 'noticeability' of specific form–meaning relationships is clearly open to empirical investigation.
5. Once this decision is made, there are a number of other design variables that relate to the framing and structuring of task input data and to task outcome, but these remain beyond the scope of the present discussion.
6. It is beyond the scope of this chapter to discuss this in the light of Loschky and Bley-Vroman's (1993) task essential/utility/natural conditions.
7. A different version of this task appears in Riggenbach and Samuda (2000).
8. Whether, as a result of task demands, learners would mine 'new' language features embedded in task input in this way (for example, in this case, the target modal auxiliaries) is open to empirical investigation, and would clearly have an impact on task design.
9. Time constraints were not built into task design, but arose from institutional demands beyond the teacher's control.

REFERENCES

Breen, M. (1989) The evaluation cycle for language learning tasks. In R.K. Johnson (ed.) *The Second Language Curriculum.* Cambridge: Cambridge University Press.
Bygate, M. (1988) Units of oral expression and language learning in small group interaction. *Applied Linguistics,* 9 (1): 59–82.
Bygate, M. (1999) Task as context for the framing, reframing and unframing of language. *System,* 27 (1): 33–48.
Bygate, M., Dörnyei, Z., Csölle, A., Király, K., Kormos, J. and Németh, N. (1998) Perspectives from a task-based instruction project. Colloquium, 32nd Annual TESOL Convention, Seattle.
Doughty, C. and Pica, T. (1986) Information gap tasks: Do they facilitate second language acquisition? *TESOL Quarterly,* 20: 305–25.
Doughty, C. and Varela, E. (1998) Communicative focus on form. In C. Doughty and J. Williams (eds) *Focus on Form in Classroom Second Language Acquisition.* Cambridge: Cambridge University Press.
Doughty, C. and Williams, J. (1998) Pedagogical choices in focus on form. In C. Doughty and J. Williams (eds) *Focus on Form in Classroom Second Language Acquisition.* Cambridge: Cambridge University Press.
Ellis, R. (1998) Teaching and research: Options in grammar teaching. *TESOL Quarterly,* 32 (1): 39–60.
Foster, P. (1998) A classroom perspective on the negotiation of meaning. *Applied Linguistics,* 19 (1): 1–23.
Foster, P. and Skehan, P. (1996) The influence of planning on performance in task-based learning. *Studies in Second Language Acquisition,* 18: 299–324.
Gass, S. and Varonis, E. (1985) Task variation and NNS/NNS negotiation of meaning. In S. Gass and C. Madden (eds) *Input in Second Language Acquisition.* Rowley, MA: Newbury House.
Gass, S. and Varonis, E. (1994) Input, interaction, and second language production. *Studies in Second Language Acquisition,* 16: 283–302.
Gibbons, P. (1998) Classroom talk and the learning of new registers in a second language. *Language and Education,* 12 (2): 99–118.
Halliday, M.A.K. (1985) *Introduction to Functional Grammar.* London: Edward Arnold.

Harley, B. (1993) Instructional strategies and SLA in early French immersion. *Studies in Second Language Acquisition*, 15: 245–60.

Harmer, J. (1991) *The Practice of English Language Teaching*. Harlow: Longman.

Hasan, R. and Perrett, G. (1994) Learning to function with the other tongue: A systemic functional perspective on second language teaching. In T. Odlin (ed.) *Perspectives on Pedagogical Grammar*. Cambridge: Cambridge University Press.

Hulstijn, J. (1995) Not all grammar rules are equal: Giving grammar instruction its proper place in foreign language teaching. In R. Schmidt (ed.) *Attention and Awareness in Foreign Language Learning*. Honolulu: University of Hawai'i Press.

Larsen-Freeman, D. (1991) Teaching grammar. In M. Celce-Murcia (ed.) *Teaching English as a Second or Foreign Language*. Rowley, MA: Newbury House.

Long, M. and Crookes, G. (1993) Units of analysis in syllabus design: The case for task. In G. Crookes and S. Gass (eds) *Tasks in a Pedagogical Context: Integrating Theory and Practice*. Clevedon: Multilingual Matters.

Long, M. and Robinson, P. (1998) Focus on form: Theory, research, and practice. In C. Doughty and J. Williams (eds) *Focus on Form in Classroom Second Language Acquisition*. Cambridge: Cambridge University Press.

Loschky, L. and Bley-Vroman, R. (1993) Grammar and task-based methodology. In G. Crookes and S. Gass (eds) *Tasks and Language Learning: Integrating Theory and Practice*. Clevedon: Multilingual Matters.

Lynch, T. (1997) Nudge, nudge: Teacher intervention in task-based learner talk. *ELT Journal*, 51 (4): 317–25.

Lyster, R. (1998) Recasts, repetitions, and ambiguity in L2 classroom discourse. *Studies in Second Language Acquisition*, 20 (1): 51–82.

Riggenbach, H. and Samuda, V. (2000). *Grammar Dimensions: Form, Meaning and Use: Book 2* (Platinum edition). Boston, MA: Heinle & Heinle.

Robinson, P. (1995) Task complexity and second language narrative discourse. *Language Learning*, 45 (1): 99–140.

Samuda, V. and Rounds, P.L. (1993) Critical episodes: Reference points for analyzing a task in action. In G. Crookes and S. Gass (eds) *Tasks in a Pedagogical Context: Integrating Theory and Practice*. Clevedon: Multilingual Matters.

Samuda, V., Rounds, P.L. and Gass, S. (1996) Structure-based tasks: Cognitive, social and linguistic perspectives. Presentation at 30th Annual TESOL Convention, Chicago.

Schmidt, R. (1990) The role of consciousness in second language learning. *Applied Linguistics*, 11: 17–46.

Skehan, P. (1996) A framework for the implementation of task-based instruction. *Applied Linguistics*, 17: 38–62.

Skehan, P. (1998) *A Cognitive Approach to Language Learning*. Oxford: Oxford University Press.

Spada, N. (1997) Form-focussed instruction and second language acquisition: A review of classroom and laboratory research. *Language Teaching*, 29: 1–15.

Swain, M. (1995) Three functions of output in second language learning. In G. Cook and B. Seidlhofer (eds) *Principle and Practice in Applied Linguistics*. Oxford: Oxford University Press.

Swain, M. (1998) Focus on form through conscious reflection. In C. Doughty and J. Williams (eds) *Focus on Form in Classroom Second Language Acquisition*. Cambridge: Cambridge University Press.

Tarone, E. and Liu, G.-Q. (1995) Situational context, variation, and second language acquisition theory. In G. Cook and B. Seidlhofer (eds) *Principle and Practice in Applied Linguistics.* Oxford: Oxford University Press.

VanPatten, B. (1996) *Input Processing and Grammar Instruction.* New York: Ablex.

Westney, P. (1994) Rules and pedagogical grammar. In T. Odlin (ed.) *Perspectives on Pedagogical Grammar.* Cambridge: Cambridge University Press.

Willis, J. (1996) *A Framework for Task-Based Learning.* Harlow: Longman.

Yule, G. (1997) *Referential Communication Tasks.* Mahwah, NJ: Lawrence Erlbaum.

Chapter 7

'A case of exercising': Effects of immediate task repetition on learners' performance

Tony Lynch and Joan Maclean

INTRODUCTION

Perspectives on tasks

Language learning tasks can be approached from a variety of perspectives, as this volume makes clear. Classroom researchers may focus on the specific effects on the negotiation of meaning of manipulating technical features of the task, such as the direction of flow of information between the learners (e.g. Pica et al., 1993) or the time allowed for planning (Crookes, 1989; Foster, 1996). Alternatively, a researcher may investigate how performance is influenced by the characteristics of the learners, such as their L1 background (e.g. Duff, 1986; Takahashi, 1989), familiarity with their partner (Plough and Gass, 1993), or L2 proficiency level (Gass and Varonis, 1985; Porter, 1986; Yule, 1994). Materials designers may investigate whether learners are successfully channelled along an intended communicative route and achieve the type or quality of outcome envisaged (Breen and Candlin, 1987; Breen, 1989; Yule and Powers, 1994), or whether the task is open to subversion – for example, by learners showing each other their pictures in a Find the Differences task. (For a recent discussion of 'subversion' in its technical sense, in the context of L2 learning tasks, see Cameron, 1999.) Teachers may be primarily interested in whether, in a wider sense, a particular task 'works' with their learners and, in judging that, different teachers will apply different criteria, such as the proportion of class time the learners spend actively using the L2 (though see Hancock, 1997) and their engagement with the task (Ellis, 1997).

In this chapter we adopt a mixed perspective. We are involved as the designers of the task we subsequently chose to investigate: the poster carousel (Lynch and Maclean, 1994). We were also the teachers of the ESP course in which we recorded learners carrying out the task, which features repetition in the form of successive cycles of talk with different speaking partners. However, the main reason for our research was an interest in analysing what individuals in the class did in and with the task; so the learner's perspective is central to our study. The questions we set out to find answers to were:

1. Do learners gain from repetition of the task?
2. In what ways do they gain?
3. Do they *think* they gain?
4. In what ways do they *think* they gain?

The poster carousel

The poster carousel was designed for a course *English for Medical Congresses*, run at the Institute for Applied Language Studies (IALS), University of Edinburgh. For a description of the history and content of the course, see Lynch and Maclean (1999). The procedure is as follows:

1. Participants are paired up and each pair is given a different research article (800–1,000 words). They have one hour to make a poster based on the article.
2. The posters are displayed round a large room. From each pair, one participant (A) – the 'host' – stands beside his or her poster, waiting to receive 'visitors' asking questions. The B participants visit the posters one by one, clockwise. They ask questions about each poster. The host is instructed not to give a mini-lecture, but to respond to questions. A limited time (approximately 3 minutes) is allowed at each poster.
3. When the B participants arrive back at base, they stay by their poster and the A participants go visiting.
4. Once the second round is completed, there is plenary discussion of the merits of the posters (by the participants) and the teachers provide feedback on general language points.

The carousel has three specific pedagogic aims: to provide a freer activity after a series of more controlled reporting tasks; to offer a lighter activity before the stresses of the final day of the course, when the participants present papers at a simulated conference; and to practise formulating and handling questions under time pressure but with the (assumed) benefit of immediate repetition.

Our research focuses on the assumption behind this third aim – whether repetition does in fact bring benefits (see Bygate in this volume for a slightly different approach to the effects of task repetition). Over the years we have had informal evidence that the carousel 'works'. Teachers believe it creates plenty of purposeful talk, involvement and apparent enjoyment. Learners' evaluations have been predominantly positive; one specifically praised what he called the 'hurry, hurry, hurry' of the carousel (cf. *real operating conditions* in Johnson, 1996). On the other hand, there have been occasional criticisms that poster preparation takes too long for too little pay-off, and this was one of the reasons for our decision to study the task: what exactly *is* the pay-off of repetition, from the learner's point of view?

The poster carousel contrasted with tasks in the literature

The carousel differs in a number of ways from oral communication tasks more typical of the 'task-based learning' literature. First, any textual *input* to such speaking tasks is usually rather limited. Prompt materials may be non-verbal (e.g. strip cartoons, videos) or very brief (under 50 words, for example, in Foster and Skehan, 1997). The carousel, on the other hand, is based on medical journal articles of 800–1000 words, converted into poster format.

Second, the effect of planning has been investigated in studies such as the Thames Valley University series (e.g. Foster in this volume; Foster and Skehan, 1996; Skehan and Foster, 1997; Skehan, 1998). Although the carousel does involve substantial planning time (an hour), the nature of the planning is different: the learners are primarily wrestling with the content of their article and its expression in a poster, but not preparing its realisation in speech.

Third, the carousel instructions are oral; there is no written guidance of the type illustrated in Skehan (1998: 137–45). Apart from strictly procedural information, the only instruction for the carousel is that the poster 'hosts' should not launch into a pre-emptive mini-presentation, but wait for the visitor to ask questions.

Fourth, previous studies of the effects of repetition (e.g. Bygate, 1996 and Chapter 2 in this volume) have focused on monologue, with learners talking to a listener – often the researcher – who provides little or no response. This has allowed the researcher to maintain experimental control, but at the cost of ignoring what McNamara, writing from the oral testing perspective, has called the 'inextinguishable presence of interaction' (McNamara, 1997: 447). In the carousel, interaction is central: the communicative initiative lies with the visitor, while the host's role is to respond appropriately and persuasively to the visitor's questions.

Fifth, in other investigations of repetition effects, the intervals between first and second performance have been relatively long – days or weeks (Brown et al., 1984; Nobuyoshi and Ellis, 1993). In the poster carousel, repetition is immediate, at three-minute intervals. It is also the case that 'repetition' is a less accurate term than 'recycling', the visitors' questions should shape the host's response. The host cannot – or should not – simply repeat what he or she has said in the previous cycle.

The final difference is that, as well as not including explicit pre-task plan-ning of speech, the carousel allows no rehearsal, in the sense of a private performance before a public one (Skehan, 1996). The conversation with the first visitor is not a 'dry run' for the later visitors; each of the six cycles is a performance in its own right.

METHOD

Participants

The learners we studied were 14 oncologists and radiotherapists taking a course in *English for Cancer Conferences* at IALS in April 1997. This was a more

specialised version of the *English for Medical Congresses* course. The participants came from six European countries and ranged in age from their late
twenties to late fifties. All were experienced in presenting conference papers
in their own language and most had also already presented in English. At the
start of the course they completed a listening test and a lexico-grammar test;
their scores indicated a proficiency range within the group equivalent approximately to TOEFL 400–600.

Our preliminary study (Lynch and Maclean, 1999) investigated linguistic
changes in the performances of Alicia and Daniela, who represented respectively the bottom (TOEFL 400) and the top (TOEFL 600) of the range. Under
'Results and discussion' below, we provide a brief summary of our findings,
to which we then add our analysis of recordings of three more participants –
Susanna, Olga and Carla. (These and the other names used in our reports of
this research are pseudonyms.)

Data

We collected two types of data. First, we recorded all six conversations between every host/visitor pair by placing an audiocassette recorder near each
poster. Recording and playback of performance is routine in the course and
so the participants were used to being recorded. All 14 sets of six interactions
were transcribed. Our second source of data was a self-report questionnaire,
which participants completed after the carousel but before they heard our
comments on their performances. Its purpose was to get them to reflect on
their experience of 'the-task-as-action' (Breen, 1989). For reasons of space
we will make only brief mention of the questionnaire comments at relevant
points in this chapter.

RESULTS AND DISCUSSION

Summary of Study 1 (Lynch and Maclean, 1999)

Our analysis of Alicia's and Daniela's performances as poster hosts found
evidence of *attention to language*: self-corrections of vocabulary and pronunciation (Daniela); corrections of pronunciation and grammar prompted by
the interlocutor (Alicia); correct fluent use of some language forms after
initial difficulty (Alicia); correct use of forms introduced and practised earlier in the course (both). *Attention to content* was evidenced by: slower speed of
speaking at conceptually difficult points, with frequent pausing (Daniela);
incorporation of content introduced by previous interlocutors (Alicia). Both
learners made *linguistic improvements* over successive cycles of the task: Alicia,
who had severe language problems, made some errors (e.g. SVO order) less
frequently with task repetition; Daniela's performances showed an increase
in the quantity of information she provided and greater precision in her
choice of words. Our provisional conclusion was that these two individuals

used the carousel task in different ways, and that this was related to their markedly different levels in English.

Study 2

To investigate further the relationship between repetition, performance and level, we then carried out a follow-up study of another three course participants, whose entry test scores fell between those of Alicia and Daniela. All three chosen were female, which removed the gender variable as a possible influence in our analysis of learner behaviour during the carousel.

Susanna

Susanna scored 36% on the listening test and 12% on grammar (approximately TOEFL 450). She had a rather hesitant speaking manner and did not volunteer contributions in open-floor talk in other course sessions. Her comparatively limited lexical knowledge appears to have made it difficult for her to respond flexibly to comprehension and production problems during the carousel. However, her performances as host included changes in three areas: phonology, syntax and lexis. She showed uncertainty about syllable-stress in a number of words, one of which was 'survival': sometimes she pronounced it with the main stress on the first syllable. The series of extracts below[1] shows where she pronounced it with incorrect stress (indicated by capital letters).

Cycle 1	V	aesthetic ok but it didn't + and you get a got a significant + I see correctly + a significant increase in <u>survival</u>?
	S	uh yes uh you see the uh overall survival and disease-free <u>survival</u> was higher in the + group who had intraportal infusions or not adjuvant
Cycle 2	V	uh how long was the follow-up of the study? the follow-up?
	S	yes the follow-up is five years disease-free <u>SURval</u> and overall <u>SURVal</u> it's the five years
	V	five years
	S	hmhm
	V	+ + + have you compared this + what do you think if you compare these cases with adjuvant intraportal chemotherapy + with a group + with uh general chemotherapy + with adjuvant therapy but not intraportal?
	S	hmhm but I think that intraportal + uh will be better because + uh it's more effective in prolonging free-disease <u>SUR-- survival</u> and overall <u>survival</u>
Cycle 3	V	yes I think it's + an important conclusion that adjuvant intraportal chemotherapy was + effective in prolonging disease-free <u>survival</u> but + what about the complications? Were there any problems with . . . ?
	S	yes + the complications is to determine + the effectiveness and to show their dependent its effectiveness intraportal chemo + chemotherapy with + um disease-free survival and overall <u>survival</u> + +

Cycle 6 S   the middle follow-up is eight years
        V   eight years
        S   eight years like + disease-free <u>survival</u> and + overall <u>survival</u>
        V   survival + is different + + + very interessant (*laughs*)

It may be that, as we found with Alicia, Susanna was making use of cues in her interlocutor's speech to guide her own production. Visitor 1 pronounced 'survival' correctly and Susanna also got the stress right. In cycle 2 it was Susanna who initiated use of the word but, without a model to follow, she wrongly stressed the first syllable and elided the second, ending up with what sounded like 'SURval'. However, when she next said the word (in her third speaking turn in cycle 2) she seemed to recognise that her previous version had been wrong, because this time she stopped in mid-word and self-corrected. In cycle 3 her visitor was the first to mention 'survival' and Susanna imitated/produced it correctly. In cycle 6 she again pronounced it accurately, even without a cue from her visitor – an apparent advance on her output in cycle 2.

There is some evidence that Susanna also used interlocutor cues to improve her syntax; a case in point was difficulty with the construction 'I think' followed by a verb clause, which varies over four cycles:

Cycle 1 V   (*reads aloud*) what stages of colorectal can be included? What stages?
        S   uh
        V   advanced? more advanced? More
        S   <u>I think so it's different stages</u> but + + + I think so that all patients hadn't uh metastatic disease + only the primary tumours

Cycle 2 V   + + + have you compared this + <u>what do you think</u> if you compare these cases with adjuvant intraportal chemotherapy + with a group + with uh general chemotherapy + with adjuvant therapy but not intraportal?
        S   hmhm but <u>I think that intraportal + uh will be better</u> because + uh it's more effective in prolonging free-disease SUR-- survival and overall survival

Cycle 3 V   yes <u>I think the outline of the poster is very [?] very nice</u> + I like it
        S   no no not about the poster + but you understand this really? + not about the poster + yes?
        V   the content? yes
        S   + + because <u>I think it's not very easy to understand</u> because we was very hurry when we did it

Cycle 5 V   do you use this kind of therapy as a routine + at home? Adjuvant chemotherapy?
        S   no + <u>I think so it's only intraportal chemotherapy</u>
            [. . .]
        V   not of the {yes yes} chemotherapy but of the technique
        S   I understand
        V   bleeding
        S   you see I don't + <u>I think that in one or two cases we had their vein thrombosis</u>

In that series we again see a possible interlocutor cue effect. See Swain and Lapkin, this volume, for additional discussion of scaffolding interaction of this sort. When following up the visitor's use of the correct form (cycles 2 and 3) Susanna correctly omitted 'so'. But when she herself initiated the expression (cycles 1 and 5) she got it wrong, though in cycle 5 she was able to get it right on the second occasion.

We referred earlier to Daniela's increased fluency and precision of expression of the same facts. A similar practice effect may have been at work in Susanna's case, in relation to the way she described the criteria for including subjects in the study featured in her poster. Her expression became less awkward and more precise over the six cycles.

Cycle 1   S   I think so it's different stages but + + + I think so that <u>all patients hadn't uh metastatic disease</u> + only the primary tumours

Cycle 4   S   <u>no uh we had only patients without metastasis</u> only with + primary tumours after operation

Cycle 6   S   you see and uh + <u>we had only patients + after operation and no reparation evidence of metastatic disease</u>

Susanna also self-corrected errors made in an earlier cycle, even in the absence of any (audible) negative feedback – whether implicit, in the form of communication breakdown, or as explicit correction. One example is her selection of the verb *take* instead of *put*, when she was referring to the fact that she and her partner had omitted the number of patients from their poster:

Cycle 1   S   but also we forgot to <u>take</u> here the number of patients + it was five hundred five patients

Cycle 4   V   yeah + thank you + + how long? uh + + + ok + + + how many patients were included in the . . . ?

              S   five hundred five patients we forgot yes we forgot (*laughs*) to <u>put</u> there

This improved lexical selection may have been the result of practice – and monitoring – since the omitted numbers of patients in the study was not mentioned in either of the intervening cycles 2 and 3.

Like Alicia, Susanna was hindered by her limited English in the way she was able to respond to the content of the questions and criticisms. Four visitors asked the same question – about side-effects of the treatment. In two cases she misinterpreted the question, and in different ways, apparently because visitors 3 and 5 used the word *complications*.

Cycle 1   S   five days and all this time the ca-- caTHETer was in the portal vein

              V   was inside there?

              S   yes

              V   for five days?

              S   yes

              V   and that didn't cause any problems like thrombosis or something like this?

              S   aest-- aestet--

              V   aesthetic ok but it didn't + . . .

Cycle 3	V	what about the complications? + were there any problems with . . . ?
	S	yes + the complications is to determine + the effectiveness and to show their dependent its effectiveness intraportal chemo + chemotherapy with + um disease-free survival and overall survival + + + and + uh we wanted to see the differentiation between the whole-body chemotherapy the normal chemotherapy and intraportal
	V	+ + do you have problems for example as infection or haemorrhage or so + by + the chemotherapy?
	S	+ + let me [?] but in this article it's not explained
Cycle 5	V	did you have any complications from the intraportal chemotherapy?
	S	no only colorectal cancer
	V	no I mean complications + side-effects of the
	S	ah + I see
Cycle 6	V	and [??] any secondary effects?
	S	um
	V	it's not included in this study
	S	yes yes + it's not included

The questions from visitors 1 and 6 were handled without obvious difficulty; she found their expressions 'problems' and 'secondary effects' transparent, it seems, whereas 'complications' caused her to give incorrect (and different) answers. She appears to have interpreted 'complications' as referring to the *complexity* of the study in cycle 3 and to the patient's existing *condition* in cycle 5. It is also noticeable that even though visitor 3 tried to help her by reformulating 'complications' as 'problems', Susanna did not recognise that potentially helpful move.

Olga

Olga's scores (71% on listening and 36% on grammar) placed her mid-way between Susanna and Daniela (TOEFL 525, approximately). She was an effective communicator in English and a relatively fluent speaker; in the carousel she contributed an overall 65% of the words produced in her six cycles as host. We have found evidence of improvement in her syntax, lexical selection and phonology. There is, however, no evidence that she adopted or adapted any English expressions used by her interlocutors, though there is some indication that the traffic was in the other direction – cases where she monitored and corrected the visitor's pronunciation.

The research article on which her poster was based compared three forms of breast cancer treatment: mastectomy, lumpectomy and lumpectomy plus irradiation. The study was a reanalysis of previously published research, made necessary because the data from one of the centres involved, St Luc Hospital in Canada, had included false biopsy results. In explaining the aim of the study, Olga progressively improved in syntactic accuracy (of the expressions underlined):

| Cycle 1 | O | . . . . it was in totally two + thousand one hundred five patients + and + eh for <u>the excluding three hundred twenty two woman</u> from St Luc |

Hospital + eh that is about 15% of total patients + it can't change the em final results

Cycle 2   O   the point of the whole study was to see + whether + this false result from this hospital St Luc Hospital + would + change the final results of the analysis of multi-centric analysis of this number of patients + and + to this analysis they have come that <u>the excluding of this number of woman</u> didn't change the final results +

Cycle 3   O   the real results + is that <u>this exclusion of these patients</u> three hundred twe-- thirty two patients + didn't influence on final results +

There we can see a move away from a syntactically inaccurate combination in cycle 1 ('the excluding' plus object) to an acceptable one in the next ('the excluding of . . .') and finally to the form most appropriate to professional discussion ('this exclusion of . . .'). There were no further refinements after cycle 3, because she used finite verbs to refer to the St Luc data ('they excluded . . .' in cycle 5, and 'they have excluded . . .' in cycle 6).

At various points we find evidence of Olga monitoring her own production, for example her on-line correction or improvement of word-choice (original and corrected words underlined below),

Cycle 1   V   yeah + I think you have performed a very important work
　　　　　 O   yes + I think it also + because it is 12 years of follow-up on such <u>big</u> em group of patients + <u>large</u> group of patients + and it is only possible to make real conclusion ah which eh could have influence in the future + treatment <u>on</u> + <u>through</u> such sorts of studies

and her self-correction in a subsequent task cycle:

Cycle 1   O   and the final results + is + that + this <u>spare</u> surgery + a lumpectomy with additional + radiotherapy can improve . . .

Cycle 6   O   but it is no doubt that it is necessary after spare eh <u>sparing</u> surgery to have + irradiation therapy

Olga also corrected 'woman' to 'women' over four cycles: 'three hundred twenty two *woman* from St Luc Hospital' (cycle 1), 'the excluding of this number of *woman*' (cycle 2) and 'three hundred twenty two *women* from that' (cycle 5). It is not clear whether this was a correction of phonological form or of lexical selection, but the upshot was that her third realisation was more accurate than the other two.

As well as listening out for points for linguistic improvement during the carousel, Olga appeared to be seeking ways of enhancing the *information* content of her utterances, by finding a more precise formulation:

Cycle 1   O   and the final results + is + that + this spare surgery + a lumpectomy with additional + radiotherapy <u>can improve</u> + is the <u>best + + possible treatment</u> in the moment + to prevent recurrence or to give a <u>local control</u> + the <u>better rates of local control</u>

Cycle 4   O   the part of post-lumpectomy irradiation is very important in preventing
　　　　　 V   in all possibility
　　　　　 O   in preventing eh recurrence disease + to have a <u>local control</u> + to have a <u>proper local control</u>

Olga seems to have aimed in each case for greater precision in her message; the changes were made to content, not form.

In general terms, however, her English remained rather inaccurate and hesitant, with frequent superficial errors (e.g. subject/verb concord and article use). Unlike Alicia and Susanna, she did not pick up more accurate forms from her interlocutors' speech during the task. One example of that was the syntax of 'influence' (as verb and noun).

Cycle 1   O   patients + large group of patients + and it is only possible to make real conclusion ah which eh <u>could have influence</u> in the future + treatment on through such sorts of studies

Cycle 3   O   and the purpose of this study was to see whether the smaller number of patients <u>would have influence at the final conclusion</u> which were already done ++ before [. . .] and you can see how much <u>influence on the recurrence</u> has radiotherapy for the probability of recurrence + so it is very

Cycle 5   O   you can't believe them + and + the aim of the study was to see whether this number could eh
　　　　　V   (*sotto voce*) influence the results
　　　　　O   <u>make any influence of the final results</u> + but + the other aim + was also to see + how can radiotherapy + improve the local control
　　　　　V   mm + yes

Cycle 6   O   and it was eh em the co-- a co-- it was concluded that has <u>no influence of the final conclusion</u> + that + it is + you have + whether a mastectomy but with same results you have lumpectomy with irradiation

In that series Olga used three different prepositions after 'influence' – *at, of* and *on*. Her interaction with visitor 5 had the potential to help her notice the gap between her expression and his, but she seems not to have heard his accurate completion of her utterance ('influence the results'), either because he said it too quietly or because her attention was focused on formulating what she was going to say next.

One of the problems of L2 pair work is that even if a learner 'notices' that his or her partner has produced an L2 form that differs from learner's own way of saying it, he or she may decide that the other person's version is incorrect – an assumption that might not be made if the partner were a native speaker of English. This may have been the case with Olga's non-adoption of visitor 5's completion; apart from being rather reserved and quietly spoken (if volume was the problem), he had weaker English than she did, and so it could be that she consciously disregarded what he had said. There is other evidence, in her final cycle, that Olga was not a particularly 'open' listener, in the sense of being prepared to notice and accept others' expressions as correct:

Cycle 6   O   there is only the open question of the post-irradiated dose that has to be given
　　　　　V   + I see
　　　　　O   but <u>it is no doubt that</u> it is necessary after spare eh sparing surgery to have + irradiation therapy

V   yes + I think <u>there's no doubt</u> yes + I agree + I agree
O   <u>it is no doubt</u> + it now it is the cosmetic results + are cosmetic results
     as a question and the dose +

In that case, visitor 6 had a better command of English, with test scores only slightly lower than Daniela. We also know from a later episode in their conversation (which we will come back to in 'Discussion') that Olga respected this visitor's professional and intellectual abilities. So rather than interpreting this incident as an example of Olga taking a conscious decision to ignore his recast ('there's no doubt') it seems more likely that she did not notice the opportunity for linguistic correction. However, there is evidence that she was willing to correct the errors of others (e.g. visitor 2's pronunciation of 'recurrence') and to *self*-correct.

Carla

Carla's test scores were virtually the same as Olga's (74% on listening; 44% on grammar) at around TOEFL 525. Her six poster conversations reveal a number of changes – increased precision of information (like Daniela) and self-corrections (like Olga) – but her opportunities to make L2 gains from this type of communicative task appear to be restricted by her interactional behaviour.

Carla was Alicia's partner in poster production, so she shared the poster topic of the meta-analysis of breast cancer research comparing the effectiveness of less extensive surgery, more extensive surgery, and surgery plus radiotherapy. The first way in which Carla's performance changed over the 25 minutes of the carousel was that she presented the information more fluently, as we have seen with Daniela and Susanna. Compare the way she dealt with the initial request for a summary of the research with the way she responded to her final visitor:

Cycle 1 V   (*reads*) the difference between the two studies is what?
             C   uh surgery + + so {hm} in the surgery but here it is the bulk of the
                  studies analysed + thirty six studies
             V   hm
             C   and they uh it was for + only surgery + more extensive surgery + uh
                  <u>I think</u> mastectomy <u>probably</u> {yes yes} versus less extensive tumour-
                  ectomy and segmentectomy <u>and things like that</u>
Cycle 6 V   (*reads*) + + + well you only say surgery + what kind of surgery is meant
                  please?
             C   all the types of uh surgery + um localised uh localised tumourectomy
                  segmentectomy or radical mastectomy

Carla's response to visitor 6 was less hesitant and less vague than in the first cycle (cf. Bygate in this volume), where she included various markers of uncertainty ('I think', 'probably' and 'and things like that').

There are also signs, in the form of lexical and phonological self-corrections, that Carla was monitoring her own performance. In cycle 2, for instance, she corrected an L1-influenced word choice:

Cycle 2 C   it should be an arrow here + to sign that + it's forgotten we had

   V   good + there are mo- more deaths?

   C   significatively more {in which group please?} <u>significantly</u> more deaths

Later she corrected her syllable stress placement in 'comparison':

Cycle 3 C   all types + + and then different types they have made different types
of compaRI- <u>comPArisons</u> + between surgery alone + every type of
surgery {I: no yes all this is clear but} here clear but

Then in cycle 5 she corrected an error of lexical selection – 'inside' to
'included':

Cycle 5 C   I think it's a problem of this study + I am not uh have not present at
the moment when the years that were inside <u>included</u> in this study it
was published in 93

Two aspects of Carla's performance were especially striking and unlike those
of others we have analysed: her attitude to the task and her interactional style.
In Tarone's phrase, she did not 'buy in' to the role expected of her as poster
host (Tarone, 1999). Throughout her tenure as host, she made it clear that
she wanted to distance herself from the article that she and Alicia had summarised in their poster. Lexically, she showed that she did not own the
research study, by using 'they' to refer to the authors of the original article;
in the other poster conversations, the hosts either identified themselves with
the researchers ('we', 'our', etc.) or adopted a neutral stance ('the data', 'the
study', 'the conclusions' and so on). Nevertheless, the fact that she maintained and marked this distance from the task material did not appear to
restrict her attention to the task.

The following extracts from the first three cycles give a flavour of Carla's
view of the study featured in her poster:

Cycle 1 C   more deaths from non-breast cancer related problems but uh + <u>they</u>
<u>have not exactly made a discrimination</u> {but} about which type of sur-
gery + of radiotherapy + if it was lymph nodes or [?] lymph nodes
included in the radiotherapy or not + I think it would be important
{yes} at least in the future {V: to know the} to do all these study
because if we know {the effect on + heart disease} irradiation of the
heart likely give a lot of problems + I think <u>they should perhaps tell a</u>
<u>little bit about</u>

Cycle 2 C   in this group {in this one} it has an arrow + an arrow {deaths from
non-breast cancer reasons} really + <u>they have not specified</u> {yes I see}
<u>they have not specified if which type</u> of radio- + <u>I think they should</u>
<u>have done here a distinction</u> between those who have been irradiated
{hm} for internal mammary [?] too {yes} and only for axillary

Cycle 3 C   yes that's very important + I think it's something they should I think
<u>it's something they should</u> {in the radiotherapy group} <u>they have to</u>
<u>study more</u> because <u>they don't say</u> which groups have done internal
mammary radiotherapy and which groups have not done that + and
which causes of the death + cardiac failure

When her next visitor asked his opening question, Carla launched into an extended turn – by far the longest in our data, at just under 200 words – and presented a thorough critique of 'them' and 'their' work.

Cycle 4 V   I have a question + why do you think it is the reason of this conclusion that in the radiotherapy group more died of non-breast cancer?

C   it's a problem for everybody because it's a contingent test and <u>they don't give us clues</u> to + to think why + and <u>they don't discriminate</u> the type of radiotherapy they did + if they irradiated internal mammary nodes then everybody tells or some opinions tell that give more problems to the heart in future + or <u>they have not discriminated</u> the type of failure the patient had + if he died of uh heart failure or pulmonary fibrosis or + which kind of failure + so it's uh + I think <u>they should have done</u> a little more + and perhaps as someone told + <u>they should discriminate</u> a little more in which type of early breast cancer + but at the moment we can discriminate a little more + the study was published in 93 + uh but at the moment I have not present the years the study include + and at the moment <u>I think a study should not be done like this</u> [??] or I should say a meta-analysis can be done but a study to evaluate these things should clarify much more the type of nodes involved and the type of radiotherapy + but *I think it should have a new study* to evaluate all this + + this + +

V   so I have another question uh . . .

The second distinctive characteristic of Carla's performance was her turn-taking. At times she did not yield to the visitor, but pressed on with her current speaking turn – 'overriding' her interlocutor (the term used by Vasseur et al., 1996: 77). In the next extract we have highlighted in bold the visitor's bids to speak, to help convey how Carla declined to cede her turn, despite what were (to us observers) clear signals that he wanted to speak. Visitor 5 made two attempts to begin a turn, but he did not succeed until Carla had added a new point that she wanted to make. At that point, he finally managed to complete what he had tried to open with his first 'because'.

Cycle 5 V   do you think + um + radiotherapy + as has been done with many of these these uh studies can be compared with or can meet the standards for radiotherapy in + nowadays?

C   I don't think so I'm not a radiotherapist I should say so and I'm not very (*laughs*) [??] with radiotherapy too but uh + I think it's a problem of this study + I am not uh have not present at the moment when the years that were inside included in this study it was published in 93 but perhaps it came long before the beginning **{yeah of course the}** and radiotherapy has changed a lot this time **{because}** and other thing that's not present in this study and somebody has told here it's what is the early breast cancer in this study? + + there's early breast cancer as cancer with different uh different prognosis

V   yeah because many of these trials in fact . . .

In a number of similar situations, Carla appeared unaware that her interlocutor was bidding to speak; either that, or she was actually ignoring that bid.

Even the two most proficient members of the class had difficulty in getting Carla to recognise and accept their bids. Below we see one of them adopting the tactic of raising his voice to ensure that he was heard:

Cycle 2 C   there's more deaths from non-breast cancer situations in this group
         V   yes
         C   it should be an arrow here + to sign that + it's forgotten we had
         V   good + there are mo- more deaths?
         C   significatively more
         V   in which group please?
         C   significantly more deaths
         V   in WHICH GROUP please? In this group?
         C   in this group . . .

However, we should stress that Carla did not dominate *throughout* her six conversations; the total word count for her six cycles shows that her overall contribution to the conversations was 58% – hardly one-sided, and rather less than Olga (65%). Twice Carla even invited her visitors to offer their comments on the issue or problems they had raised, once she had made her point, as shown here:

Cycle 2 C   as you are a radiotherapist <u>perhaps you could tell me something</u> about your opinion

Cycle 6 V   well you know results of the literature so this is very um + a very difficult result I think
         C   so uh <u>what would you suggest</u>?
         V   well I think that we would expect . . .

One possible explanation for Carla's unusual turn-taking (unusual in this group of learners) emerged in her course evaluation questionnaire. Of another course session, in which pairs of participants had had to summarise different journal articles for the rest of the class, she said

> I couldn't follow the other groups. I would like to have from the beginning of the course all the articles to be discussed and perhaps mine only to be chosen at the session. It would oblige me to pay attention to all the others.

Perhaps the problem was, then, that she found it hard to understand other learners of English, or indeed to *concentrate* on what they were saying. If so, then it may be that Carla's tendency to override her interlocutor arose from a difficulty in hearing or understanding what he or she was saying, rather than an insistence on having her say.

On the other hand, we have some evidence she was actively monitoring the *content* of what her visitors say, as we noted was also true of Daniela and Olga. In the extract below she explicitly recycles a point from an earlier conversation:

Cycle 5 C   and other thing that's not present in this study <u>and somebody has told here</u> it's what is the early breast cancer in this study? + + there's early breast cancer as cancer with different uh different prognosis

It may be significant that we have found no examples of Carla taking up language from her interlocutor. There are a number of possible explanations for this. It could be because her English was relatively accurate – compared for example with Olga, despite their similar test scores. Carla's performances on the task contained few systematic errors that might have allowed her to notice and correct by comparing with her visitors' English. On the other hand, it may have been that she did not consider it *useful* to look for and adopt new language from her interlocutors. She may have seen it as her communicative goal to focus on her own performance, rather than the performances of others.

Discussion

Our earlier study (Lynch and Maclean, 1999) found that Alicia and Daniela both made their speech more accurate and more fluent during their time as poster hosts. They did so in different ways, which we concluded were related to their very different levels of English. This second analysis of the three further recordings confirms that general finding: Susanna, Olga and Carla also selected and produced more accurate L2 forms in successive cycles. All five learners whose conversations we have analysed improved in terms of phonology (segmental or stress) and vocabulary (access or selection); all but Alicia increased the semantic precision of what they were saying; and three made improvements in syntax.

There is evidence that both the type of change and these individuals' awareness of change may be linked with their L2 level. While the three learners with the lowest grammar scores of those studied so far (Alicia, Susanna and Olga) made improvements in syntactic accuracy, the higher-scoring individuals (Carla and Daniela) did not. That is not in itself surprising, but we find it interesting that the adjustments made by the two weakest individuals (Alicia and Susanna) came in response to cues in the speech of their interlocutor, whereas Olga was able to self-correct by monitoring her own speech.

It is encouraging that the task provided an opportunity for different types of improvement from different learners across a wide proficiency range. The carousel required each learner to interact with six visitors, with the inevitable result that the gap in proficiency in some pairings was considerable. This issue of grouping learners for paired tasks has been the subject of debate (e.g. Porter, 1986; Yule and Macdonald, 1990; Lynch, 1996), particularly in view of the risk that when the difference between partners' proficiency is substantial, the higher-level learner may be frustrated, even if the lower-level partner stands to benefit. So the fact that all the learners we have studied made changes and improvements is welcome confirmation of earlier findings on more controlled tasks (Porter, 1986).

A further risk with disparate pairs is that the more proficient partner will dominate, particularly when assigned the informationally authoritative role in an information gap task (Yule, 1994). However, in the case of the carousel, the shared professional expertise of the course participants means that both partners are able to draw on their pre-existing specialist knowledge in discussing the research featured in the poster, and this precludes one having sole access to task-relevant information.

How exactly did the task assist or enable the learners to make progressive changes? In our earlier study we reported that two of the three most proficient members of the class said that they felt more 'relaxed' as the carousel went on, and certainly that subjective perception is important. In addition it has been argued, from a cognitive rather than an affective perspective, that task repetition facilitates more accurate L2 production by allowing a shift of attention:

> this shift, from a preoccupation with finding the expressions to a greater capacity for monitoring formulation, may be precisely what teachers might wish to encourage since it may enable learners to pay more attention to the task of matching language to concepts, and possibly to improving their knowledge and organization of the language.   (Bygate, 1996: 144)

There are parallels between the findings of our study and those from the Australian *access* oral interaction testing research (e.g. O'Loughlin, 1995; Wigglesworth, 1997). This has included comparisons of the spoken performances by language learners on direct (face-to-face) and semi-direct (recorded) speaking tests. Among other things, these studies have found that candidates achieved higher lexical density in their responses in semi-direct tests, which may have resulted from the longer planning time available; this appeared to allow or encourage candidates to produce more 'literate' spoken performances than in the face-to-face test (O'Loughlin, 1995). Wigglesworth (1997) analysed direct and semi-direct test performances by candidates' proficiency level and, again, found evidence of the benefits of planning: higher-proficiency candidates were able to perform better on measures of accuracy and complexity in the semi-direct tests. In both cases, this (implicit and unfocused) planning led to improved spoken performances. So it could be that in the poster carousel the recycling and practice available through the series of visitor cycles offer a sort of 'planning', which brings benefits that are realised – in two senses – by the more proficient learners.

We now turn to the question of whether the learners were *aware* of the changes and improvements in their successive performances. The questionnaire responses provide some insights into individual perceptions during the carousel task, though they are more limited than we had hoped for: while they identified types of change they had made, for example, in grammar or pronunciation, none of the participants gave any specific examples of such changes. At the lower end of the range, Alicia was definite that she had neither planned nor noticed any changes during the task; and Susanna wrote that she could not remember doing either. Yet, as we have seen, both did in fact correct and improve aspects of their English, even if they were not aware of it. Of the three higher-level learners, both Olga and Daniela reported that they consciously planned changes to their English during the carousel and Daniela said she had also noticed making unplanned changes. Again, this is arguably evidence for an effect of level; as teachers we face the paradox that weaker learners like Alicia and Susanna may be so concerned with making themselves understood that they do not have the chance to monitor the changes and improvements they are in fact making to their L2 output.

So, although we observed improvements in the performances of Alicia and Susanna, the least proficient learners in the group, we found that they were *not aware* of those changes. The conclusion we draw from that finding is that teachers should design and include post-task activities to help them to monitor ways in which their performances had in fact become more accurate, but which they were too preoccupied to notice in the heat of communication. For example, Johnson (1996), Lynch (1996) and Skehan and Foster (1997) have proposed the use of task transcripts to help learners to 'see' their own L2 speech in a concrete and noticeable form. An ongoing study of self-transcribing (Lynch, in press) suggests that L2 learners are prepared to spend (surprisingly) long periods of time transcribing their own performances and then discussing and editing their transcripts, in return for teacher feedback on their final version.

The type of interaction built into the carousel task is, we think, of particular importance from the pedagogic point of view. The cyclical task structure means that each visitor presents the hosts with a relatively natural opportunity to recycle some of what they have said before, but at the same time the hosts have to tailor their answers to the specific questions asked. In this sense, talk during the carousel is genuinely *co-constructed*, with 'distributed responsibility among interlocutors for the creation of sequential coherence, identities, meaning, and events' (Jacoby and Ochs, 1995, cited in McNamara, 1997: 456). The visitor is not simply a listener, but a full communicative partner, initiating topics-for-talk and evaluating the comprehensibility and adequacy of the responses.

As we have noted, the learners at the bottom of our range, Alicia and Susanna, were also able to exploit the interactive nature of the task by using their visitors as sources of new or more accurate expression in English. Their role in their conversations was more reactive (receiving corrections and recasts from their visitors), while Olga, Carla and Daniela used talk proactively as a means of self-correction.

Naturally, individuals will differ in their openness to the learning potential in communicative events. Our analysis of Carla's performances has hinted at the complexities underlying an individual learner's actions within this particular task. At times her overriding gave the impression that she wanted to prevent or pre-empt participation from her interlocutor; yet, as we noted earlier, her overall contribution was not much above 50% of the words exchanged. What made her speaking different from the others was not so much her relative contribution to the conversations, but rather the way she maintained her turn at specific points. In a different way, Olga was also less open than Alicia and Susanna to learning opportunities because she did not take up – or did not notice – the chance to adopt correct L2 forms used in her visitors' speech.

This issue of openness brings us to a more general need suggested by our study: to help learners to appreciate what they stand to gain from conversation with other learners. Even if many SLA researchers (e.g. Gass and Varonis, 1985; Pica et al., 1996) are optimistic about the availability and longer-term value of negotiated input and output with other non-native speakers in the classroom, that view is not shared by all researchers (for a recent discussion, see Foster, 1998), and certainly not, in our experience, by many L2 learners. Some learner-training materials (e.g. Anderson and Lynch, 1996) have explored this area, highlighting the potential learning opportunities in both NS–NNS and NNS–NNS conversations inside the classroom and beyond, but a great deal remains to be done to raise learners' – and teachers' – awareness of ways of using those opportunities.

Our final point is that the carousel task is structured without teacher intervention. The learners' changes to their English came about not in response to external intervention before or during the task, but in pursuit of communication with a series of different visitors. In his experimental study of task repetition with the same partner, Bygate (1996) speculated that there might be benefits in getting students to repeat a similar task with a different partner, on the basis that 'different people will do tasks in different ways and a variety of partners could provide valuable learning opportunities' (Bygate, 1996: 145). Our findings support his view. What makes the carousel successful as a communicative task is the particular combination of text input, task structure and learner interaction, which pushes the hosts towards more accurate performance. (It is possible that learners also make changes to their English when in the *visitor* role, but that remains to be investigated.)

Given our interest in the learners' perspective, we would like to leave the last word to two learners with their own views on the value of practice, both in the carousel and more widely, apparently. In the extract below, Olga (host) and Michael (visitor) discover that they have said all they need to say about the points Michael has raised, so for once they have the luxury of a few moments before the whistle signals the end of the cycle:

> O we are finished too early + you are too clever Michael
> M why?
> O because you see immediately what is going on
> M mm
> O and we have to speak
> M mm + it's only a case of exercising
> O yes + yes + everything is a case of exercising
> M no not every + but a lot of things
> O most
> M mm
> O most + most (*laughs*)

They, at least, are convinced of the fundamental value of the 'exercising' built into the carousel. Clearly, learning a language requires much more than simple practice, yet successive cycles of classroom activity under varied conditions may have an important part to play in proceduralisation of the L2 (Johnson, 1996) – in other words, the process by which access to and use of L2 knowledge becomes automatic. We would agree that 'it is optimistic to suppose that retrial *alone* will efficiently eradicate mistakes' (Johnson, 1996: 129, our emphasis), but we conclude from our two studies that learners gain from the particular sort of retrial available to them during the carousel, even without teacher intervention.

CONCLUSION

In most walks of life, people equate 'repetition' with boredom; in the TESOL context, 'repetitious' and 'repetitive' are hardly the most exciting adjectives to apply to a classroom task. Despite the evidence that immediate task repetition led these learners to change and improve their spoken English, the notion of repetition as a useful classroom procedure will require some 'selling', both to our professional colleagues and to language learners. These findings may be a small step in that process of persuasion.

The evidence we have presented here comes from a highly specific teaching context, and we do not claim to have demonstrated the benefits of task repetition in general. Our claims are limited to the positive changes we have identified in the English produced by learners on this particular task. We believe that they maintained their level of interest and engagement over the six cycles of the carousel precisely because they *did not perceive* the task to be repetitive. The recycling built into the task seemed natural and plausible to them, since it derived from a professional genre, poster discussion, of which they had first-hand experience at medical congresses. In addition, it could well be that aspects of the ESP context – e.g. the learners' specialist knowledge, the currency of the poster topics, the additional 'edge' of having to defend the study they had turned into a poster – also contributed to their commitment to the task. Clearly, if recycling tasks of this type are to be seen as useful and interesting for general-purpose learners, they must be carefully designed and managed.

We have discussed ways in which successive cycles of performance allowed learners to make L2 changes over a relatively short period of 20–25 minutes, but have avoided making claims about longer-term learning. Our data do not allow us to say whether the adjustments that Alicia and Susanna made to incorporate their interlocutors' expressions into their own output represented longer-term learning, or temporary loans. We mentioned the paradox that these weaker learners, who may have had the most to gain from this sort of practice, reported they were *unaware* of the changes. Our investigation of this specific classroom task underscores the crucial importance of developing effective techniques to help learners to exploit the potential of task-based interaction by monitoring changes in their own performances and noticing useful L2 features in the performances of others.

ACKNOWLEDGEMENT

We would like to thank all 14 participants in the *English for Cancer Conferences* course for allowing us to record their carousel performances for this research.

NOTE

1. Explanation of symbols used in extracts: underlining is used to highlight the focal or key expression in the extract under discussion; + short pause; ++ medium pause; +++ long pause; -- false start, hesitation; [. . .] some turns omitted; [??] indecipherable.

REFERENCES

Anderson, K. and Lynch, T. (1996) *PROFILE: Principles, Resources and Options for the Independent Learner of English.* Institute for Applied Language Studies, University of Edinburgh.

Breen, M. (1989) The evaluation cycle for language learning tasks. In R. Johnson (ed.) *The Second Language Curriculum* (pp. 187–206). Cambridge: Cambridge University Press.

Breen, M. and Candlin, C. (1987) Which materials? A consumer's and designer's guide. In L. Sheldon (ed.) *ELT Textbooks and Materials: Problems in Evaluation* (pp. 13–28). ELT Documents 126. London: Modern English Publications.

Brown, G., Anderson, A., Shillcock, R. and Yule, G. (1984) *Teaching Talk.* Cambridge: Cambridge University Press.

Bygate, M. (1996) Effects of task repetition: appraising the developing language of learners. In J. Willis and D. Willis (eds), pp. 136–46.

Cameron, L. (1999) Subverting the task: the impact of divergent motivations on the dynamics of classroom interaction. Leeds/Budapest Symposium on Task-based Learning. University of Leeds, 14–15 January 1999.

Crookes, G. (1989) Planning and interlanguage variation. *Studies in Second Language Acquisition,* 11 (3): 367–83.

Day, R. (ed.) (1986) *Talking to Learn: Conversation in Second Language Acquisition.* Rowley, MA: Newbury House.

Duff, P. (1986) Another look at interlanguage talk: Taking task to task. In R. Day (ed.), pp. 147–181.

Ellis, R. (1997) The empirical evaluation of language teaching materials. *ELT Journal,* 51 (1): 36–42.

Foster, P. (1996) Doing the task better: how planning time influences students' performance. In J. Willis and D. Willis (eds), pp. 126–35.

Foster, P. (1998) A classroom perspective on the negotiation of meaning. *Applied Linguistics,* 19 (1): 1–23.

Foster, P. and Skehan, P. (1996) The influence of planning on performance in task-based learning. *Studies in Second Language Acquisition,* 18 (3): 299–324.

Foster, P. and Skehan, P. (1997) Modifying the task: the effects of surprise, time and planning type on task-based foreign language instruction. *Thames Valley Working Papers in ELT,* 4.

Gass, S. and Varonis, E. (1985) Task variation and nonnative/nonnative negotiation of meaning. In S. Gass and C. Madden (eds) *Input in Second Language Acquisition* (pp. 149–61). Rowley, MA: Newbury House.

Hancock, M. (1997) Behind classroom code-switching: layering and language choice in L2 learner interaction. *TESOL Quarterly*, 31 (2): 217–35.

Jacoby, S. and Ochs, E. (1995) Co-construction: An introduction. *Research on Language and Social Interaction*, 28(3): 171–83.

Johnson, K. (1996) *Language Teaching and Skill Learning.* Oxford: Blackwell.

Lynch, T. (1996) *Communication in the Language Classroom.* Oxford: Oxford University Press.

Lynch, T. (in press) Seeing what they meant: Transcribing as a route to noticing. *ELT Journal* 55.

Lynch, T. and Maclean, J. (1994) Poster carousel. In K. Bailey and L. Savage (eds) *New Ways of Teaching Speaking* (pp. 108–9). Washington, DC: TESOL.

Lynch, T. and Maclean, J. (1999) The benefits of 'natural' repetition of a classroom task. Leeds/Budapest Symposium on Task-Based Learning. University of Leeds, 14–15 January 1999.

McNamara, T. (1997) 'Interaction' in second language performance assessment: Whose performance? *Applied Linguistics*, 18 (4): 446–66.

Nobuyoshi, J. and Ellis, R. (1993). Focused communication tasks and second language acquisition. *ELT Journal*, 47 (3): 203–10.

O'Loughlin, K. (1995) Lexical density in candidate output on direct and semi-direct versions of an oral proficiency test. *Language Testing*, 12 (2): 217–37.

Pica, T., Kanagy, R. and Falodun, J. (1993) Choosing and using communicative tasks for second language instruction. In G. Crookes and S. Gass (eds) *Tasks and Language Learning: Integrating Theory and Practice* (pp. 9–34). Clevedon, Avon: Multilingual Matters.

Pica, T., Lincoln-Porter, F., Paninos, D. and Linnell, J. (1996) Language learners' interaction: How does it address the input, output and feedback needs of language learners? *TESOL Quarterly*, 30 (1): 59–84.

Plough, I. and Gass, S. (1993) Interlocutor and task familiarity: Effect on interactional structure. In G. Crookes and S. Gass (eds) *Tasks and Language Learning: Integrating Theory and Practice* (pp. 35–56). Clevedon, Avon: Multilingual Matters.

Porter, P. (1986) How learners talk to each other: input and interaction in task-centered discussions. In R. Day (ed.), pp. 200–22.

Skehan, P. (1996) A framework for the implementation of task-based instruction. *Applied Linguistics*, 17 (1): 38–62.

Skehan, P. (1998) *A Cognitive Approach to Language Learning.* Oxford: Oxford University Press.

Skehan, P. and Foster, P. (1997) Task type and task processing conditions as influences on foreign language performance. *Language Teaching Research*, 1 (3): 185–211.

Takahashi, T. (1989) The influence of the listener on L2 speech. In S. Gass, C. Madden, D. Preston and L. Selinker (eds) *Variation in Second Language Acquisition: Discourse and Pragmatics* (pp. 245–79). Clevedon, Avon: Multilingual Matters.

Tarone, E. (1999) Adolescents at play with tasks: The role of parody/travesty in task-based learning. Leeds/Budapest Symposium on Task-based Learning. University of Leeds, 14–15 January 1999.

Vasseur, M.-T., Broeder, P. and Roberts, C. (1996) Managing understanding from a minority perspective. In K. Bremer, C. Roberts, M.-T. Vasseur, M. Simonot and

P. Broeder (eds) *Achieving Understanding: Discourse in Intercultural Encounters* (pp. 65–108). Harlow: Longman.

Wigglesworth, G. (1997) An investigation of the effects of planning time and proficiency level on oral test discourse. *Language Testing*, 14 (1): 85–106.

Willis, J. and Willis, D. (eds) (1996) *Challenge and Change in Language Teaching*. London: Heinemann.

Yule, G. (1994) ITAs, interaction and communicative effectiveness. In C. Madden and C. Myers (eds) *Discourse and Performance of International Teaching Assistants* (pp. 189–200). Alexandria, VA: TESOL.

Yule, G. and Macdonald, D. (1990) Resolving referential conflicts in L2 interaction: The effect of proficiency and interactive role. *Language Learning*, 40 (4): 539–56.

Yule, G. and Powers, M. (1994) Investigating the outcomes of task-based interaction. *System*, 22 (1): 81–91.

Part III

TASK-BASED APPROACHES TO TESTING

The three chapters on testing have a considerable degree of common concern. They all focus on the assessment of *spoken* language performance, reflecting the interest that this area of assessment has consistently provoked, as well as the difficulty it entails. They also, in common, address the fundamental testing concept of validation. Traditionally, testers address validation issues through statistical means, exploring what relationships from batteries of tests reveal about the underlying structure of abilities, and about the ways different test formats interrelate. Correlation and factor analysis are basic investigative methods for such studies. Usually missing in such endeavours is much focus on the nature of speaking itself, of models which may account for it, or of any fine-grained analysis of what different speaking formats entail. The three chapters, in contrast, make the nature of speaking more prominent, and make the fundamental assumption that tasks which are used to elicit spoken language may introduce artefactual influences on the performance that results. One may, as a result, question the judgements which are made about test candidate performance, since reliance on procedures which systematically influence performance may introduce error into the measurement process.

Following this concern for validation, all three chapters use statistical methodologies which are not routinely used in testing research. They explore the effects of different test characteristics through careful research designs, as well as evaluation procedures such as *t*-tests and analyses of variance (Skehan), Rasch item–response analysis (Wigglesworth), and multidimensional scaling (Chalhoub-Deville). The focus is not on correlations or factor analyses to examine inter-test relations; rather the intention is to establish whether the different characteristics of tests have significant effects on performance, of the sort which would be important in any test interpretation and standardisation. Each chapter reports a number of findings of this type, arguing persuasively that to choose a particular task is not a neutral, technical decision: tasks introduce effects upon performance, and an unawareness of such effects may introduce error (and potential unfairness) into measurement procedures.

All three studies report analyses of considerable quantities of data, whether from a series of studies, or from a single large-scale project.

There are also some contrasts between the chapters. Skehan and Wigglesworth rely upon a model of spoken language test performance developed by Skehan from work by Kenyon (1992) and McNamara (1996). The model attempts to schematise the influences on the test score that is awarded, in order to better identify sources of potential error. These include the raters, the rating system, the nature of the interactional encounter, and the *tasks* which are used, as well as the *conditions* under which the tasks are completed. The value of the model is that it allows knowledge to accumulate about these various effects so that we can improve our ability to standardise test design and target it to focus better on particular aspects of proficiency. In this respect, the chapter by Skehan focuses on task characteristics and their influence on scores, while Wigglesworth examines task characteristics *and* task conditions.

While Skehan and Wigglesworth take as their unit of analysis the task itself, Chalhoub-Deville, in contrast, does not take such an atomistic perspective. Instead, she examines complete tests, comparing three publicly administered spoken language test formats. The three formats each purport to test spoken language, and so should be broadly equivalent. Chalhoub-Deville, in contrast, asks the question: do these different formats measure different things? In this respect, one can consider that each test format is a 'bundle' of test characteristics, performance conditions, interactional conditions, and ratings. Rather than take the more 'first principles' componential stance of Skehan and Wigglesworth, Chalhoub-Deville explores the way tests operate in the real world, under routine conditions, to see whether they are the neutral, transparent instruments that they claim to be.

Both Wigglesworth and Chalhoub-Deville rely on data largely or wholly derived from performance *ratings* by judges. In this way, the data underlying the studies is exactly the sort of data that real-world language testers often work with for oral language assessment. In contrast, Skehan, reflecting the experimental atomistic approach he takes to investigating task characteristics, reports on detailed indices of performance based on coded versions of transcripts of the performances concerned. He reports statistics for measures of fluency, accuracy, and complexity, reflecting the way these three areas have come to be fairly typical of much task-based work (see also the chapters by Bygate and Foster in this volume). So the data used in this chapter are more fine-grained and painstaking to compute, rendering them unusable in normal testing contexts, even though revealing for the more experimental meta-study that he reports.

Perhaps a concluding point that can be made about this part of the volume is that it represents an interesting contribution to the literature, linking second language acquisition and testing research. By drawing on theorising from outside testing, the chapters help to reconceptualise the nature of test validation, as they show how conventional statistical procedures are of limited value. In this they suggest how language testing, as a discipline, needs to make connection with neighbouring areas if it is to maintain vitality. SLA researchers are making major contributions to clarifying how tasks and elicitation devices influence the data on which assessment decisions may be made. But the scope for influence between these two fields is reciprocal, since testers have much to contribute to the methods of SLA. Language testing draws upon a range of statistical methodologies, and these can help SLA researchers to refine their understanding of the possible complex processes underlying their data. The chapters by Wigglesworth and Chalhoub-Deville are instructive in this regard in their use of techniques such as Rasch analysis and Multidimensional Scaling to reveal aspects of task difficulty. If, as a result, task researchers are able to draw upon more powerful statistical techniques in the future, then this will be no small contribution.

REFERENCES

Kenyon D. (1992) Introductory remarks at symposium on development and use of rating scales in language testing. 14th Language Testing Research Colloquium, Vancouver, 27 February to 1 March.

McNamara T. (1996) *Measuring Second Language Performance*. London: Longman.

Chapter 8

Tasks and language performance assessment

Peter Skehan

Developments over the last 15 years or so have suggested that pedagogy can fruitfully be organised by means of tasks that learners transact, and that tasks can be used as the basis for syllabus organisation as well as the unit for classroom activities. As Chalhoub-Deville (Chapter 10) points out, however, such developments constitute a source of difficulty for achievement testing. Conventional approaches to testing link with sampling frames which can be organised around some structural organisation for a syllabus. Tasks, in contrast, are centrally concerned with the learner achieving some purpose and outcome, and do not directly require the use of conformity-oriented language (Willis, 1991), of the sort that it would be convenient to engage if a syllabus is to be tested systematically.

A move towards tasks also poses problems for abilities-oriented *proficiency* testing. The most influential approaches of this type (Canale and Swain, 1980; Bachman, 1990; Bachman and Palmer, 1996) posit an underlying structure of the components of competence, and then propose mediating mechanisms by which such competences will impact upon performance. In principle, such an approach might be extremely rewarding but, in practice, the codifying nature of the underlying competence-oriented models has not interfaced easily with effective predictions to real-world performances (Harley et al., 1990; Skehan, 1998). At the most general level, the problem is that underlying and generalised competences do not easily predict across different performance conditions or across different contexts. Moving from underlying constructs to actual language use has proved problematic.

In response to these difficulties, a number of investigators have proposed alternative models of how spoken language might be conceptualised and measured. These models attempt to portray the assessment event in more comprehensive ways which (a) incorporate a larger number of performance elements directly, and (b) clarify how research studies might be organised and integrated more effectively to give an empirical basis for the claims that are made about spoken language assessment. The model shown as Figure 8.1 is based on work by Kenyon (1992), McNamara (1995) and Skehan (1998). It is useful to discuss the various components of this model briefly before turning to the factor which is the main focus of this chapter – the influence

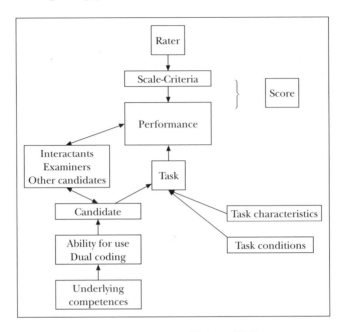

Figure 8.1   A model of oral test performance (Skehan, 1998)

of the task itself on assessment procedures. The model in general clarifies the potential fallibility of a test score as an indicator of underlying abilities. The section on tasks explores whether there are systematic influences on the nature of the performance which is elicited arising from task characteristics themselves.

Figure 8.1 shows that a test score is most immediately influenced by the rating procedures which have been used. The oral performance which has been elicited will have been judged by raters. In addition, the performance which is being rated will be filtered through a rating scale. Such scales vary in their origin, in their characteristics, and in their purposes (see Alderson, 1991; Fulcher, 1996a). As a result of these rater and scale factors, we have to consider the possibility that the score assigned to a candidate may not reflect candidate performance only, but may partly be based on biases and limitations arising from raters and scales.

Working systematically through the model, we can identify a number of additional influences on the score which is assigned. These fall into three major headings:

- the interactive conditions under which performance was elicited;
- the relevant abilities of the candidate;
- the task which was used to generate the performance, as well as the conditions under which the task was completed.

The interactive conditions under which performance is elicited have posed problems to oral language assessment that have been recognised for many years. For example, in a conventional assessor–assessed arrangement, the power relations between the participants are manifestly unequal, and the asymmetry which results distorts the language subsequently used (Van Lier, 1989). It is also likely that there is important restriction in the functions of language which can be probed in any meaningful way. For these reasons, alternative organisational arrangements for oral testing have been tried in recent years, such as group-based encounters. At the cost of standardisation, they enable a wider range of language functions and roles to be engineered to provide a better basis for oral language sampling with less asymmetry between participants (Van Lier, 1989). At a more theoretical level, the group format enables us to portray the interaction in terms of co-construction, since participants will have some degree of mutual equality, and so the direction the discourse develops will not be pre-ordained and orchestrated by the assessor.

We turn next to the abilities of the candidate. Measuring these, one might say, is the major goal of the actual assessment procedure, so the first value of the dynamic represented in Figure 8.1 is to show how this ability may not have a dominant effect upon the score that is awarded because so many other factors intrude and in potentially unsystematic ways. Again, it is not the focus of this chapter to cover this area in detail, and so only a brief account will be given here. The model in Figure 8.1 suggests that we need to consider underlying competences *and* ability for use. The former is represented in models such as those proposed by Canale and Swain (1980) and Bachman (1990). Competence-oriented models describe different components of communicative competence and their interrelationships. They also propose some method by which such underlying competences might influence actual performance. The relevant section of Figure 8.1, however, takes this competence-to-performance linkage further, and proposes the construct of *ability for use* as a set of abilities which mediate between underlying competence and actual performance conditions in systematic ways (Skehan, 1995, 1998). It is then the goal of assessment techniques to devise methods of assessing this construct as well as the underlying competences.

Figure 8.1 describes what is largely a programmatic model. There has been significant research in the area of rater and rating scale influences (Lumley and McNamara, 1995; North, 1996). Further, proposals to describe underlying competences have received considerable theoretical and empirical attention in recent years, but the inclusion of interactive conditions and ability-for-use in the model is rather speculative at this point, and unconnected to any testing-oriented evidence. The same has been true of the influence of tasks until recently. The remainder of this chapter will be concerned with relevant research which tries to clarify how the task component of the model is increasingly susceptible to empirical investigation.

ASSESSING TASK DIFFICULTY: INTRODUCTORY ISSUES

This section will prepare the ground for a meta-analysis of a number of separate studies of task-based performance. Such an examination of a number of different studies with common features is revealing about the way we might understand the impact of task characteristics on test performance. The section first discusses some measurement issues, and then describes the datasets used in the meta-analysis.

Measuring task performance

At the outset, one general issue needs to be clarified concerning the way task performance has been generally measured. Figure 8.1 has shown that it is typical, in assessing spoken performance, to use a rating scale approach. Such scales may be global scales, or they may be more analytic, with separate ratings for areas such as range, accuracy and fluency. In task-based research, in contrast, such rating scale measures are not typical (but see Wigglesworth, 1997 and this volume, for exceptions). Instead, reflecting the different psycholinguistic research tradition to which they belong, researchers into tasks have tended to use more precise operationalisations of underlying constructs.

In general, there is some consensus that measures are required in the three areas of complexity,[1] accuracy and fluency. These three areas are theorised to have important independent functioning in oral performance (Skehan, 1998).[2] In addition, they enter into competition with one another, with higher performance in one area seeming to detract from performance in others (Skehan and Foster, in press). So, for example, greater accuracy may well be achieved at the expense of greater complexity, and vice versa. Research is continuing to establish just how these three areas interrelate; however, a growing number of investigations into the task-based area are based on carefully computed indices in each of these three areas, and the competition between them will have an important impact in decisions that are made about task difficulty.

The datasets for the present research

The meta-analysis of task characteristics and their influence on task performance is based on six research studies conducted at Thames Valley University, with Pauline Foster as co-investigator. At the outset, it is essential to give a brief overview of the tasks that were used, and the purpose of the various studies (see Table 8.1).

ASSESSING TASK DIFFICULTY: TASK CHARACTERISTICS AND CONTRASTS

At the beginning of the series of research studies, the conceptualisation of task type was in terms of a contrast between personal, narrative and decision-making tasks. (These task types were chosen as maximally representative of tasks used in language-teaching coursebooks.) As the research programme has developed, however, it has become clear that this contrast between task

Table 8.1 Overview description of the six studies

Description	Tasks
Study 1: Comparison of the effects of planning on performance on personal, narrative and decision-making tasks (Foster and Skehan, 1996)	(a) *Personal*: Students* have to instruct their partner how to return to their homes, and then turn off an oven which has been left on. (Oven task) (b) *Narrative*: Students have to devise a story to a set of pictures: the pictures have common characters, but no obvious storyline. (Weave a story task) (c) *Decision*: Students are given a series of 'crimes', and have to agree on judicial sentences for these crimes, e.g. woman discovers husband in bed with another woman, and stabs and kills him. (Judge task)
Study 2: Comparison of the effects of planning on performance on personal, narrative and decision-making tasks, together with a comparison of the effects of a post-task and no post-task (Skehan and Foster, 1997)	(a) *Personal*: Students have to compare things that surprise them, pleasantly and unpleasantly, about life in Britain. (Surprise task) (b) *Narrative*: Students have to tell the story to a cartoon strip of pictures. The pictures have clear structure and an amusing ending. (Sempé task) (c) *Decision*: Students have to agree on advice to give letter writers to an Agony Aunt column. Each letter conveys a difficult problem, e.g. father is worried about his child living with mother and new partner in a drug-suspected communal house. How should he act? (Agony Aunt task)
Study 3: Comparison of the effects of planning on a decision-making task, together with comparison of the effects of introducing surprise information mid-task (Foster and Skehan ms)	*Decision*: Judge task, as in Study 1
Study 4: Comparison of four different conditions for video narrative retelling, with different processing loads. Three conditions require different versions of simultaneous tellings, i.e. telling the story while the video is playing, while the fourth is a delayed condition. Comparison of two tasks, one more structured and one less structured (Skehan and Foster, 1999)	(a) *Unstructured narrative*: Mr Bean video of Crazy Golf. In this video Mr Bean plays a round of golf, in which various mishaps occur. The events are an essentially disconnected series. (Golf task) (b) *Structured narrative*: Mr Bean video of restaurant meal. Mr Bean has a restaurant meal in which various amusing events occur, but against the background of a typical restaurant 'script'. (Restaurant task)

Table 8.1 *(cont'd)*

Description	Tasks
Study 5: Comparison of four different planning conditions: teacher-fronted, solitary, group-based and control (Foster and Skehan, 1999)	*Decision-making*: Balloon debate, with occupants to defend of actor, politician and EFL teacher. Students are assigned pre-task groups for teacher and group conditions where particular planning conditions are implemented. Then, students are assigned new groups and have to argue a position as to who should be thrown from the balloon. (Balloon task)
Study 6: Comparison of two different experimental post-task conditions (based on the need for participants to complete a transcription of their own recorded task-based performance) and a control group (Skehan and Foster, ms)	(a) *Decision-making*: Agony aunt task, as above (b) *Narrative*: Picture cartoon strip. (Sempé task, as above)

* All studies were completed with students working in pairs, except for Study 4, where groups of four students were involved.

types, although useful, is not the whole story, by any means. It was originally thought that it would be possible to generate a number of (roughly equivalent) personal, narrative and decision-making tasks. As the research results accumulated, however, it became clear (somewhat unsurprisingly, in retrospect) that not all exponents of each of these task types were indeed the same as regards the complexity, accuracy and fluency of the language produced. It became clear, in other words, that other, finer-grained features, operating at a more basic level, were influential. Where there were differences between the more global task types that had been the starting point for the research, this was probably due to the combination of finer-grained factors that happened to be shared.

On the basis of the emerging results, Skehan (1998) proposed the following set of task characteristics which might impinge upon the nature of performance (in each case, the studies from the Thames Valley programme which bear upon the variable in question are indicated):

• *Familiarity of information*: Tasks vary as to whether they require information that is familiar to the participants because it is part of their personal experience, compared to tasks which require the assimilation of material presented by the experimenter. Tasks based on familiar information are Study 1(a), and Study 2(a), where, in each case, the retrieval of personally relevant information, which is well known to the participants, becomes the basis for completing the task. In Study 1(a) participants' contributions are based on their route home from college and house layout. In Study 2(a) participants describe what surprises them about life in Britain, pleasantly and unpleasantly. Both these tasks (and all others) were piloted, and in the piloting performance gave no indications of effortful retrieval – such material as participants wanted to use seemed instantly available to them.

- *Dialogic vs monologic*: Some tasks require interaction, and a discourse style that leads participants to alternate in who holds the floor, compared to others where extended turns are required, with little need to interact other than listen and wait for one's turn. A sub-set of monologic tasks are narratives, where one participant tells a story. Clear dialogic tasks are the Judge task (Study 1(c) and Study 3), and the Agony Aunt task (Study 2(c) and Study 6(b)). Each of these is a decision-making task. There was one other such task, the Balloon debate, (Study 5), but in this case although the task was completed in groups of four, there was little dialogic performance when the learners 'took the floor' to defend their different characters – instead learners 'declaimed' at some length. The narratives in the research were Study 1(b) (Weave a story), Study 2(b) (Sempé cartoon), Study 4 (both tasks: video-based narratives) and Study 6(a) (Sempé cartoon). These were completed by pairs of students, with each taking it in turn to tell the narrative and be asked questions.
- *Degree of structure*: Some tasks contain a clear macrostructure, with the time sequence underlying the task fairly clearly identifiable. Other tasks do not have this clear over-arching structure. Examples of structured tasks are: Study 1(a) (personal), Study 2(b) (narrative), Study 4(b) (structured narrative) and Study 6(b) (the same task as Study 2(b)). In all these cases, the time line for the information underlying the task is clear and well organised, with the different stages in each case having a clear relationship with one another.
- *Complex outcomes*: Some tasks require only straightforward outcomes, in which a simple decision has to be made. Others require multi-faceted judgements, in which the case or position a learner argues during a task can only be effective if it anticipates other possible outcomes, and other learners' contributions. In the present research, this functions as a sub-category of dialogic tasks, in that the clearest comparison is between the Agony Aunt task from Studies 2 and 6, on the one hand, and the Judge task from Studies 1 and 3, together with the Balloon debate from Study 6, on the other. The Agony Aunt task is the only one which requires joint engagement with the ideas concerned, as opposed to superficial negotiation of appropriate custodial sentences (in the Judge task) or ejection from the Balloon.
- *Transformation*: Some tasks do not require participants to operate upon the information presented or retrieved, but instead simply to reproduce it. Others require some degree of on-line computation which changes the state or the relationship of the elements in the task. Most of the tasks in the six research studies do not require transformation of this sort, emphasising instead retrieval of information or judgements about material which is presented. An exception is the narrative task from Study 1, where participants had to use their imaginations to 'impose' a story structure upon an unrelated

series of pictures. In so doing, the shared characters within the given picture set had to be transformed in their relationships with one another. In this respect, it comes close to what Brown et al. (1984) term a dynamic task, except that here the dynamic qualities are derived from the mental operations of the participants themselves, rather than from the unfolding events of a *given* story.

We now have five task characteristics which can be investigated through the six studies in the Thames Valley research. These studies can be used to explore whether these different characteristics have systematic influences upon performance. It has to be admitted, however, that these comparisons were not planned at the outset of this research programme. They are nevertheless worth pursuing since the various studies do share sufficient common features to justify the comparisons which are made. In particular, the scoring of the dependent variables was approached in a fairly consistent manner, so that the scores which are quoted below can be validly related to one another. However, the numbers and nature of the tasks which enter into the comparisons are not so systematic. The generalisations which are offered below should therefore be treated as tentative, and the basis for future, more systematically organised research studies.

ASSESSING TASK DIFFICULTY: EMPIRICAL RESULTS

The following section will detail the results for each of the five task characteristics mentioned above. In each case, three sets of measures will be used to assess the various tasks concerned. These are complexity, accuracy and fluency. Complexity is measured through a subordination index. Data are coded into communication units and clauses (Foster et al., ms), and then an index is calculated representing number of clauses per *c*-unit. This has been shown in the research programme to be a sensitive measure of the degree of subordination in spoken language. It is also taken to be a surrogate measure of general language complexity. Accuracy is calculated as the proportion of clauses which are error-free. Finally, fluency is measured by the number of pauses greater than 1 second in duration per 5 minutes of performance. Better performance is therefore indicated by *higher* complexity and accuracy scores and *lower* numbers of pauses.

In the course of the research programme a number of other measures have been explored, such as the range of different syntactic structures that are drawn on; the type-token ratio of the lexis; or dysfluency indicators such as reformulation and repetition. The measures which are actually used in these analyses are those which have proved most sensitive to experimental differences, as well as the most clearly defined for operational purposes. It is not claimed that they are definitive measures (and indeed, reviews such as Wolfe-Quintero et al. (1998) are showing the range of measures that can be used in this regard). They are now serviceable and have been used by the Thames

Valley research team, and others (e.g. Wigglesworth, 1997), with encouraging results.

Familiarity of information

Skehan (1998) hypothesises that familiarity of information will lead to greater fluency and accuracy of performance, since the easy access to information should make only limited demands on attention, allowing material to be assembled for speech more easily, and with greater attention to form. He proposes that there will be no push towards greater complexity as a result of the greater familiarity, since speakers will be likely simply to draw upon well-established language to code familiar events.

The most direct test of this hypothesis is to examine the results from Studies 1 and 2, where, in each case, tasks that are based on familiar information (the two personal tasks) can be compared with tasks that are not. The relevant results are shown in Table 8.2.

Table 8.2 Familiar information, fluency and accuracy

		Personal	Narrative	Decision	Sig.
Accuracy:	Study 1	0.68	0.62	0.67	0.05
	Study 2	0.66	0.62	0.68	0.01
Fluency:	Study 1	14.8	22.2	27.1	0.001
	Study 2	23.1	17.8	21.7	0.04

In Studies 1 and 2, the personal task does indeed generate higher accuracy than the narrative, but so does the decision task, in each case. It appears, therefore, that while the results are not inconsistent with familiar information leading to greater accuracy, the supporting evidence is not strong, since there are alternative routes to achieving greater accuracy of performance. Turning to fluency, the results from Study 1 are supportive of the original hypothesis. The personal task in this case is associated with fewer pauses and greater fluency than in the other two tasks. In this case, it does appear that familiar information is associated with less interruption to the speech flow. However, these results are not particularly supported when we look at Study 2. In this case, the personal task produces the *least* fluent performance, with the narrative generating the fewest pauses, and the decision task leading to more fluent performance. Additional analyses were carried out with the planning variable, since it is possible that there might be an interaction with planning, such that when there is time to prepare, familiar information might be selectively associated with more fluent performance. The results, however, are not supportive of this: the same patterns occur under all planning conditions.

The evidence, therefore, is not strongly supportive of an effect for familiarity of information on either accuracy or fluency. The present results are based on a meta-analysis of studies not intended to make sustained systematic comparisons, and so it may be that other correlating variables are obscuring potential relationships. The accuracy achieved from the dialogic decision-making tasks may be a case in point, since, as will be shown below, such tasks independently and consistently generate greater accuracy. The comparison made in Table 8.2 may not therefore be the best one to judge the effects of familiar information on task performance. What we can say, though, is that familiarity does not have such a strong effect on performance that higher accuracy is guaranteed. In other words, the effect seems weaker than was anticipated. Similarly, the effects upon fluency may depend on factors additional to the information itself. In the personal task in Study 2, for example, the need to retrieve information may introduce a strong processing element into performance, such that fluency is disrupted. This, however, brings us to the point made immediately above: familiar information does not guarantee more attention being available to achieve a higher level of performance.

Dialogic tasks

Skehan and Foster (in press) propose that interactive tasks are associated with greater accuracy and complexity, but lower fluency. They suggest that such effects are due to:

- *greater accuracy*
    - communication-driven push towards precision
    - 'creation' of more time to focus on form, as partner is speaking
    - recycling of partner's language, both with tendency to re-use correct language and to edit and correct it;
- *greater complexity*
    - collective reinterpretation of the task to make it more complex
    - scaffolded elaboration of partner's language;
- *lower fluency*
    - need to accommodate the unpredictability of partner's contributions, i.e. greater need to engage in on-line planning
    - uncertainty of turn-taking, and consequent disruption to fluency.

The descriptive statistics for the relevant comparisons are shown in Table 8.3. The comparisons involve:

- Studies 1 and 2, where dialogic (decision-making) tasks were contrasted with narrative and personal tasks;
- Study 6, where a dialogic (decision-making) task was contrasted with a narrative;
- Study 5 vs Studies 1, 2, 3 and 6, where the comparison was between *different* decision-making tasks, in that Study 5 used a Balloon debate, which was essentially monologic, compared to all other decision-making tasks which were much more interactive in nature.

In the first comparison, for Studies 1 and 2, a one-way within-subjects analysis of variance yields an F value of 5.64, and a significance level of $p < 0.001$. However, the significance is located in the contrast between the

Table 8.3   Accuracy, complexity and fluency on dialogic vs non-dialogic tasks

Study	Accuracy (% of error-free clauses)			Complexity (clauses per c-unit)			Fluency (No. pauses per 5 mins)		
	Decis. making	Nar.	Pers.	Decis. making	Nar.	Pers.	Decis. making	Nar.	Pers.
1 ($N = 32$)	0.67	0.61	0.68	1.32	1.35	1.16	27.1	22.3	14.8
2 ($N = 40$)	0.68	0.62	0.68	1.67	1.31	1.37	21.7	17.8	23.1
3 ($N = 60$)	0.68	–	–	1.41	–	–	22.8	–	–
5 ($N = 66$)	0.61	–	–	1.44	–	–	8.6	–	–
6 ($N = 42$)	0.68	0.56	–	1.47	1.35	–	12.8	10.8	–

narrative task accuracy level of 61% error-free clauses and the decision-making (67%) and personal (68%) tasks. In other words, while the decision-making (dialogic) task yields significantly more accuracy than the narrative task, it is not significantly different from the personal task. The other comparisons, are, however, clearer in their results. In the second comparison, the *t*-test between the decision-making task (68% accuracy) and narrative tasks (56% accuracy) in Study 6 generates a *t*-value of 4.14, translating to a significance level of $p < 0.001$. In the third comparison, the between-subjects *t*-test shows that the more monologic Study 5 decision-making task (61% accuracy) is significantly different from the other (dialogic) decision-making tasks (mean 68% accuracy), with a *t*-value of 3.56 and a significance value of $p < 0.001$. In a guarded fashion, therefore, and provided other relevant variables do not intrude, it can be claimed that dialogic tasks are associated with fewer errors.

A similar mixed picture emerges with the complexity results. The first comparison, Studies 1 and 2, does generate a significant effect for the dialogic decision-making task compared to the narrative and personal tasks ($F = 15.6$; $p < 0.001$), but this result should be modified in that the complexity mean for Study 1 narrative is actually higher than that for the decision-making task in that study (1.35 vs 1.32). The second comparison, for Study 6, does produce a clear result. The comparison yields a *t*-value of 1.84, which is significant at the $p < 0.05$ level (one-tailed test). However, the comparison between the more monologic Study 5 decision-making task and all the other (dialogic) decision-making tasks is not significant. This suggests that, as with the accuracy results, dialogic tasks *tend* to be associated with greater complexity, but this effect is mediated by other factors.

We turn finally to the fluency results. In the first comparison, for Studies 1 and 2, the dialogic task generates less fluency than the other two tasks ($F = 7.93$; $p < 0.001$). Once again, however, the results are not completely clear-cut, in that the personal task from Study 2 generates slightly less fluent performance than the dialogic decision-making task from this study. The trend, however, seems to be in the direction of lower fluency being associated with interaction. The second comparison, from Study 6, does not yield a significant result ($t = 0.66$; $p > 0.05$). The third (between-subjects) comparison between the Study 5 decision-making task and all the other decision-making tasks ($t = 8.35$; $p < 0.001$) is highly significant, with the Study 5 more monologic decision-making task generating much more fluent language than that in the more interactive tasks.

Returning to the rationale for these effects proposed at the beginning of this section, it is clear that the next stage of the research is to return to the transcripts of the different performances to see whether the factors which are proposed to account for the task difference effects can be detected in the actual data. The quantitative results are mixed, and now need to be triangulated from another data source. It is encouraging, however, that the results described here complement those reported in Bygate (this volume), especially for complexity and fluency, in relation to the narrative and interactive tasks.

Degree of structure

Skehan (1998) proposes that this variable has an effect upon the fluency and accuracy of performance. He suggests that tasks which contain clear structure, especially sequential structure, facilitate task performance by clarifying the macrostructure of the speech event. As a result, the lack of need to engage in large-scale planning frees up attentional resources for on-line planning. This additional attention, he proposes, is directed towards the immediate goals of avoidance of error and breakdowns in communicational flow, i.e. accuracy and fluency.

Three tasks, out of the total set used, were identified as containing greater structure. These were the personal task from Study 1 (turn off the oven); the narrative task from Studies 2 and 6 (the Sempé story, i.e. the same task in each study), and the 'restaurant' task from Study 4. The first source of evidence here comes from within subject comparisons from Study 1, where the personal task results can be opposed to those for the other two tasks. Regarding fluency, the within-subjects one-way analysis of variance is significant ($F = 16.6$; $p < 0.001$), with the personal task generating significantly more fluency than the other two tasks. With respect to accuracy, the corresponding analysis also indicates significance ($F = 3.58$; $p < 0.05$), but the operative contrast is between the personal *and* decision-making tasks, which are significantly more accurate than the narrative. These results, therefore, provide only partial support.

The findings for the comparison from Study 2 show similar results for fluency ($F = 4.7$; $p < 0.04$), with the narrative task (the structured Sempé story) generating significantly fewer pauses than the other two tasks. The results for accuracy from Study 2 are, however, very different. Significance is achieved ($F = 6.2$; $p < 0.01$), but the significant contrasts are in the reverse direction to those predicted, with the Sempé task associated with *lower* accuracy at 62% error-free clauses. On this occasion, at least, the structured task did not produce greater accuracy. The same two tasks were used in Study 6, where *t*-tests produced exactly the same results as for Study 2. Fluency was greater in the structured Sempé task, but this difference did not attain statistical significance ($t = 0.66$). Accuracy, however, was clearly greater in the decision-making Agony Aunt task ($t = 4.14$; $p < 0.001$). No different pattern emerges if these studies are analysed at a greater level of detail by examining the different planning conditions.

The trend towards clearer effects for fluency rather than accuracy is particularly evident in Study 4. Relevant results are shown in Table 8.4.

Table 8.4   Structured and unstructured narratives

Variable	Golf task ($N = 21$) (mean)	Restaurant task ($N = 24$) (mean)
Repetition	39.3	19.1
False starts	29.5	15.5
Reformulations	10.9	4.8
Replacements	8.2	5.2
Accuracy	47%	50%

All the fluency effects shown in Table 8.4 generate significant differences, all beyond the $p < 0.001$ level of significance. It is clear also that when fluency is operationalised in terms of repetition, etc.,[3] the structured task generated roughly *half* the amount of disfluency that the unstructured task generated. However, the accuracy effects, although showing a very slight superiority for the structured 'restaurant' task, do not remotely approach significance.

We can summarise the results in this section by saying that there is a fairly consistent pattern that tasks based on more structured information seem to be associated with greater fluency. There are some indications that accuracy might also be enhanced, but the evidence is, to say the least, mixed, and so it would be unwise at this stage to make any claims in this direction. If on-line planning and attentional availability are facilitated by structured tasks, these are directed towards fluency.

Complexity of outcome

This contrast is restricted to the decision-making tasks, and opposes the tasks which are susceptible to minimal interpretation for outcome, enabling low-level negotiation of consensus (Judge and Balloon tasks), and those which require engagement and careful examination of the different facets of a decision (Agony Aunt task). The results in this case are clear cut. Skehan (1998) predicts selectively for complexity here, and the differences found are indeed confined to this area. The relevant data are presented in Table 8.5 (overleaf).

Given that these comparisons are based on large groups (of 82 and 157 participants respectively), they represent powerful evidence that the complexity of task outcome is a major influence upon the complexity of the

Table 8.5 Complexity of outcome and task performance

Variable	Mean score complex outcome	Mean score simpler outcome	*t*-Value	Sig.
Accuracy	0.68	0.65	1.51	0.24
Complexity	1.59	1.41	5.01	0.001
Fluency	17.5	17.7	−0.127	0.90

language which is produced in a task. The less easily the consensus is achieved in a decision-making task, the more participants have to engage in subtler dialogue and the more extending is the language that is likely to be used.

Transformations of task material

The one task which required material to be transformed on-line was the narrative from Study 1. Skehan (1998) predicts that transformations will be associated with greater complexity, as learners have to wrestle with the need to bring the elements of the task into some sort of meaningful (and non-given) relationship with one another.

When one examines the results from this study, the within-subjects one-way analysis of variance for the complexity scores suggests that there are significant differences, but that the specific contrasts are between the personal task, on the one hand, and both the narrative and decision-making tasks on the other ($F = 11.3$; $p < 0.001$), with associated mean scores: 1.16 (personal), 1.32 (decision-making) and 1.35 (narrative). This only provides partial support for the hypothesis. However, a more supportive picture emerges if one examines the results when the mean scores for the different planning conditions are examined in more detail. These are shown in Table 8.6.

Table 8.6 Complexity measures for tasks requiring transformation and tasks not requiring transformation under different planning conditions

	Narrative	Personal	Decision-making
Unplanned	1.22	1.11	1.23
Undetailed planners	1.42	1.16	1.35
Detailed planners	1.68	1.26	1.52

Comparisons at each of the different levels of planning do not reach statistical significance, but the power of the comparisons is limited by the small sample sizes that result when such fine-grained comparisons are made. What is striking, however, is that the task requiring transformations always generates the highest level of complexity under planning conditions, and that *this advantage grows as the planning condition changes*. In other words, as the planning becomes more directed (Foster and Skehan, 1996, discuss this in terms of the task being interpreted as more challenging) there is an interaction with the complexity measure, such that the task requiring transformation benefits most from this opportunity to plan. In other words, requiring learners to handle tasks requiring transformations immediately does not produce significantly greater complexity. When, however, planning time is given to enable them to respond to the *potential* complexity of the task, they are able to meet the challenge more effectively and the complexity of their language is greater.

Summary of the task results

It is easier now to try to summarise the results that have been obtained for each of the characteristics by representing the data in tabular form. The summary is shown in Table 8.7.

Table 8.7 Summary of the effects of task characteristics on complexity, accuracy and fluency

Task characteristic	Accuracy	Complexity	Fluency
Familiarity of information	No effect	No effect	Slightly greater
Dialogic vs. monologic tasks	Greater	Slightly greater	Lower
Degree of structure	No effect	No effect	Greater
Complexity of outcome	No effect	Greater	No effect
Transformations	No effect	Planned condition generates greater complexity	No effect

LIMITATIONS OF THE META-ANALYSIS

The existence of the six related datasets has enabled analyses to be performed which have the advantage of linking a range of different variables. The generalisations which are then possible can be more wide-ranging in their applicability. There are, however, serious limitations to this approach. The meta-analysis has had an inevitable opportunistic quality. The six datasets in question are related, since they derive from a common research framework, but they were not *designed* to ensure principled and systematic comparisons between the range of variables involved. Where it is possible to make broader-based but still clear comparisons (e.g. the large samples underlying the *complex outcomes* comparison), the conclusions made can have some force. On occasions, the comparisons have a rather tentative character. For example, the structured tasks are 'personal' and 'narrative', and these from different studies. These tasks then enter into contrasts with a whole range of 'non-structured' tasks. Clearly, the designation 'structured' was not by original design, but through post-hoc analysis. This must inevitably limit the force of the claims which are made. On many other occasions, the variables under investigation can only be partially disentangled. For example, one of the predictions concerned accuracy. Structured tasks were predicted to generate greater accuracy. Hence the (structured) narrative in Study 2 would be predicted to be more accurately done. But it was also proposed that dialogic tasks (which narratives clearly are not) are also associated with greater accuracy. Hence, when the (structured) narrative in Study 2 was compared with the decision-making task from Study 2 (which may have been unstructured, but was dialogic) it was not possible to make an absolutely clear comparison because of the confound of variables. Other examples of this occur in the data, and clearly would suggest that the insights obtained so far should feed into the design of a more systematic study in the future. Still, the data that exist are all that can be analysed. Provided that the limitations of the dataset are understood, it is possible to draw the sort of tentative conclusions that have been proposed here, and extract some value from them.

IMPLICATIONS FOR TESTING

It is useful now to relate the findings shown in Table 8.7 to the model of oral language assessment presented in Figure 8.1. It was argued earlier that while model components from Figure 8.1, such as underlying competences and rater effects, have benefited from relevant empirical work, components such as interaction conditions, ability for use, and the role of tasks have not. It has been the goal of the present chapter to explore how this situation may be redressed by reviewing the contributions that can be made by a particular set of research studies into tasks.

Recalling that task fulfils an important mediating function which shapes the nature of the performance which will be the basis for the ultimate rating of the candidate score, we can see that the task itself is hardly a constant in this equation. The five task characteristics which have been explored show that systematic (and potentially uncontrolled and undesirable) effects are likely to follow from any task selection decision. In other words, there may be significant consequences when one task is chosen rather than another. Or to spell this out even more directly, if candidate performances are compared after having been elicited through the use of different tasks, the performances themselves may be very difficult to relate to one another. Different candidates, in other words, might be disadvantaged or advantaged by the particular task that they might have taken as part of their test, and so their performance may not be directly comparable to the other candidates.

Take, for example, the case of one candidate who was required to do a dialogic task compared to another candidate who had a narrative-based test. The above results suggest that the first candidate may well have been predisposed to achieve higher levels of accuracy and complexity than would otherwise have been the case, but lower fluency. The situation for the candidate taking a narrative-based test is exactly the reverse. The scores assigned these two candidates might then vary spuriously, even if the candidates were of a similar ability level. Public examination bodies are often attracted by narrative formats to assess spoken language since they seem to contain useful stand-ardisation potential: the present conclusions suggest that such an approach might inadvertently introduce another set of dangers.

In slight contrast, consider a situation where one candidate took a test containing clear sequential macrostructure, and another took a test in which transformations of input material were required. Assume further that in both cases there was some time for planning. The above research-based general-isations would lead us to expect an advantage in the first case for greater fluency and in the second, an advantage for complexity. If we relate these outcomes in performance to the rating scales which are used and/or the predispositions of the raters, we can see that there is even further scope for arbitrary score decisions. These may derive from the particular aspects of performance the rating scales and raters prioritise in importance, linked to the tasks which the candidates were required to do. The potential for inaccu-racy is therefore magnified.

In short, to require spoken performances – which will be the basis for scoring – to be based on tasks which vary in the sort of language that they favour may well introduce error into spoken language assessment. Unless we are able to combat this through research-based studies which inform test design decisions, we are likely to treat candidates unfairly. There is therefore a strong need for research programmes which explore just how the range of factors which impact upon the scores assigned in spoken language tests oper-ate in systematic ways. Unless this is done, incorrect decisions are likely to be made.

NOTES

1. The construct of complexity is close to what testers mean by range, in that both focus on a willingness to use a greater variety of syntactic forms.
2. They figure in other chapters in this volume, e.g. Bygate, Foster. In this section the focus is away from acquisition and towards measurement issues themselves.
3. The task required simultaneous retelling of a video-based narrative. For this reason, since the speed of the video tape influenced the performance, it was decided that measures of pausing-based fluency were inappropriate. Hence the use of alternative measures.

REFERENCES

Alderson, J.C. (1991) Bands and scores. In J.C. Alderson and B. North (eds) *Language Testing in the 1990s* (pp. 71–86). Modern English Publications and the British Council.

Bachman, L. (1990) *Fundamental Considerations in Language Testing.* Oxford: OUP.

Brown, G., Anderson, A., Shilcock, R. and Yule, G. (1984) *Teaching Talk: Strategies for Production and Assessment.* Cambridge: CUP.

Canale, M. and Swain, M. (1980) Theoretical bases of communicative approaches to second language teaching and testing. *Applied Linguistics*, 1 (1): 1–47.

Foster, P. and Skehan, P. (1996) The influence of planning on performance in task-based learning. *Studies in Second Language Acquisition*, 18 (3): 299–324.

Foster, P. and Skehan, P. (1999) The influence of source of planning and focus of planning on task-based performance. *Language Teaching Research*, 3, 3: 185–214.

Foster, P. and Skehan, P. (ms) Modifying the task: The effects of surprise, time and planning type on task based performance.

Foster, P., Tonkyn, A. and Wigglesworth, G. (in press) Measuring spoken language: A unit for all reasons. *Applied Linguistics.*

Fulcher, G. (1996a) Does thick description lead to smart tests? A data-based approach to rating scale construction. *Language Testing*, 13 (2): 208–40.

Harley, B., Allen, J.P.B., Cummins, J. and Swain, M. (1990) *The Development of Second Language Proficiency.* Cambridge: CUP.

Kenyon, D. (1992) Introductory remarks at symposium on development and use of rating scales in language testing. 14th Language Testing Research Colloquium, Vancouver, 27 February to 1 March.

Lumley, T. and McNamara, T. (1995) Rater characteristics and rater bias: Implications for training. *Language Testing*, 12: 55–71.

McNamara, T. (1995) Modelling performance: Opening Pandora's box. *Applied Linguistics*, 16 (2): 159–79.

North, B. (1996) *The development of a common framework scale of language proficiency based on a theory of measurement.* Unpublished PhD thesis, Thames Valley University.

Skehan, P. (1995) Analysability, accessibility, and ability for use. In G. Cook and B. Seidlhofer (eds) *Principle and Practice in Applied Linguistics.* Oxford: OUP.

Skehan, P. (1998) *A Cognitive Approach to Language Learning.* Oxford: OUP.

Skehan, P. and Foster, P. (1997) The influence of planning and post-task activities on accuracy and complexity in task based learning. *Language Teaching Research.* 1 (3): 185–211.

Skehan, P. and Foster, P. (1999) The influence of task structure and processing conditions on narrative retellings. *Language Learning*, 49 (1): 93–120.

Skehan, P. and Foster, P. (ms) *Using post task analytic activities to promote accuracy.* Manuscript, Thames Valley University.

Van Lier, L. (1989) Reeling, writhing, drawling, stretching, and fainting in coils: Oral proficiency interviews as conversation. *TESOL Quarterly*, 23: 489–508.

Wigglesworth, G. (1997) An investigation of planning time and proficiency level on oral test discourse. *Language Testing*, 14 (1): 85–106.

Willis, D. (1991) *The Lexical Syllabus.* London: Collins.

Wolfe-Quintero, K., Inagaki, S. and Kim, H.-K. (1998) *Second Language Development in Writing: Measures of Fluency, Accuracy, and Complexity.* Technical Report No. 17, Second Language Teaching and Curriculum Center: University of Hawai'i.

Further reading

Bachman, L. and Palmer, A. (1996) *Language Testing in Practice.* Oxford: OUP.

Berry, V. (in preparation) *An investigation into how individual differences in personality affect the complexity of language test tasks.* PhD dissertation, Thames Valley University.

Candlin, C. (1987) Towards task based language learning. In C. Candlin and D. Murphy (eds) *Language Learning Tasks.* Englewood Cliffs, NJ: Prentice Hall.

Chalhoub-Deville, M. (in press) Task-based assessment: A link to second language instruction.

Fulcher, G. (1996b) Testing tasks: Issues in task design and the group oral. *Language Testing*, 13 (1): 23–52.

Long, M. and Crookes, G. (1991) Three approaches to task-based syllabus design. *TESOL Quarterly*, 26 (1): 27–55.

Lowe, P. Jr (1982) *ILR Handbook on Oral Interview Testing*, Washington, DC: DLI/LS Oral Interview Project.

Lumley, T. and Brown, A. (1996) Specific purpose language performance tests: task and interaction. In G. Wigglesworth and C. Elder (eds) *The Language Testing Cycle: from Inception to Washback* (pp. 105–36). *Australian Review of Applied Linguistics*, Series 8, No. 13.

Mosenthal, P.B. (1998) Defining prose task characteristics for use in computer-adaptive testing and instruction. *American Educational Research Journal*, 35 (2): 269–307.

Norris, J., Brown, J.D., Hudson, T. and Yoshioka, J. (1998) *Designing Second Language Performance Assessments*. Technical Report No. 18, Second Language Teaching and Curriculum Center: University of Hawaii.

Nunan, D. (1989) *Designing Tasks for the Communicative Classroom*. Cambridge: CUP.

Robinson, P. (1995) Task complexity and second language narrative discourse. *Language Learning*, 45 (1): 99–140.

Shohamy, E. (1994) The validity of direct vs semi-direct oral tests. *Language Testing*, 11: 99–124.

Skehan, P. (1996) A framework for the implementation of task based instruction. *Applied Linguistics*, 17 (1): 38–62.

Skehan, P. (ms-a) *Assessing ability for use*. Manuscript, Thames Valley University.

Skehan, P. (ms-b) *Task characteristics, fluency, and oral performance testing*. Manuscript, Thames Valley University.

Chapter 9

Influences on performance in task-based oral assessments

Gillian Wigglesworth

INTRODUCTION

One focus of the research into tasks to enhance language learning has been the examination of different types of task with respect to how they influence the language output of second language learners. Different types of task can affect both the quality and quantity of linguistic output and much recent investigation has addressed the impact on the language of different conditions and/or different characteristics. The study reported here[1] is an attempt to investigate the kind of impact such task variations might have on learners' performances in relatively informal classroom-based assessments.

The majority of the work on task variability and its effects on learner language has focused on classroom-based tasks, with a few studies examining tasks in the context of assessment. Various aspects of tasks have been analysed, with those relevant to this study including the cognitive difficulty of the task, whether the interlocutor is a native speaker or a non-native speaker, and the presence or absence of planning time.

A number of factors may influence cognitive load. Chronological sequencing reduces cognitive demand, whereas multiple actions and actors increase it (Candlin, 1987). Such features have provided a starting point for the operationalisation of cognitive difficulty. Empirical investigation has suggested that cognitive load, or difficulty, does influence performance, although not always negatively. Robinson et al. (1995) found that the more cognitively demanding task produced higher accuracy rates in the use of articles and higher levels of lexical density. Similarly, Wigglesworth (1997) found that more accurate language was produced by high intermediate level students under test conditions where the task was more cognitively demanding and yielded a higher difficulty value in the statistical analysis.

Investigation of the differences between non-native speaker and native speaker interlocutors has shown that negotiation is more likely in NNS/NNS interaction than in NS/NNS interaction (Gass and Varonis, 1985; Yule and McDonald, 1990; Young and Milanovic, 1992). Plough and Gass (1993) suggest that the less shared background exists between conversational partners (linguistically and culturally) the greater the frequency and complexity of negotiation routines. Plough and Gass (1993) also investigated the effect of interlocutor familiarity. They analysed the discourse on a number of measures related to the co-operative nature of the discourse, and found while interlocutor familiarity had little effect on the use of back channel cues, it affected sentence completions, interruptions and overlaps. Interviewer familiarity also affected the way comprehensibility and misunderstanding was dealt with, with a higher incidence of comprehension checks and clarification requests in the familiar dyads. Where the interlocutors were unfamiliar, echoic repetitions of the interlocutor speech appeared to be used to avoid potential misunderstandings. With respect to task familiarity, lack of familiarity resulted in greater numbers of interruptions showing greater involvement and commitment, but where tasks were familiar, there was greater negotiation in the form of confirmation checks and clarification requests. Overall, however, the interlocutor variable had a greater influence on the language output than did task familiarity.

The third variable, planning time, has been the focus of a number of studies, with the measures of accuracy, fluency and complexity having been used to analyse the discourse. Ellis (1987) found greater accuracy in the use of the past tense where planning time was provided. Crookes (1989) found no effect for accuracy with planning time. Wigglesworth (1997), however, found a variable effect, with one minute of planning time appearing to influence accuracy only for high intermediate candidates on more cognitively demanding tasks. Foster (1996) found a trend towards increasingly accurate language where planning time was available, but the differences were not significant. Mehnert (1998), in a study in which different amounts of planning time were manipulated with intermediate university students, found accuracy to be significantly improved with one minute of planning time, but no further benefit for accuracy with longer amounts of planning time provided although complexity improved where ten minutes planning was provided. Somewhat variable results have been reflected in a series of studies in which both the type (detailed versus non-detailed) and amount (length of time in minutes) of planning time were examined with three different task types (Foster and Skehan, 1996; Skehan, 1996; Skehan and Foster, 1997). The analyses undertaken in this series of studies suggested that time and task type influence different aspects of language. For example, the narrative task elicited more complex language at the expense of accuracy, while the personal information exchange task elicited more accurate language (based on error-free clauses) but not more complex language. This trade-off effect between accuracy and complexity may result from differences in the perceived goals of the task (Skehan, 1996). Skehan argues that the provision of structure and planning time are resources the second language learner may draw on to reduce the processing load on a limited capacity processor.

While these studies have all employed detailed analyses of the spoken language performance, cross-study comparisons must be conservatively made. Generally, there has been little consistency in the analytical approaches adopted, and in particular to the operationalisation of the critical constructs (usually accuracy, fluency and complexity). For instance, a well-defined unit for the analysis of language data is crucial if significant comparisons are to be made across different studies (see Foster et al., 1998, for further discussion of this issue). It is therefore difficult to summarise and draw conclusions. However, we may tentatively conclude that there is a complex interaction between task type, cognitive load and planning time.

In this chapter, we attempt to quantify the effect of a range of variables on assessment task difficulty. Assessment tasks aim to elicit an adequate sample to make an appropriate assessment of the linguistic skill of the candidate. However, the range of tasks used in assessment situations inevitably vary in terms of their difficulty and the type of language they elicit. Unless this is controlled it may result in samples of language from different tasks which are variable in terms of key assessment criteria, such as grammatical accuracy, syntactic complexity and fluency. In the assessment situation, the extent and the degree of influence of such variables on task output needs to be clearly identified. The next section considers some of the implications of variability in task type on the assessment process.

ERROR AND VARIABILITY IN THE ASSESSMENT SITUATION

Variability in the assessment process

One goal of any assessment procedure is to ensure fair and equitable treatment of all learners. However, any measurement necessarily includes some degree of error, and there are a number of sources and levels at which this error may impact upon the measurement of a particular skill. In the language assessment situation, the goal is to reduce all sources of error which are external to the learner's language performance to the greatest possible degree. This is done in order to ensure that the score the learner obtains is, to the greatest extent possible, a true reflection of his or her ability to use the language for the purposes required in the assessment process.

The sources of error which are external to the learner are many. For example, in an oral interview, the interviewer may vary in the manner in which the interview is conducted and this may affect the learner's ability to demonstrate his or her range of linguistic knowledge. In a task-based oral interview, the nature of the task may impact upon the final score obtained by the learner in that it may be a more or less difficult task. The person who is rating the performance (who may or may not be the interviewer) will also influence the score – one rater may be more or less lenient than another rater. In addition to these, there are affective variables and personal attributes which may influence the learner's performance (Bachman, 1990).

In order to reduce variability related to factors extraneous to the test score, it is important to consider all the factors which may impact upon the final score and increase possible error. The focus of this study was the examination of one source of variability: task variability.

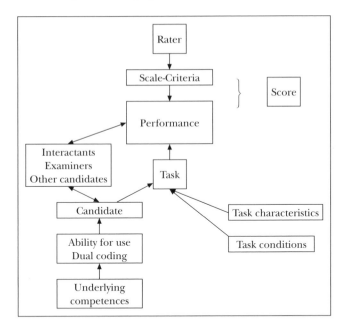

Figure 9.1   A model of oral test performance (Skehan, 1998)

Task variability

While task-based curricula lay claim to providing more authentic interactions within language pedagogy, the use of tasks in test design is a reflection of a move towards a more communicatively oriented approach to language assessment.

Figure 9.1 (reproduced here, and also used in the chapter by Skehan in Chapter 8), draws on a language-testing model first proposed by Kenyon (1992). This has been widely cited and was extended initially by McNamara (1996) and later by Skehan (1998). The model shows how a variety of different factors impact upon the performance by the candidate, and that all of these, including rater interactions with the scale or criteria used in the marking process, contribute to the score achieved by the candidate. Skehan argues that aspects of the task which are variable are both the characteristics inherent in the task, which may systematically influence the language output of the test candidate, and aspects of the conditions under which the tasks are administered.

The characteristics of the task (features internal to the task such as structure, cognitive load, familiarity of content) and the different conditions under which tasks are administered (such as availability of planning time, NS/NNS characteristics of the interviewer) are variables which need to be taken into account in both the testing and the classroom situation. Investigation of these will contribute to our understanding of the kinds of qualities and conditions which may influence second language learners in their acquisition of another language. In this project, the findings from previous studies on the effect of task variables on language output were drawn upon and used to identify a series of variables contributing to the characteristics of the tasks and the conditions under which they were administered. These were then manipulated and empirically examined in order to determine their effect on the performances of the learners on a range of further tasks.

All tasks were competency based assessment tasks which are used routinely for evaluating achievement in the Australian Adult Migrant Education Program. These are normally administered for assessment purposes by teachers in the classroom context.

METHODOLOGY

Five task types at two different levels were identified. Task types reflected competences required at each level and tasks were developed from a range of tasks sent in by teachers from three Australian States. Task types 1–3 were to assess learners at the functional level of proficiency, and task types 4–5 were designed to assess learners at a vocational level of proficiency.[2] The task types were as follows:

- *Level 1*
  Task type 1: giving instructions
  Task type 2: negotiating an oral transaction to obtain information
  Task type 3: negotiating an oral transaction for goods and services

- *Level 2*
  Task type 4: obtaining information through a telephone enquiry
  Task type 5: negotiating a complex/problematic spoken exchange

Two or three examples of each task type were developed for use in the project. The tasks were required to conform to certain criteria: contextual material that needed to be pre-taught was kept to a minimum; the context of the tasks needed to be universally familiar to learners; the tasks needed to limit the use of skills other than the one being tested; the tasks needed to be relevant to learner needs. Outlines of the tasks are given in Appendix 9.1.

Once the tasks had been developed, one task for each competency was selected as a control task. This task was not manipulated in any way. The remaining tasks were manipulated using specifically identified variables in either an independent two-way or four-way design.

Identification of variables

Two task characteristics and two task conditions were identified as variables. The task characteristics were:

- *Structure*: The task was developed either with or without structure. This was operationalised in terms of the amount of information provided to the learners to assist them in doing the task. Specifically where structure was present the learners were provided with five specific prompts to direct them in their interaction with the interlocutor. Where structure was not provided, one general statement was provided to guide the learners in the task.

- *Familiarity of activity*: This was operationalised by varying the extent to which the activity involved in the task consisted of some activity or undertaking with which the learners would reasonably be expected to be familiar.

The task conditions were:

- *Native versus non-native speaker interlocutor*: This was operationalised by selecting whether the interlocutor involved in the exchange was a native speaker of English or a non-native speaker.
- *Planning time*: Planning time was operationalised as either five minutes planning or no planning time. Planning was always manipulated in conjunction with one of the task characteristics.

These variables were assigned to the tasks as shown in Table 9.1. Eighty learners at each level participated in the project. Learners were drawn from

Table 9.1   Allocation of variables by task and task type

Level 1			
Task type 1	Task 1	No variation	
	Task 2	+ planning	+ familiar activity
	Task 3	− planning	+ familiar activity
	Task 4	+ planning	− familiar activity
	Task 5	− planning	− familiar activity
Task type 2	Task 1	No variation	
	Task 2	+ structure	
	Task 3	− structure	
	Task 4	− complex	
	Task 5	+ complex	
Task type 3	Task 1	No variation	
	Task 2	+ structure	
	Task 3	− structure	
	Task 4	NS interlocutor	
	Task 5	NNS interlocutor	
Level 2			
Task type 4	Task 1	No variation	
	Task 2	− planning	+ structure
	Task 3	+ planning	+ structure
	Task 4	− planning	− structure
	Task 5	+ planning	− structure
Task type 5	Task 1	No variation	
	Task 2	NS interlocutor	
	Task 3	NNS interlocutor	
	Task 4	+ structure	
	Task 5	− structure	

different ESL centres. As shown in Table 9.2, each learner was administered task 1 for each competency. In addition, each learner was administered one of the manipulated tasks for each competency. Due to occasional errors in the administration of the tasks, each manipulated task was not always administered to exactly 20 learners.

Table 9.2   Task and subject assignment

	Task 1	Task 2	Task 3	Task 4	Task 5
Level 1					
Task type 1	80	20	20	19	20
Task type 2	80	20	20	20	20
Task type 3	80	20	19	21	20
Level 2					
Task type 4	80	20	20	19	21
Task type 5	80	21	20	20	19

Thus, at each level, the unmanipulated task (Task 1) was administered to all 80 learners. The learners were then randomly assigned one of the remaining four tasks at the appropriate level. Thus approximately 20 learners were each administered one of the remaining (manipulated) tasks.

Tasks were administered in various AMEP centres in three states in Australia by trained and experienced teachers. Each learner undertook four (level 2) or six (level 1) tasks individually over a two- or three-day period. All performances were tape-recorded for rating at a later stage. Once the learners had completed the four (for level 2) or six (for level 1) assigned tasks they were asked to rate, on a five-point Likert scale, the difficulty of the tasks in which they had participated.

Rating procedure

In order to ensure that measures of task difficulty were optimally sensitive to the range of possible variation within any particular feature of performance, an analytic scale was used for the rating. The scales had previously been extensively trialled, had been used in the assessment of the English language proficiency of adult immigrants, and were familiar to raters. Each of the rating scales was accompanied by a set of descriptors covering four criteria at each of seven levels. The criteria used were related to those used at the different levels, and were not thus identical. The criteria are given in Table 9.3 (overleaf). All performances were double rated by randomly assigning the performances across the sixteen trained and experienced raters.

Table 9.3 Assessment criteria

Level 1	Task type 1	Grammar
		Fluency
		Cohesion
		Communicative effectiveness
	Task types 2 and 3	Grammar
		Fluency
		Vocabulary
		Communicative effectiveness
Level 2	Task types 4 and 5	Grammar
		Fluency
		Intelligibility
		Communicative effectiveness

ANALYSIS

Three separate quantitative evaluations were made in an attempt to identify variations in the difficulty level of each of the oral tasks. This was necessary as the numbers were relatively small and robust differences were unlikely to emerge. Firstly, analyses of variance (for four-way comparisons) and *t*-tests (for two-way comparisons) were performed on the raw scores provided by the raters.

Secondly, the data were subjected to a Rasch analysis, using the statistical modelling program, FACETS (Linacre, 1990). This program produces an estimate of candidate ability based on all the available information – that is, the different facets of the assessment situation – which may be considered to impact most seriously upon the assessment environment. In this case, the information included in the analysis consisted of four facets: the candidate, the task, the rater, and the rating criteria. The program is designed to take account of all the available information provided by these facets, and it uses this to model an estimated ability value for each of the candidates. This is expressed in a unit called a *logit* which results from an analysis of the interaction between all facets of the assessment situation. In addition to the ability estimates, the analysis provides a logit value for each of the facets identified: the difficulty of the task, the relative leniency or harshness of the rater, and the relative difficulty of the criteria. Thus it is possible to compare the relative difficulty within each facet – in this case of the tasks.

While Rasch analyses are optimal where *N* sizes are substantial (e.g. in excess of 100) and such analyses are not usually performed with the relatively small numbers used here (approximately 20 in each group), there are precedents for using Rasch techniques as research tools with small *N* sizes (see, for example, Lumley and McNamara, 1995). However, as the number of candidates who undertook each of the manipulated tasks was small, the additional measures of task difficulty were considered essential.

The third measure of task difficulty came from the learner evaluations of the difficulty of the tasks they had undertaken. This was calculated by determining the proportion of the learners who graded each task they had taken on a five-point Likert scale from very easy to very difficult.[3]

To summarise: the first analysis measured subject performance, the second analysis provided a measure of task difficulty and the third analysis provided a measure of the subjects' evaluation of the task difficulty.

RESULTS

The first analyses of the oral data investigated whether there were any significant differences in the performances of learners from the different centres by analysing the scores they achieved on task 1, the baseline task, which was common to all learners. There were no significant differences for learners participating at either level, and although significant differences across the tasks were identified, no interaction effect was present in the way particular centres interacted with particular tasks. We can conclude, therefore, that the different groups of learners were comparable to one another.

The discussion below focuses on the manipulated tasks (tasks 2–5) within each task type. The level 1 tasks are discussed first, followed by those for level 2.

LEVEL 1

Task type 1: giving instructions

This task type involved a four-way manipulation with planning time and familiarity. For tasks 2 and 3, the learner was required to give instructions about how to use a bank automatic teller machine. For tasks 4 and 5, the learner was required to explain to a 12-year-old child how to change a light bulb. The manipulations for each task are given in Figures 9.2(a)–(c), which also present the mean scores for the three analyses. Figure 9.2(a) shows the raw scores.

Where the *raw* scores are concerned, the higher the score, the easier the task is likely to be. Therefore, in order to ensure that the polarity of the three tables (raw scores, Rasch, student evaluations) was in the same direction the average raw scores for each task were subtracted from 28, the total possible score (4 criteria × 7 rating points). Figure 9.2(a) gives the total raw scores for all four criteria averaged over the sample size. Task 3 (the more familiar task *operating the ATM* without planning time) appears to be the easiest task, although this difference is not significant ($F(3,147) = 2.077$, $p = 0.106$). Differences between the raw scores obtained for the other three tasks are negligible.

Figure 9.2(b) gives results of the Rasch analysis.

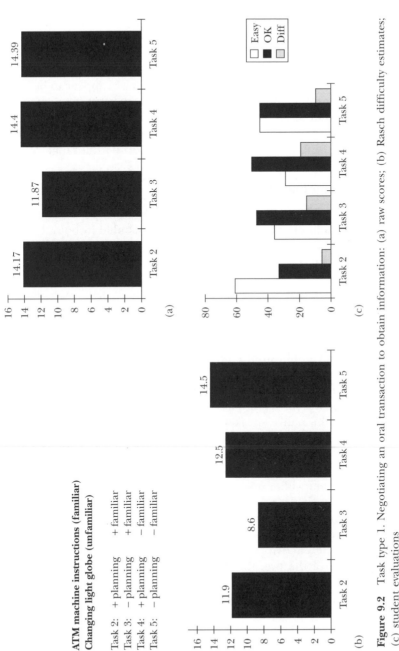

ATM machine instructions (familiar)
Changing light globe (unfamiliar)

Task 2: + planning   + familiar
Task 3: − planning   + familiar
Task 4: + planning   − familiar
Task 5: − planning   − familiar

Figure 9.2   Task type 1. Negotiating an oral transaction to obtain information: (a) raw scores; (b) Rasch difficulty estimates; (c) student evaluations

Once again, it appears that task 3 is the easiest of the tasks, supporting the view that the unfamiliar task is the most difficult. In this analysis, planning time appears to provide a small advantage where the task is unfamiliar, but a disadvantage when the task is familiar. This latter finding is in line with previous results from the literature and is discussed further below. Figure 9.2(c) gives the learner evaluations of the task.

The learner evaluations suggest that task 2 (familiar with planning) was the easiest of the four tasks. The three remaining tasks appear to be assessed as having similar difficulty levels by the learners with most learners assessing the task in the 'OK' category. It is important to bear in mind, however, that this is a somewhat rough measure as the learners have only completed the control task and one of the manipulated tasks, not the full range of tasks.

Task type 2: negotiating an oral transaction to obtain information

Two different variables were investigated for this task type. In tasks 2 and 3 structure was manipulated, with planning time included in both. For tasks 4 and 5, familiarity was manipulated (here operationalised as the learner being required to either obtain information about a language school for themselves [more familiar] or about a high school for their child [less familiar]). Thus the more familiar task involved obtaining, for oneself, information of immediate relevance to the learners, whereas the less familiar tasked involved obtaining less familiar information related to another person.

In all four of these tasks, the specified interlocutor was a native speaker. Unfortunately, an administrative error meant that the majority of candidates were administered task 5 (less familiar) with a non-native speaker interlocutor. Since this applied to the majority of learners taking this task, it was decided to remove the scores for the few learners who had had a native speaker interlocutor so that the native speaker/non-native speaker interlocutor was not confounded within task 5. However, this meant that the NS/NNS variable was confounded across tasks 4 and 5, since candidates doing task 4 (more familiar) interacted with a native speaker, whereas candidates doing task 5 (less familiar) interacted with a non-native speaker. This position was adopted to ensure that the variables were clear in the analysis.

Figure 9.3(a) suggests that there is little difference between the structured and unstructured tasks (tasks 2 and 3) where the raw scores are concerned, but a notable difference in tasks 4 and 5, with the less familiar task appearing to be the easier of the two, the difference being significant ($t = 2.589$, $p < 0.05$, df = 33).

Examining the Rasch logit estimates in Figure 9.3(b), there is a clear difference between the structured (task 2) and unstructured (task 3) with the unstructured task being the more difficult. While for the other two tasks (4 and 5) the differences in this analysis are small, task 5 (the less familiar task) again appears marginally easier. This had not been anticipated and we will return to address this issue in more detail below. The learner evaluations (see Figure 9.3(c)) support this view with task 3 (unstructured) being

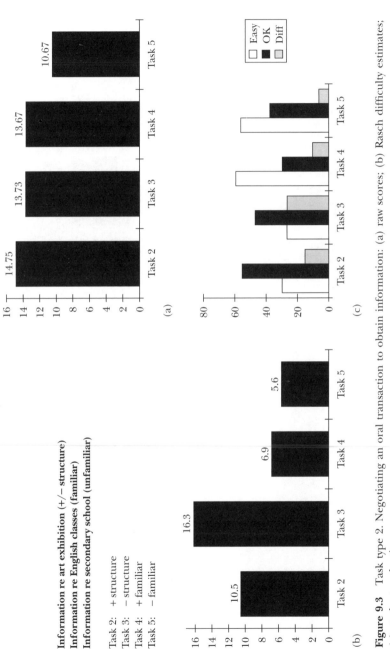

Information re art exhibition (+/– structure)
Information re English classes (familiar)
Information re secondary school (unfamiliar)

Task 2: + structure
Task 3: – structure
Task 4: + familiar
Task 5: – familiar

Figure 9.3 Task type 2. Negotiating an oral transaction to obtain information: (a) raw scores; (b) Rasch difficulty estimates; (c) student evaluations

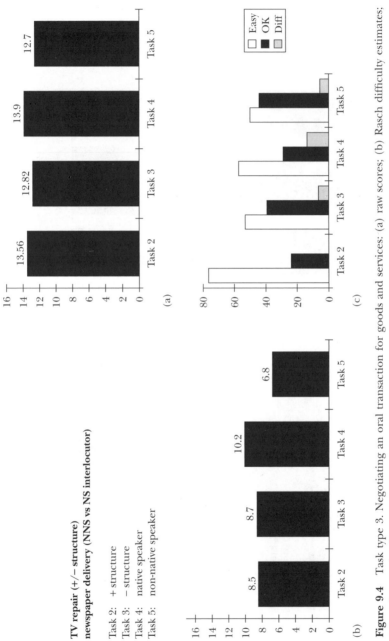

Figure 9.4 Task type 3. Negotiating an oral transaction for goods and services: (a) raw scores; (b) Rasch difficulty estimates; (c) student evaluations

designated as the most difficult and task 4 (more familiar) being slightly more difficult than the less familiar task 5.

Task type 3: negotiating an oral transaction for goods and services

In this task type, structure was manipulated in tasks 2 and 3 and interlocutor (NS vs NNS) in tasks 4 and 5. The NNS interlocutor in task 5 was a non-native speaker at a similar level of proficiency to the learner taking the task. As a few candidates on tasks 2 and 3 interacted with a NNS interlocutor rather than a NS interlocutor, these learner scores were removed for the purposes of this analysis.

Turning first to tasks 2 and 3, the raw scores (Figure 9.4(a)) suggest minimal differences between the structured and the unstructured task, and the Rasch analysis (Figure 9.4(b)) supports this view. For tasks 4 and 5, where the interlocutor was either a native speaker or another non-native speaker, the non-native speaker interlocutor appears to make the task easier.

The Rasch analyses agree with the raw score tallies for these two tasks, indicating that the non-native speaker interlocutor makes the task easier. However, these effects are small. The learner evaluations support the view that the presence of a native speaker interlocutor makes the task more difficult. However, given the small differences in the values we need to treat this finding with some caution.

LEVEL 2

Task type 4: obtaining information through a telephone enquiry

For this task type, the same task was used for all four versions and manipulated with structure and planning time. The results are shown in Figure 9.5.

Figure 9.5(a) suggests that task difficulty increases across the tasks, although these differences are small across the raw scores. The differences are not significant for the raw scores, but the general pattern suggests that the presence of structure advantages learners, while the presence of planning time disadvantages them. This same general pattern is exhibited for the Rasch analysis (Figure 9.5(b)) and also for the learner evaluations (Figure 9.5(c)).

Thus for this series of tasks, we may rather tentatively propose that the unstructured tasks are the most difficult with the presence of planning time appearing to increase the difficulty.

Task type 5: negotiating a complex/problematic spoken exchange

The final series of tasks was again subdivided into two groups of two (Figure 9.6). Tasks 2 and 3 were identical except that the interlocutor in task 2 was a native speaker and in task 3 was a non-native speaker. In tasks 4 and 5,

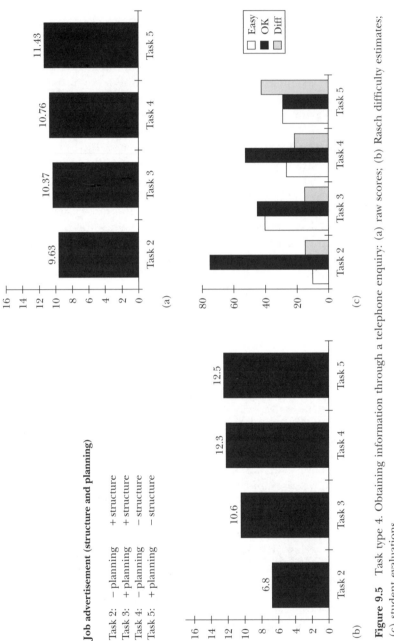

Job advertisement (structure and planning)

Task 2: − planning   + structure
Task 3: + planning   + structure
Task 4: − planning   − structure
Task 5: + planning   − structure

(a)

(b)

(c)

Figure 9.5 Task type 4. Obtaining information through a telephone enquiry: (a) raw scores; (b) Rasch difficulty estimates; (c) student evaluations

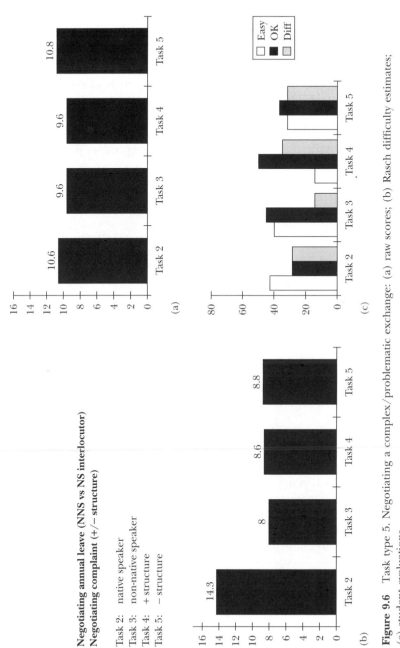

Negotiating annual leave (NNS vs NS interlocutor)
Negotiating complaint (+/- structure)

Task 2: native speaker
Task 3: non-native speaker
Task 4: + structure
Task 5: - structure

Figure 9.6 Task type 5. Negotiating a complex/problematic exchange: (a) raw scores; (b) Rasch difficulty estimates; (c) student evaluations

structure was manipulated. Planning time was present in both cases (Figure 9.6(a)).

While the differences in the raw scores were not significant, the non-native speaker interlocutor apparently made the task the easier in tasks 2 and 3. For tasks 4 and 5, there is again a small difference in the raw scores with the unstructured task being the more difficult.

The FACETS (Figure 9.6(b)) difficulty estimates also suggest that interaction with a native speaker task (task 2) is more difficult than with a non-native speaker (task 3). This is supported by the learner evaluations (Figure 9.6(c)). More learners found task 2 difficult than was the case with task 3. The FACETS analysis reveals no difference for tasks 4 and 5. Compared to the student evaluations of the other task types, the learner evaluations here suggest that all these tasks are perceived as relatively difficult. This suggests that it is this task type (negotiating a complex/problematic exchange) that is difficult.

Summary of results

These results are not conclusive in a statistical sense. This, no doubt, results partly from the fact that the numbers of learners taking the different variations of the tasks were small. However, we may draw some tentative conclusions based on the fact that the differences are in most cases consistently in the same direction on all three types of analyses and across the different tasks. To summarise, we find that for the task characteristics:

1. *Structure*: The weight of the evidence points towards structure making the task easier in three of the task types (task types 2, 4 and 5). The exception is task type 3, where the raw scores suggest that the unstructured task is slightly easier.
2. *Familiarity*: The results for this variable were problematic. In task type 1, where the activity was more familiar, the task appeared to be easier. However, where familiarity was manipulated in task type 2 the less familiar of the two tasks appeared to be easier. However this task (the less familiar task) was somewhat compromised by the use of non-native speaker interlocutors, so it is not possible to clearly tease out whether the effects found are related to the variable (familiarity), or result from the nature of the interlocutor (a non-native speaker). This is discussed further below.

For task conditions we may summarise as follows:

1. *Native speaker vs non-native speaker*: Where the interlocutor is a non-native speaker the task appears to be easier (task type 3; task type 5).
2. *Planning*: Planning time was manipulated in two 2 × 2 designs: with familiarity in task type 1 and with structure in task type 4. The results tentatively suggest that a familiar activity is easier where planning time is not present. Further, planning time appears to adversely influence performance in both structured and unstructured tasks.

DISCUSSION

Five oral task types at two levels were investigated. Two task characteristics (structure and familiarity) and two task conditions (native speaker versus non-native speaker and planning time) were manipulated.

In general the results for the structured versus the unstructured tasks had been anticipated – structure makes the task easier, although this was more apparent where the learner was required to obtain information (task types 2 and 4) than where the interaction was negotiated (task types 3 and 5). We may postulate that the presence of structure in the task reduces the cognitive load placed on the speaker by providing scaffolding upon which to build language. This provides a framework at the global level which in turn allows the learner to pay more attention to the local linguistic content of the response. Of the four tasks in which this variable was manipulated, two involved obtaining information while the other two required negotiation. The results were most consistent for the tasks which required learners to obtain information. However, one aspect of the task which may contribute to the difference in the role of structure is the degree to which the role of the interlocutor is specified.

In the tasks which require negotiation (task types 3 and 5), the interlocutor role is fairly precisely specified, identifying for the interlocutor a list of items to be discussed with the student. This means that although in the unstructured versions of the task the student has not been provided with structured input, the interlocutor nonetheless is able to provide a strong framework for them since the interlocutor's card itself is to some degree structured. We speculate that this might mean that the interlocutors, either consciously or unconsciously, provided more structure by their input than was the case in the less negotiable task type. Such structured input would apply regardless of whether the task was a structured one or not, and thus may negate the effect of the structure with the result that the effect for structure is less obvious in negotiated exchanges. Examination of the discourse supports this. The content of the unstructured dialogues in task types 3 and 5 is very similar to that of the structured dialogues in these tasks, as the learners respond to information-seeking questions (for further discussion of this see Wigglesworth (in press)). This tends to reinforce the view that the interlocutor contributes to the structure and content of these role plays which require negotiation to take place.

In the tasks which require the students to obtain information (task types 2 and 4) learners perform better where structure is present. However, in these cases, the students are required to ask the questions. In the more negotiated exchanges, both interviewer and learner can ask and answer questions, and therefore it is much easier for the interviewer to consciously or unconsciously structure the interview for the students. Thus structure can be either built into the task, or provided by the interlocutor. What is important is that there is recognition of the influence it may have.

The familiarity of the activity appeared to make the task easier in task type 1. We had expected to find the more frequently performed activity to be easier to access and report on. For the other tasks in which familiarity was manipulated, however, the less familiar task was the easier task and in fact this advantage was apparent on all criteria in the raw score analysis and to a small extent in both other analytic approaches. In one particular case we had expected that obtaining information for oneself in a habitual environment (the English language school) would be easier than obtaining information for a third party in a less familiar environment. However, there are two points that need to be raised in consideration of this task. Firstly, the task was to some extent compromised by the use of NNS interlocutors for the less familiar task (telephoning the high school), but NS interlocutors for the more familiar task (telephoning the language school). As we saw in the results section above, where NS versus NNS was intentionally manipulated as a variable, NNS interlocutors appeared to make the task easier. Thus it may be that the unintended use of NNS interlocutors in the less familiar task affected the results obtained for the high school task. Secondly, upon examining the task in more detail, it was found that this task also included many more cues about the types of information to be elicited – thus it incorporated more structure into the task than was the case for the more familiar task. This suggests that structure and/or NS vs NNS interlocutors have a particularly strong impact on the outcome. We return to a discussion of the NS/NNS dimension below. Meanwhile, we have postulated above that structure is an important factor in making tasks easier, particularly in tasks where information must be obtained, as was the case with these tasks. We now turn to the task conditions.

Two task conditions were manipulated: NS vs NNS interlocutor, and planning time. The finding for native vs non-native speaker was not as we had anticipated. We had anticipated that in assessment tasks of this type, the native speaker teacher would make the task easier – in fact, this was not the case – the native speaker interlocutor made the task more difficult in all analyses across both task types. There are a number of reasons that this might be the case. Firstly, the learners may be more relaxed in discussion with an NNS interlocutor, with the effect that this makes the task easier. Secondly, raters may compensate for a perceived disadvantage in having an NNS interlocutor. A third alternative is that where the interlocutor is a NNS, the learner tends to produce less (and less complex) language. We may postulate that the NS interlocutor may force the learner to produce more language generally, thus increasing the learner's opportunities to display the full extent of their language competence. However, there was a substantial range of NNS interviewer proficiencies used in administering these tasks and where NNS interlocutors are used, careful consideration needs to be given to the effect this kind of variable proficiency may have on the learner's performance. Finally, it should be pointed out that there was a 'power' differential at play here. The native speaker was a teacher, but the non-native speaker was another learner; thus the social status of the two relationships was not equivalent, and this may be an intervening variable. In order to identify more precisely the effects of this variable, more detailed investigation is required, which would need to focus on a detailed analysis of the discourse.

Finally we turn to planning time. Planning time was not manipulated on its own, but in conjunction with structure in one case, and familiarity of activity in another. It was found that a structured task was easier, and that planning time appeared to increase difficulty in both the structured and the unstructured tasks. A familiar activity was also easier without planning time but, where the task was unfamiliar, planning time had no effect either way. We may postulate that planning time encourages learners to attempt to introduce more complex ideas, or more complex structures and that when this is translated into linguistic output, the learner's performance is adversely affected resulting in less fluent and perhaps less grammatically accurate language. However, it must be noted that we are discussing small differences, although we may gain some confidence from the fact that all three approaches to the analysis generally agree over different tasks.

These results for planning are somewhat inconsistent with previous findings in the literature, where planning has been shown to increase accuracy under a range of conditions (Foster and Skehan, 1996; Skehan and Foster, 1997; Wigglesworth, 1997; Mehnert, 1998). However, it should be noted that the measures for evaluation in these other studies has not been external ratings by qualified assessors who must assess the material on a single hearing. Instead, these studies have used linguistic measures either in the form of error-free clauses, or specific measures of linguistic accuracy at the morphological or syntactic level – requiring a rather different approach with detailed and time-consuming application of measures to transcripts. Thus, the operationalisation of 'accuracy' is quite different. The study by Wigglesworth (1997), where both specific linguistic measures and rater assessments were used, found differences apparent on the specific linguistic measures although these were not manifest at the level of the rater assessments.

CONCLUSIONS

The findings presented here raise a number of issues. For the oral data, the relatively small changes in the characteristics and/or conditions of the task can be shown to influence the scores obtained despite the small number of subjects undertaking the tasks. This suggests that in the process of designing tasks as assessment instruments, it is important to pay considerable attention to very precise parameters of the task. In addition, the findings point to the importance of extensive trialling of all tasks on a range of learners, and ideally, with a range of interlocutors, before they are used as assessment instruments. Bachman and Palmer (1996) argue that task characteristics will inevitably influence test scores to some degree, and for that reason it is essential to understand the effect of that influence. Clearly task conditions also have a role to play. This project was designed to investigate these issues and attempt to make some contribution to our knowledge of the factors that must be taken into account in task design, and there are a number of points which suggest the necessity for further research. Specifically, we need to identify how particular features of language – accuracy, fluency, discourse organisation, etc. – change under differing conditions and characteristics of tasks. This means that more attention needs to be paid (a) to the way in which tasks are developed and classified, (b) to how their differential development may influence the quantitative scores obtained by candidates on tests, and (c) to how the language output of the candidate may be influenced by the task.

Different factors influence different types of tasks to differing degrees. For example, in a task where the learner is required to obtain information, structure appears to be quite influential in its effect on the discourse since it provides a framework for the learner to use. In more negotiated interaction, such as that found in task types 3 and 5, where questions may be asked and answered by both the learner and the interviewer, structure is not as influential. Here, on the other hand, the interlocutor variable is crucial, not only because the interlocutor may provide structure for the learner, but also because this type of task allows much more leeway for the interlocutor to dominate the interaction, to assist or to problematise the task (the issues related to interviewer variability are discussed further in Wigglesworth (in press)).

For this reason, in oral assessments, close attention needs to be paid not only to possible variables which can be incorporated or not into the task, but also to the role of the interlocutor. This role is central in ensuring that learners obtain similar input across similar tasks. To this end, in developing task-based assessments – particularly those for use in the classroom – training needs to include an awareness of the ways in which interlocutors can affect tasks positively and negatively. The clearer the specifications for assessment task development, and the clearer the specifications for the role of the interlocutor, together with expectations of his or her input, then the more reliable will be the assessment tasks employed.

ACKNOWLEDGEMENTS

I am very grateful to Helen Slatyer and Helen Price for their assistance with the organisation of the data collection, and its subsequent transcription. I would also like to express my gratitude to Chris Howell and Mary Anne Brown (AMES Vic), Jennifer Riatti (AMES WA) and Sue Hood and Judy Christie (AMES NSW) who co-ordinated the data collection in each of the states, and to the teachers and students who so willingly agreed to participate in the interviews.

NOTES

1. This research was carried out as part of an NCELTR Special Project funded by the Department of Immigration and Multicultural Affairs.
2. Functional proficiency is approximately equivalent to FSI (Foreign Service Institute) level 2, and vocational is roughly equivalent to FSI 3.
3. For the purposes of the analysis, the 'very easy' category and the 'very difficult' category were collapsed with the 'easy' and 'difficult'.

REFERENCES

Bachman, L. (1990) *Fundamental Considerations in Language Testing.* Oxford: Oxford University Press.

Bachman, L. and Palmer, A. (1996) *Language Testing in Practice.* Oxford: Oxford University Press.

Candlin, C. (1987) Toward task-based learning. In C. Candlin and D.F. Murphy (eds) *Language and Learning Tasks.* Englewood Cliffs, NJ: Prentice Hall.

Crookes, G. (1989) Planning and interlanguage variation. *Studies in Second Language Acquisition,* 11: 367–83.

Doughty, C. and Pica, P. (1986) 'Information gap' tasks: Do they facilitate second language acquisition? *TESOL Quarterly,* 20 (2): 305–25.

Ellis, R. (1987) Interlanguage variability in narrative discourse: Style shifting in the use of the past tense. *Studies in Second Language Acquisition,* 9: 1–20.

Foster, P. (1996) Doing the task better: How planning time influences students' performance. In J. Willis and D. Willis (eds) *Challenge and Change in Language Teaching.* London: Heinemann.

Foster, P. and Skehan, P. (1996) The influence of planning and task type on second language performances. *Studies in Second Language Acquisition,* 18: 299–323.

Foster, P., Tonkyn, A. and Wigglesworth, G. (in press) Measuring spoken language: A unit for all reasons. *Applied Linguistics.*

Gass, S. and Varonis, E. (1985) Task variation and non-native/non-native negotiation of meaning. In S. Gass and C. Madden (eds) *Input in Second Language Acquisition.* Rowley, MA: Newbury House.

Kenyon, D. (1992) Introductory remarks at symposium on development and use of rating scales in language testing. 14th Language Testing Research Colloquium, Vancouver, 27 February to 1 March.

Linacre, J.M. (1990) *FACETS: Computer Program for Many Faceted Rasch Measurement, Version 2.36.* Chicago, IL: Mesa Press.

Lumley, T. and McNamara, T. (1995) Rater characteristics and rater bias: Implications for training. *Language Testing,* 12: 55–71.

Mehnert, U. (1998) The effects of different lengths of time for planning on second language performance. *Studies in Second Language Acquisition,* 20 (1): 83–108.

McNamara, T. (1996) *Measuring Second Language Performance.* London: Longman.

Plough, I. and Gass, S. (1993) Interlocutor and task familiarity: Effects on interactional structure. In G. Crookes and S. Gass (eds) *Tasks and Language Learning: Integrating Theory and Practice.* Clevedon, Auon: Multilingual Matters.

Robinson, P. and Ross, S. (1996) The development of task-based assessment in English for academic purposes programs. *Applied Linguistics,* 17 (4): 455–76.

Robinson, P., Ting, S. and Urwin, J. (1995) Investigating second language task complexity. *RELC Journal,* 25: 35–57.

Sajjadi, S. and Tahririan, M.H. (1992) Task variability and interlanguage use. *IRAL,* 30: 1.

Skehan, P. (1996) A framework for the implementation of task-based instruction. *Applied Linguistics,* 16 (3): 38–62.

Skehan, P. (1998). *A Cognitive Approach to Language Learning.* Oxford: Oxford University Press.

Skehan, P. and Foster, P. (1997) Task type and task processing conditions as influences on foreign language performance. *Language Teaching Research,* 13: 185–211.

Wigglesworth, G. (1997) An investigation of planning time and proficiency level on oral test discourse. *Language Testing,* 14 (1): 101–22.

Wigglesworth, G. (in press) Issues in the development of oral tasks for competency based performance assessments. In G. Brindley (ed.) *Studies in Immigrant English Language Assessment* (Volume 1). Sydney: NCELTR.

Young, R. and Milanovic, M. (1992) Discourse variation in oral proficiency interviews. *Studies in Second Language Acquisition,* 14 (4): 403–24.

Yule, G. and McDonald, D. (1990) Resolving referential conflicts in L2 interaction: The effect of proficiency and interactive role. *Language Learning,* 40 (4): 539–56.

APPENDIX 9.1: EXAMPLES OF TASKS USED (WITHOUT MANIPULATIONS INCLUDED)

Level 1 tasks

Task type 1

- *Task 1* You invite a friend from your class to visit you. Give instructions on how to get from where you are now to where you live.

- *Tasks 2 and 3* Your friend has a new flexi card for an Automatic Teller Machine (ATM). Explain how to use the card to get money from the ATM.

- *Tasks 4 and 5* The bulb in your kitchen light doesn't work. It is on a high ceiling. Give instructions to your 12-year-old child on how to change it.

Task type 2

- *Task 1* You want to visit Alice Springs for 1 week in September. Call the airline company and ask about a plane trip to Alice Springs.

- *Tasks 2 and 3* There is an exhibition of Aboriginal paintings at the museum which you would like to see. Call the museum and obtain information about the exhibition.

- *Task 4* You want information about English classes for yourself. Enquire at a local teaching centre.

- *Task 5* Your family has moved to a new suburb. You want information about the local high school for your 13-year-old child. Phone the school.

Task type 3

- *Task 1* Your washing machine doesn't work. Call a repair service and ask for someone to come and fix it.

- *Tasks 2 and 3* Your television doesn't work – you can't get the ABC. Call the television repair service.

- *Tasks 4 and 5* You want to have *The Australian* newspaper delivered to your home on Saturdays. Call your newsagent.

Level 2 tasks

Task type 4

- *Task 1*   Ring the TAFE Information Centre and enquire about computer courses. Say what type of course you are interested in.

- *Tasks 2 to 5*   Read the job advertisement below. Call the contact person and obtain information about the position.

Task type 5

- *Task 1*   You have an appointment for a job interview with an employment agency tomorrow. The time that has been arranged is not convenient for you. Go to the agency, introduce yourself and explain the situation. Try to arrange another time for the interview.

- *Tasks 2 and 3*   You have four weeks annual leave available this year. You would like to take three weeks leave now, even though it is a busy time at your workplace. Talk to your manager about this situation, explain why you want to take the leave now and negotiate a solution.

- *Tasks 4 and 5*   You are an employee in a department store. A customer approaches you with a complaint about a faulty cassette recorder that they bought. The shop's policy is to only give credit for returned goods and not to give money back. Attend to the customer's complaint.

Chapter 10

Task-based assessments: Characteristics and validity evidence

Micheline Chalhoub-Deville

INTRODUCTION

Test validation has evolved in the last few decades from an emphasis on the test item itself as the basis for validity to construct-based investigations that focus on test score interpretation and use. Many researchers have even questioned the value of content-related validity because of its failure to account for test-takers' performance (Deville, 1996). A validation approach that concerns itself solely with aspects of the test and neglects test scores is especially questionable for educational tests that are intended to inform instruction and learning. According to Geisinger (1992), the discrepancy has prompted some researchers to dismiss content evidence as a legitimate source of validity evidence. As Messick (1989) argues, however, content-related evidence cannot be dismissed in an overarching conceptualisation of validity but must be examined in conjunction with evidence provided from test score data. The present chapter presents issues related to second language (L2) task-based assessment within this coherent framework of validity, exploring both content-related test attributes as well as construct-related evidence obtained from performance data. These assessment issues are informed by the L2 teaching and SLA (second language acquisition) literature on tasks.

In the last two decades, L2 instruction has become more communicative with greater emphasis placed on students' ability to use the L2 in real-life situations. Crookes and Gass (1993a) indicate that task-based instruction is one increasingly popular approach to communicative language learning. According to Loschky and Bley-Vroman (1993), tasks have gained support in the L2 teaching community because they 'have often been seen principally as devices to allow learners to practice using the language as a tool of communication rather than as a device to get learners to focus on grammatical features of the language' (p. 124). A very important assumption in task-based learning, as stated by Skehan (1998), is that this focus on meaning 'will engage naturalistic acquisitional mechanisms, cause the underlying interlanguage system to be stretched, and drive development forward' (p. 95). In short, task-based pedagogy moves away from the traditional focus on form to an approach that promotes, in addition to grammatical skills, the ability to interact to achieve communicative goals in the real world.

210

While the L2 literature includes numerous investigations of task-based instruction and learning investigations (e.g. Crookes and Gass, 1993a, 1993b; Skehan, 1998), a cursory examination of testing publications shows that task-based assessment work is scarce (one example, however, is Wigglesworth, 1997). In fact, at first glance it may appear that the term 'task', except for denoting an activity or exercise such as in performance assessments, is relatively new in the L2-testing field. Where the term 'task' is used in testing, it has been closely connected with the notion of test method (Bachman, 1990). Although the terms 'task' and 'test method' do share some attributes, a closer examination of the two terms leads one to argue that the two are not identical. Test method has been used to refer to a variety of exercises ranging from paper-and-pencil, indirect measures such as cloze, multiple choice, etc., to performance-based and direct activities, e.g. the oral proficiency interview (OPI), tape-mediated interviews, etc. (see Bachman and Palmer, 1981; Shohamy, 1984). So, the emphasis has been on testing formats, irrespective of their real-life connection, and the systematic effect these may have on the resulting scores. The term 'task', on the other hand, has been used in SLA and instructional domains, for the most part, to refer to activities that simulate those in the real-world outside the classroom and promote interlanguage development (e.g. Krahnke, 1987; Long and Crookes, 1992).

The fact that the language-testing literature has not been discussing task-based assessment does not denote that L2-testing efforts have not been addressing issues comparable to those considered in task-based instructional approaches to L2 learning. In fact, the push for communicative competence in the 1970s, the proficiency movement in the 1980s, and more recently the call for more performance-based testing, have all been accompanied by a concomitant emphasis by language testers on assessments that share features considered core in the L2 instructional task. Additionally, L2 testers are increasingly promoting the use of the term 'task'. For example, Bachman and Palmer (1996: 60), state:

> First, this [task] refers directly to what the test-taker is actually presented with in a language test, rather than to an abstract entity. Second, the term 'task' is more general, and relates more directly to the notion of task as it is currently used in the contexts of language acquisition and language teaching.

As can be seen, part of the increased motivation and push to use the term 'task' is to enhance the link between L2 assessment and instruction. L2 testers recognise the need to align not only testing practices but also their terminology with that of both the SLA and L2 instruction communities. In short, SLA specialists and L2 teachers have been discussing task-based instruction for over a decade. In comparison, L2 testers are only now beginning to use the term and to make connections with researchers in adjacent areas.

The purpose of the present chapter is to investigate issues related to the design and construct validation of task-based L2 oral assessments. First, the chapter identifies characteristics reported in the literature as core to the instructional task and links these characteristics to attributes commonly present in L2 assessments. The chapter then discusses these attributes in relation to popular foreign language oral assessments, emphasising their importance from a content validation standpoint. The chapter moves on to argue, however, that content-related evidence is not sufficient in today's conceptualisation of validation research. 'It is clear that content-related evidence cannot stand alone, but we need to examine how it functions in concern with construct-related evidence in a unified validity framework' (Messick, 1989: 42). The chapter, therefore, presents an empirical study that addresses construct validity evidence. The study investigates the structure of language abilities underlying oral scores obtained using instruments that incorporate attributes shared with L2 instructional tasks.

INSTRUCTIONAL TASK CHARACTERISTICS

Based on a review of task-based resarch and literature, Skehan (1998: 95) presents several core features of a task in instruction:

- meaning is primary
- there is some communication problem to solve
- there is some sort of relationship to real-world activities
- task completion has some priority
- the assessment of the task is in terms of outcome.

In order to further clarify the concept of 'task', Skehan (1998: 95) lists characteristics that show what a task is not. Tasks:

- do not give learners other people's meanings to regurgitate
- are not concerned with language display
- are not conformity-oriented
- are not practice-oriented
- do not embed language into materials so that specific structures can be focused upon.

These characteristics are also discussed by several other authors, for example, Berwick (1993), Candlin (1987), Long (1989), Nunan (1989, 1993) and Willis (1996).

These task-based characteristics, discussed so extensively in SLA and pedagogy publications, bear a relationship with concepts found in the L2-testing literature. Nevertheless this relationship with L2 testing is to be inferred as it has never been stated explicitly – one might even argue that the relationship may even be accidental, rather than conscious. If we examine several L2 assessment instruments developed in the last two decades (e.g. the oral proficiency interview (OPI), the simulated oral proficiency interview (SOPI), the contextualised speaking assessment (CoSA), and the video/oral communication instrument (VOCI)), we can explore the extent to which the SLA and teaching tasks on the one hand, and the assessment tasks on the other, share like characteristics. For example, features listed above as core to the instructional task – such as focus on meaning, individual expression, emphasis on genuine communication, real-world connection, etc. – correspond to characteristics such as learner-centredness, contextualisation and authenticity.[1] Before moving to the sections that discuss these three characteristics, however, a brief description of the assessment instruments focused upon in this chapter is provided.

POPULAR FOREIGN LANGUAGE ORAL ASSESSMENTS

The assessment instruments chosen to explore the correspondence of task-based features in instruction and assessment include the OPI, the CoSA (patterned after the simulated oral proficiency interview – SOPI (Stansfield, 1996)), and VOCI.[2] At least one or a modified version of these assessments is used in most foreign language programs in the USA (see Harlow and Caminero, 1990; Omaggio Hadley, 1993).

The OPI, developed in the early 1980s, is modelled after the Foreign Service Institute (FSI) oral interview in its structure, rating criteria and level descriptions. The OPI is a structured, live conversation between a trained interlocutor/rater and a test-taker on a series of topics of varied language difficulty, with the goal of establishing the test-taker's proficiency level (Omaggio Hadley, 1993). The interviewer initiates the interactions and builds on the responses of the interviewee. The tester uses the ACTFL Guidelines for scoring the interview. These guidelines include nine-level descriptions ranging from the Novice to the Superior. For detailed information about the OPI see Liskin-Gasparro (1987), Omaggio Hadley (1993) and Kuo and Jiang (1997).

As Chalhoub-Deville (1997b) and Stansfield (1996) point out, the OPI is limited in terms of practicality. The limitations include the need to have the interviewer and the interviewee present in the same place in order to administer an OPI. Also, it is not feasible to administer the OPI to more than one person at a time, which is quite costly when one has a large group of students whose oral abilities need to be evaluated. As a result, a number of more practical surrogates to the live OPI have been developed, such as the CoSA and VOCI instruments.

Similar to the OPI, the CoSAs, and VOCIs attempt to involve the learner in relatively personalised exchanges, which are set in various everyday communicative situations typically encountered by learners in real life. While patterned after the OPI, these instruments are intended to circumvent the practicality concerns regarding the OPI. These instruments engage the learner using pre-recorded segments. The CoSA segments are tape-mediated and the VOCI are video-based. Test-takers' timed responses on each of the CoSAs, and VOCI are audio-taped. Responses are evaluated using scoring rubrics based on the ACTFL Guidelines. For more information about the CoSA see Chalhoub-Deville (1997b, 1999), and for the VOCI see Higgs (1995). For a review of the limitations of the interview format and the ACTFL Guidelines, see Lantolf and Frawley (1985), Bachman and Savignon (1986), Shohamy (1988), Van Lier (1989), North (1993) and Chalhoub-Deville (1997a).

ORAL TEST TASK DEVELOPMENT CHARACTERISTICS

The OPI, CoSA, and VOCI instruments incorporate attributes shared by the task-based instructional characteristics listed above. In discussing these characteristics, however, terms commonly referred to in assessment are employed, i.e. learner-centred features, contextualisation, and authenticity (Underhill, 1987; Brindley, 1989; Bachman, 1990; Cohen, 1994; Bachman and Palmer, 1996). The following sections address the significance of each characteristic in the area of assessment. Although they are interrelated, for the purposes of explication here the three attributes are discussed sequentially.

Learner-centred properties

Instructional tasks personalise language interaction by not giving 'learners other people's meanings to regurgitate', being 'conformity-oriented', or 'practice-oriented' (Skehan, 1998: 95). Correspondingly, learner-centred assessments emphasise interactions that encourage test-takers' individual expression and activate their background knowledge and experiences. An important feature of learner-centred assessments is the promotion of test-takers' individual expression, as accomplished when using open tasks. In open tasks, Loschky and Bley-Vroman (1993) argue that 'the information which learners must exchange is relatively unrestricted or indeterminate', as opposed to closed tasks where 'the information needed for task success is very determinate or discrete' (p. 125). In L2 oral performance assessment, where the focus is to get an accurate picture of students' communicative abilities and when the purpose is often to generalise about students' ability beyond the learning/ testing situation to real-life communication, open tasks allow test-takers to take interest in the interaction, display more language, and have relatively more control over the language produced (Douglas and Selinker, 1985).

In addition, learner-centred assessments give test-takers the opportunity to utilise their background knowledge and experiences in the testing situation (Douglas and Selinker, 1985). Such assessments enhance test-takers' ability to be active and autonomous participants in a given communicative interaction. Tasks present test-takers with relatively novel situations together with context descriptions or visuals that enable them to activate and rely upon appropriate schemata to achieve their communicative goals.

The OPI, because the interlocutor/interviewer is actively interacting with the test-taker, can provide a high degree of personalisation and learner-centredness. The interviewer typically introduces a topics that he or she discerns from the conversation are familiar and of interest to the interviewee, leading to involved interaction on the part of the test-takers. In comparison, the CoSA and VOCI, which are tape- or video-mediated instruments, are quite limited in their ability to provide on-line interactions that adapt to personalised communication. Test developers of these instruments, however, attempt to circumvent this problem by selecting topics, settings, interlocutors, etc., deemed appropriate and meaningful to the targeted test-takers.

Finally, except for the VOCI instrument at the Novice level, which includes situations that require test-takers to produce memorised language, these instruments typically do not present test-takers with situations that elicit rehearsed materials, specific structures, or vocabulary. On the contrary, the instruments attempt to present test-takers with interactions, similar to open tasks described above, that encourage fresh but familiar communicative exchanges.

Contextualisation

Anastasi (1986), a noted measurement expert, argues for the importance of testing in context. She writes (p. 484): 'when selecting or developing tests and when interpreting scores, consider context. I shall stop right there, because those are the words, more than any others, that I want to leave with you: *consider context*' (italics in original). Anastasi contends that context is important for test development as well as for test score validation. In the L2 field, Omaggio Hadley (1993) maintains that language use occurs in contexts 'where any given utterance is embedded in ongoing discourse as well as some particular circumstance or situation' (p. 125). This definition underscores two aspects to contextualisation: discourse and situational embeddedness, a conceptualisation echoed by several researchers (Bachman, 1990; Berwick, 1993). For example, Bachman maintains that 'the full context of language use [includes] the context of discourse and situation' (p. 82).

With regard to discourse embeddedness, Widdowson (1978: 2) states that 'normal linguistic behaviour does not consist of the production of separate sentences but in the use of sentences for the creation of discourse'. Contextualised tasks should present test-takers with, and invite the use of, cohesive and coherent discourse that conveys the expressions, conventions and structures typically encountered in non-testing real-world language. Indeed, the OPI, VOCI and CoSA assessments not only require test-takers to produce discourse resembling that typically encountered in real-life communication, but also present test-takers with extended discourse to help to prompt such a communicative interaction.

As for situational embeddedness, contextualisation implies the need to use meaningful situations in language testing. In this regard, Berwick (1993) appropriately cites Brown, Collins and Duguid: 'situated cognition and invention is based on the premise that "knowledge is situated in activity and that is used and made sense of within specific contexts and cultures"' (p. 100). In other words, discourse should be situated in a focused and appropriate sociolinguistic context.

The OPI can provide a high degree of situational embeddedness. For example, the exchange between the interviewer and the interviewee typically helps to establish the language and content appropriate for the given communication. The CoSAs, in order to compensate for the absence of one-on-one interaction, embed the various language situations within an overall setting. Specifically, each CoSA instrument is thematically based. In considering the interest and experiences of the targeted test-takers, CoSA test developers include themes such as a summer camp, study abroad trip, student gathering, etc. As a result, the thematic structure provides test-takers with a focused and meaningful overall context that helps test-takers to discern the relevant and appropriate interaction. The CoSAs provide further contextualisation at the task level. Task segments, which include a wide range of situations that focus on different language interactions, provide detailed description of the situation in which the interaction is supposed to take place. The description includes information about the speakers involved in the interaction, the place, the time, the topic, the rationale for the interaction, and other variables relevant to the immediate setting in which the test-taker is asked to operate.

Situational embeddedness in the VOCI is more limited. In comparison to the OPI and CoSA instruments, the VOCI provides less description to help situate the interaction. The main advantage of the VOCI over the CoSA, however, is its video-delivery. The test-taker is not required to process the printed and/or taped information in order to visualise the language setting. The video provides test-takers with a richer depiction of the socio-linguistic elements of the interaction, especially non-verbal language and cues.

Authenticity

The third feature that has received considerable attention in task-based language instruction and testing is authenticity, i.e. the establishment of a more direct relationship between language use and activities employed in instruction and assessment. In the L2 task-based literature, proponents of authenticity such as Nunan (1989) assert the importance of engaging learners in real-world activities for these learners to be able to operate in the real world outside the classroom. In the language-testing field, this interest in authenticity is evidenced in the publication of an entire issue of *Language Testing* on the topic (*Language Testing, 2* (1), 1985). In general, the discussion of authenticity has evolved over the years, moving from a focus on differentiating between intact versus adapted texts to a more involved conceptualisation attempting to identify the relationship between language included in tests versus language use in the real world. (The reader is referred to Lewkowicz, 2000, who documents the evolution of authenticity in the last two decades.)

Bachman (1990) provides one of the most critical and comprehensive reviews of authenticity in L2 tests. Bachman maintains that two approaches to authenticity have been in contention: the real-life (RL) perspective, which considers authenticity more in terms of replication of real-world language performance, versus the interactional/ability (IA) approach, which emphasises an abilities-based characterisation of test performance. According to Bachman (1990), test developers using the IA may invest considerably in creating instruments that incorporate real-life features that make these instruments look similar to ones created using the RL task-driven approach. The starting point and score interpretation of the ability-driven instrument, however, are different. IA test developers typically identify the abilities of interest for a particular testing situation and proceed to create assessments that involve those abilities. While connection to the real world may be built into the ability-based assessment, a distinction between the abilities being measured and the observed performance is emphasised. It follows, then, that the interpretation of scores obtained from IA assessments attempts to delineate and characterise test-takers' abilities to use the language. For examples of ability-driven assessments, see Bachman and Palmer (1996).

The RL approach has been typically adopted in the development of foreign language oral assessment instruments such as those under investigation in the current chapter. The RL approach conceptualises authenticity in terms of performance in the real world. Test developers following this RL approach tend to focus on constructing test tasks that replicate those in real life and rate test-takers' performance according to which tasks can be accomplished.

The emphasis on the replication of real life is best exemplified in the OPI format and procedures, which are said to resemble a genuine conversation in the real world (Clark and Lett, 1988; Kuo and Jiang, 1997). Such live interaction is lacking in the tape-mediated CoSA and video-based VOCI instruments. Much like the OPI, however, these instruments do incorporate a variety of topics and language tasks typically encountered in diverse real-life settings based on the ACTFL Guidelines. The ACTFL Guidelines outline the topics, types of tasks and contexts in which test-takers are expected to perform at different proficiency levels. For example, at the Intermediate level, test-takers perform tasks typically encountered on a daily basis. The Intermediate Mid level specification is: 'Can talk simply about self and family members. Can ask and answer questions and participate in simple conversations on topics beyond the most immediate needs; e.g. personal history and leisure time activities' (Omaggio Hadley, 1993: 504). Additionally, in terms of evaluating test-takers' performance, all three instruments utilise the ACTFL Guidelines as criteria. The guidelines emphasise the effectiveness of integrating language abilities to accomplish the communicative goal of the task.

TASK-BASED ASSESSMENT: VALIDATION RESEARCH

The present chapter makes the argument that learner-centredness, contextualisation and authenticity are important because they overlap with task features identified in the L2 instructional field as conducive to enhancing learning, and also because they can help to produce assessments that allow the elicitation of rich language samples from test-takers. These three attributes, which pertain to test design and construction, address content validity issues. As Messick (1996: 245) states, however: '[V]alidity is not a property of the test or assessment as such [content validity], but rather of the meaning of the test scores.' While it is not prudent to dismiss content-related evidence as it underscores the importance of considering validity from the outset of test development, content validation needs to be complemented with investigations that focus on test performance, i.e. construct validity research. According to Moss (1992: 233), the primary 'purpose of construct validity is to justify a particular interpretation of a test score by examining the behaviour that the test score summarises'. In the present context, construct validation research requires investigating the performance ratings on the OPI, CoSA and VOCI to uncover the language abilities underlying scores obtained from these instruments. The following sections report such a study.

UNDERSTANDING THE ABILITIES[3]

The purpose of the present study is to investigate the structure of abilities underlying test-takers' performances on three oral testing instruments: an OPI, a CoSA and VOCI.[4] Because, as mentioned above, both the CoSA and VOCI are intended to be practical variations of the live OPI, and given that the instruments share similar design attributes, it is hypothesised that comparable structure of language abilities underlie test scores from these three instruments.

The research questions addressed in the present study include:

1. How comparable are the dimensions of language abilities underlying holistic oral ratings obtained from each of the OPI, CoSA and VOCI instruments for three language groups: French, German and Spanish?
2. What are the dimensions of language abilities underlying holistic oral ratings obtained from each of the OPI, CoSA and VOCI instruments for three language groups: French, German and Spanish?

Participants' profile

Two different groups participated in the present study: the test-takers who provided the speech samples, and the raters who provided the ratings of test-takers' oral performance. The test-takers were US university students enrolled in a third or fourth quarter French, German or Spanish language class at the time of the study.

There were about 14 test-takers in French, 15 in German and 14 in Spanish. The French and German test-takers took the OPI and the CoSA, and the Spanish test-takers took all three instruments, including the VOCI. As mentioned above, the VOCI was only available in Spanish at the time of the study.

Three rater groups provided the ratings of the speech samples. There were 13 raters in French, 12 in German and 14 in Spanish. At the time of the study these raters were teaching at the high school or post-secondary level in the state of Minnesota.

There were 28 speech samples available for rating in French (14 test-takers performing on the OPI and CoSA), 30 in German (15 test-takers performing on the OPI and CoSA) and 42 in Spanish (14 test-takers performing on the OPI, CoSA and VOCI). Given the multidimensional scaling (MDS) analyses employed in the present study (see *Multidimensional scaling analyses* below), the number of speech samples included is more than adequate to uncover multiple dimensions of language abilities. Kruskal and Wish (1978) recommend three to five stimuli (speech samples) for every derived dimension. According to Schiffman et al. (1981: 24), 'ideally one should have about 12 stimuli [speech samples] for two-dimensional solutions and 18 stimuli for three-dimensional solutions'. Even using this more stringent requirement from Schiffman and colleagues, the speech samples available in each of the three languages are enough to derive a number of stable dimensions.

Speech samples and ratings

For each test-taker, speech segments of approximately two minutes for each assessment were put on stimulus tapes and given to raters. According to Brown et al. (1984: 75), 'it is possible for teachers to reach a reliable consensus about the relative abilities of a group of school pupils based on a relatively brief tape recording of performance in a verbal task'. The authors describe 'brief' as 'one or two minutes long' (p. 80). Moreover, other studies reported in the literature such as those by Fayer and Krasinski (1987), Albrechtsen et al. (1980) and Chalhoub-Deville (1995a, 1995b) have also used speech samples of this length. In order to minimise a carry-over of one test-taker's rating on a certain task to a following test-taker, samples from any one assessment instrument or test-taker were randomised on the stimulus tape.

After listening to each speech sample, raters provided two types of ratings: (1) a global rating that reflected their overall impression of the speech samples; and (2) ratings on specific analytic scales typically used in L2 oral assessment (see Chalhoub-Deville, 1995a, 1995b, 1997a). These analytic scales include variables such as fluency, comprehensibility, grammatical accuracy, vocabulary, language appropriateness, confidence, etc. (see Table 10.1 (overleaf)). Therefore, each test-taker received from each rater on each task both a global rating and a set of 14 ratings, one for each of the analytic scales. Nine-point scales were used for the ratings, 1 indicating minimal proficiency and 9 superior proficiency.

Multidimensional scaling analyses

MDS techniques were used to analyse the present data, in part because '[t]here exists substantial evidence in the literature supporting the . . . validity of MDS solutions. . . . Some studies . . . demonstrated a close correspondence between subjects' verbal reports of their judgemental process and MDS results' (McCallum, 1988: 441). Additionally, the rationale for selecting MDS over factor analysis is best summarised by Snow et al. (1984: 88) who maintain that 'although factor analysis and multidimensional scaling provide much of the same information, the scaling representation leads to more direct consideration of the relations among tasks, and to the various dimensions or facets

Table 10.1 Scales included in the rating instrument

1. Global Proficiency Rating
2. Analytic Proficiency Ratings:
   - Fluency
   - Your comprehension of student's speech
   - Pronunciation
   - Confidence
   - Creativity
   - Grammatical accuracy
   - Student's comprehension of questions/prompts
   - Length of student's responses
   - Appropriateness of the language used
   - Varied grammatical structures
   - Student's attempts to get the meaning across (e.g. circumlocution)
   - Varied vocabulary
   - Linguistic maturity (simple vs complex)
   - Providing detail

along which tasks can differ simultaneously'. Similarly, Davison and Skay (1991: 551) argue that '[f]actor analysis is more oriented towards individual differences, whereas MDS is more oriented toward variation in task content or task demands . . . MDS [has] been favored over factor analysis by researchers, such as Guttman (1970) and Snow et al. (1984), who were heavily concerned with task structure'.

Within each language, the averaged holistic scores provided by raters were used to construct proximity matrices[5] that were analysed using two MDS techniques: replicated multidimensional scaling (RMDS) and individual differences scaling (INDSCAL). The basic assumption in RMDS 'is that the stimulus configuration X applies with equal validity to every matrix of data. Thus, the implication is that all the data matrices are, except for error, the same; they are replicates of each other . . .' (Young and Harris, 1992: 178). RMDS was employed to answer research question #1, i.e. examine the comparability of the abilities underlying performance on each of the OPI, CoSA and VOCI. More specifically, RMDS indicates the extent to which the ability structure underlying performance ratings on the OPI and CoSA is similar in each of French and German, and the structure underlying ratings on all three instruments is similar in Spanish.

INDSCAL analyses help to uncover dimensions from the proximity matrices. In addition, INDSCAL provides weights that represent 'the information that is unique to each individual [method] about the structure of the stimuli, a notion that we did not have in RMDS' (Young and Harris, 1992: 189). The INDSCAL analyses were employed to answer research question #2, i.e. to extract the dimensions underlying the performance ratings. Finally, to help to interpret the derived INDSCAL dimensions, the mean ratings for each of the analytic language scales were regressed on the MDS dimension co-ordinates.

RESULTS

Descriptive statistics

Before reporting the results of the MDS analyses, descriptive statistics regarding rater reliability and the correlations among the OPI, CoSA and VOCI instrument scores are provided. Table 10.2 provides the results of intra-class[6] rater reliability analyses. As Table 10.2 shows, the indices are above 0.91, except for the German CoSA, which is 0.79. This lower index for the German CoSA may be due to the more homogeneous student performance, as indicated by the relative lack of variability among student scores in the sample. Nonetheless, all these reliability estimates indicate that raters used the holistic scale in a relatively consistent fashion within each language group for each task.

Table 10.2   Rater reliability

	OPI	CoSA	VOCI
French	0.96	0.95	*
German	0.90	0.79	*
Spanish	0.98	0.96	0.91

The correlations of test-takers' scores on the OPI, CoSA and VOCI for each language are reported in Table 10.3. These correlations are somewhat modest. The restricted proficiency range of the test-taker students in the present study is likely to have contributed to these modest correlations. The correlation between the OPI and CoSA in German is low. This, again, could be attributed to the relatively more homogeneous student performances in that group. Also, the lower rater reliability index reported above is a factor that can influence this correlation. (While this correlation is surprisingly low, it is important to note that the MDS analyses of the German data result in solutions comparable to those in French and Spanish. These analyses are presented below.) In short, the correlations indicate that test-takers' rankings differ across the various instruments.

Table 10.3   Correlations among the instruments for each language

French	CoSA/OPI	0.63		
German	CoSA/OPI	0.15		
Spanish	CoSA/OPI	0.50	CoSA/VOCI	0.65
	VOCI/OPI	0.63		

Multidimensional scaling

This section reports the results of the MDS analyses, beginning with the RMDS results. The RMDS technique is used to investigate the likelihood that comparable language structures underlie test-takers' performance ratings across the various oral assessment instruments. Selecting the RMDS solution that best represents the underlying structure is typically done using two principal statistical criteria: stress, which is the lack of fit index, and R^2, which is the amount of variance accounted for. A low stress index together with a high R^2 would provide evidence to support the comparability of the language structure underlying test-takers' performance ratings across the instruments – across the OPI and CoSA in each of French and German, and across the OPI, CoSA and VOCI in Spanish.

Table 10.4 reports the fit indices for the RMDS solutions. As seen from the table, for each of the French, German and Spanish solutions the fit indices generated are poor; the stress indices are higher and the R^2 are lower than desired for each of the 2-, 3- and 4-dimensional solutions. The fit indices were not much better for the 5- and 6-dimensional solutions. For each language, these poor fit indices indicate that it is relatively implausible that the same ability structure underlies performance ratings on the instruments across the tasks. In other words, each task is tapping language abilities differentially.

Table 10.4   The fit indices for the RMDS solutions for each language

Language	4 Dimensions		3 Dimensions		2 Dimensions	
	stress	R^2	stress	R^2	stress	R^2
French	0.16	0.66	0.19	0.65	0.27	0.61
German	0.19	0.42	0.24	0.36	0.32	0.37
Spanish	0.19	0.50	0.23	0.48	0.30	0.48

The INDSCAL model provides, as mentioned above, both a co-ordinate configuration of the language dimensions that underlie test-takers' performance ratings, and weights that indicate the extent to which the underlying dimensions are salient in the various assessment instruments. The results of the INDSCAL analyses are reported in Table 10.5.

Table 10.5   The fit indices and weights of the INDSCAL solutions for each language

	French		German		Spanish		
	⇓		⇓		⇓		
	2 Dimensions		2 Dimensions		3 Dimensions		
	Stress	R^2	Stress	R^2	Stress	R^2	
	0.15	0.92	0.19	0.88	0.14	0.94	
	⇓		⇓		⇓		
	Weights*		Weights*		Weights		
	D-1	D-2	D-1	D-2	D-1	D-2	D-3
OPI	0.97	0.00	0.97	0.05	0.97	0.02	0.02
CoSA	0.12	0.94	0.05	0.91	0.08	0.97	0.01
VOCI	–	–	–	–	0.13	0.07	0.95

* The VOCI was not available in French or German.

The fit indices in Table 10.5 indicate that the 2-dimensional solution provides an acceptable fit to the French rating data. A similar pattern is noted with regard to the German group, where the 2-dimensional solution again provides an acceptable fit to the rating data. As for Spanish, an acceptable data fit is observed with the 3-dimensional solution. The relatively low stress and high R^2 support the selection of these solutions. The weights of the INDSCAL solutions follow a definitive pattern within each language whereby variability along the derived dimensions is related to a specific assessment instrument.

In an effort to interpret the derived dimensions, regression analyses are used. Within each language and for each instrument, standardised mean ratings for each of the analytic scales are regressed on the (already standardised) INDSCAL dimensional loadings, yielding beta weights that are essentially correlation coefficients. The goal is to identify which of the analytic scales correlate highly with the derived dimensions. Highly correlated scales help to explicate the nature of the derived dimensions. Within each language, all instrument-specific analytic scale scores (e.g. fluency, pronunciation, etc.) correlated highly with the co-ordinates of the one dimension weighted by the particular instrument. This lack of differentiation among the abilities as represented by the analytic scales, coupled with the distinctive pattern of weights, indicates a strong method effect.

To examine the hypothesis of a method effect, the INDSCAL dimension loadings are correlated with test-takers' mean scores on each instrument. The results are reported in Table 10.6. As can be observed, all the correlations for French, German and Spanish are 0.94 and above. Dimension 1, for all three language groups, correlates strongly with test-takers' mean scores on the OPI. Similarly, dimension 2, for all three language groups, correlates strongly with test-takers' mean scores on the CoSA. And for the Spanish group only, dimension 3 correlates strongly with test-takers' mean scores on the VOCI. These correlations provide additional strong evidence for a method effect. In other words, the method chosen for assessing test-takers' oral performance strongly influences their oral ability scores.

Table 10.6   Correlations of INDSCAL dimension loadings and test-takers' mean scores for each instrument and each language

Language	Dimension 1 OPI	Dimension 2 CoSA	Dimension 3 VOCI
French	0.99	0.99	–
German	0.97	0.94	–
Spanish	0.98	0.99	0.94

DISCUSSION

Not only do the MDS analyses provide evidence indicating that performances on the three instruments cannot be said to be comparable and, subsequently, scores obtained on these various instruments cannot be used interchange-ably, but the analyses also show that it is not feasible to document the specific language abilities underlying performance across these oral assessment instru-ments. These findings have two principal implications for L2 test researchers and practitioners. First, the implausibility of the notion that similar language abilities underlie ratings of students' performances on the OPI, CoSA and VOCI indicates that test users should be careful in generalising scores obtained from these instruments to a universe of similar, face valid oral instruments. Second, the inability to uncover the specific language abilities underlying performance on the OPI, CoSA and VOCI, coupled with the strong method effect on test-takers' performance, undermines meaningful interpretation of test scores.

In terms of pedagogy, the present findings are problematic. To a large extent, the interest in assessment is because it can help to inform the instruc-tion/learning process. Assessment scores are of little pedagogic value if not accompanied by appropriate and meaningful interpretations regarding learners' abilities on various linguistic and non-linguistic variables that in-form teachers as to how instruction might be structured to promote student learning.

The findings of the present study speak to the SLA field as well. Instruments used for eliciting speech samples from language learners play a critical role in the type of data used to make inferences about the L2 learning process. SLA researchers need to reconsider the notion of elicitation instruments as a monolith, be aware of instrument effect on the abilities under investigation, and exercise caution when generalising findings, without verification, based on one task type to others considered comparable. The message is, as Duff (1993: 57) writes:

> to consider how various common, relatively open-ended tasks influence the production of IL structures, and whether the failure to treat tasks as distinct from one another obscures task-related variability in an individual subject's IL performance, which is important when the aim of L2 is to account for a learner's demonstrated ability (or proficiency) at a given point in time.

In conclusion, it is important for SLA researchers to investigate and docu-ment the knowledge and skills that underlie L2 ability as observed on various tasks.

CONCLUSION

The chapter acknowledges the communicative task as the most promising pedagogic approach to enhancing the development of learners' language and proceeds to document features core to the instructional task. These task features, it is argued, bear relationship with three attributes in the testing literature: learner-centredness, contextualisation and authenticity. The chapter discusses these attributes in the context of three foreign language oral instruments: the OPI, the CoSA and VOCI. It is argued, however, that the incorporation of these attributes, which pertain to test design, address content validity issues. Content validity provides an excellent, although not a sufficient, springboard for establishing validity evidence. Validation research emphasises the importance of construct-related evidence utilising test score data. As Messick (1996) asserts, in validation it is important to provide 'empirical evidence of response consistencies or performance regularities reflective of domain processes [i.e. language proficiency]' (p. 249). The findings of the performance-based study reveal a strong method effect with each of the three language groups across the various tasks. Method effects mask the knowledge and skills that underlie performance ratings and undermine appropriate interpretation and use of test scores, keeping educators from utilising test results to design and plan instruction around identifiable L2 abilities.

The results of the study prompt test developers and researchers to consider, in addition to important content attributes, the language abilities their assessments intend to measure. Language testers and researchers need to expand their test specifications to include the knowledge and skills that underlie the language construct. Such specifications should be informed by theory and research on the language construct and the language-learning process as well as by systematic observations of the particulars in a given context (see Chalhoub-Deville, 1997a). In other words, referring back to Anastasi (1986), we must consider the interaction between context (e.g. tasks) and language abilities in order to better understand the language-learning process and better validate our tests.

NOTES

1. These terms were introduced in a presentation by Chalhoub-Deville and Tarone at the annual meeting of the American Association for Applied Linguistics March, 1997, in Orlando, Florida.
2. The OPI is arranged by Language Testing International, the testing office affiliated with ACTFL – www.actfl.org/htdocs/programs/opi.htm. The CoSA instruments are available from the Center for Advanced Research on Language Acquisition at the University of Minnesota. The VOCI assessments are available from the Language Acquisition Resource Center at San Diego University.
3. This study was presented at the annual meeting of the American Association for Applied Linguistics, March 1998, in Seattle, Washington.
4. The study was originally carried out as part of a research agenda designed for documenting the properties of the CoSA (see also Chalhoub-Deville, 1999).
5. A proximity matrix represents the amount of difference/distance between the speech samples, as perceived by the raters. In the present study the dissimilarity option was chosen because, according to Young and Harris (1992: 170), 'similarities are not as robust as dissimilarities for the SPSS Multidimensional Scaling procedure'.
6. The intraclass coefficient is a reliability estimate of ratings data based on mean squares. The procedure is an extension of analysis of variance (ANOVA).

REFERENCES

Albrechtsen, D., Henrisksen, B. and Faerch, C. (1980) Native speaker reactions to learners' spoken interlanguage. *Language Learning*, 30: 365–96.

Anastasi, A. (1986) Evolving concepts of test validation. *Annual Review of Psychology*, 37: 1–15.

Bachman, L.F. (1990) *Fundamental Considerations in Language Testing*. New York: Oxford University Press.

Bachman, L.F. (1991) What does language testing have to offer? *TESOL Quarterly*, 25: 671–704.

Bachman, L.F. and Palmer, A. (1981) A multitrait–multimethod investigation into the construct validity of six tests of speaking and reading. In A. Palmer, P.J.M. Groot, and G.A. Trosper (eds) *The Construct Validation of Tests of Communicative Competence* (pp. 149–65). Washington, DC: TESOL.

Bachman, L.F. and Palmer, A. (1996) *Language Testing in Practice*. New York: Oxford University Press.

Bachman, L.F. and Savignon, S. (1986) The evaluation of communicative language proficiency: A critique of the ACTFL oral interview. *Modern Language Journal*, 70: 380–90.

Berwick, R. (1993) Towards an educational framework for teacher-led tasks. In G. Crookes and S. Gass (eds) *Tasks in a Pedagogical Context: Integrating Theory and Practice* (pp. 97–124). Clevedon: Multilingual Matters.

Brindley, G. (1989) *Assessing Achievement in the Learner-centred Curriculum*. Sydney, Australia: National Centre for English Language Teaching and Research, Macquarie University.

Brown, G., Anderson, A., Shillcock, R. and Yule, G. (1984) *Teaching Talk: Strategies for Production and Assessment*. New York: Cambridge University Press.

Candlin, C. (1987) Towards task-based language learning. In C. Candlin and D. Murphy (eds) *Language Learning Tasks*. Englewood Cliffs, NJ: Prentice-Hall.

Chalhoub-Deville, M. (1995a) Deriving oral assessment scales across different tests and rater group. *Language Learning*, 45: 251–81.

Chalhoub-Deville, M. (1995b) A contextualised approach to describing oral language proficiency. *Language Testing*, 12: 16–33.

Chalhoub-Deville, M. (1997a) Theoretical models, operational frameworks, and test construction. *Language Testing*, 14: 3–22.

Chalhoub-Deville, M. (1997b) The Minnesota articulation project and its proficiency-based assessments. *Foreign Language Annals*, 30: 492–502.

Chalhoub-Deville, M. (1999) Investigating the properties of assessment instruments and the setting of proficiency standards for admission into university second language courses. In K. Heilenman (ed.) *Research Issues in Language Program Direction*. Boston, MA: Heinle & Heinle.

Clark, J.L.D. and Lett, J. (1988) A research agenda. In P. Lowe Jr and C. Stansfield (eds) *Second Language Proficiency Assessment: Current Issues*. CAL/ERIC *Language in Education: Theory and practice, 70* (pp. 53–82). Englewood Cliffs, NJ: Prentice-Hall.

Cohen, A. (1994) *Assessing Language Ability in the Classroom* (2nd edition). Boston: Heinle & Heinle.

Crookes, G. and Gass, S. (eds) (1993a) *Tasks and Language Learning: Integrating Theory and Practice*. Clevedon: Multilingual Matters.

Crookes, G. and Gass, S. (eds) (1993b) *Tasks in a Pedagogical Context: Integrating Theory and Practice*. Clevedon: Multilingual Matters.

Davison, M. and Skay, C. (1991) Multidimensional scaling and factor models of test and item responses. *Psychological Bulletin*, 110: 551–6.

Deville, C. (1996) An empirical link of content and construct evidence. *Applied Psychological Measurement*, 20: 127–39.

Douglas, D. and Selinker, L. (1985) Principles for language tests within the 'discourse domains' theory of interlanguage: Research, test construction and interpretation. *Language Testing*, 2: 205–26.

Duff, P. (1993) Tasks and interlanguage performance: An SLA perspective. In G. Crookes and S. Gass (1993a).

Fayer, J.K. and Krasinski, E. (1987) Native and non-native judgements of intelligibility and irritation. *Language Learning*, 37: 313–26.

Geisinger, K.F. (1992) The metamorphosis of test validation. *Educational Psychologist*, 27, 197–222.

Guttman, L. (1971) Measurement as structural theory. *Psychometrika*, 36: 329–47.

Harlow, L. and Caminero, R. (1990) Oral testing of beginning language students at large universities: Is it worth the trouble? *Foreign Language Annals*, 23: 489–501.

Higgs, T. (1995) *Introducing the VOCI*. San Diego, CA: San Diego State University National Language Resource Center.

Krahnke, K. (1987) *Approaches to Syllabus Design for Foreign Language Teaching.* Englewood, NJ: Prentice Hall.

Kruskal, J.B. and Wish, M. (1978) *Multidimensional Scaling.* Beverly Hills, CA: Sage Publications.

Kuo, J. and Jiang, X. (1997) Assessing the assessments: The OPI and the SOPI. *Foreign Language Annals*, 30: 503–12.

Language Testing (1985) 2 (1).

Lantolf, J.P. and Frawley, W. (1985) Oral proficiency testing: A critical analysis. *Modern Language Journal*, 69: 337–45.

Lewkowicz, J. *Authenticity in language testing: Some outstanding questions*, Unpublished manuscript, University of Hong Kong: English Centre.

Liskin-Gasparro, J.E. (1987) *Testing and Teaching for Oral Proficiency.* Boston, Mass.: Heinle & Heinle.

Long, M.H. (1989) Task, group, and task-group interaction. *University of Hawaii Working Papers in English as a Second Language*, 8: 1–26.

Long, M.H. and Crookes, G. (1992) Three approaches to task-based syllabus design. *TESOL Quarterly*, 26: 27–56.

Loschky, L. and Bley-Vroman, R. (1993) Grammar and task-based methodology. In G. Crookes and S. Gass (1993a).

McCallum, R. (1988) Multidimensional scaling. In J.R. Nesselroade and R.B. Cattell (eds) *Handbook of Multivariate Experimental Psychology* (pp. 421–45). New York: Plenum.

Messick, S. (1989) Validity. In R. Linn (ed.) *Educational Measurement* (pp. 13–103). New York: American Council on Education and Macmillan.

Messick, S. (1996) Validity and washback in language testing. *Language Testing*, 13: 241–56.

Moss, P. (1992) Shifting conceptions of validity in educational measurement: Implications for performance assessment. *Review of Educational Research*, 62: 229–58.

North, B. (1993) *The Development of Descriptors on Scales of Language Proficiency.* Washington, DC: National Foreign Language Center.

Nunan, D. (1989) *Designing Tasks for the Communicative Classroom.* Cambridge: Cambridge University Press.

Nunan, D. (1993) Task-based syllabus design: Selecting, grading and sequencing tasks. In G. Crookes and S. Gass (1993b).

Omaggio Hadley, A. (1993) *Teaching Language in Context* (2nd edition). Boston, MA: Heinle & Heinle.

Schiffman, S.S., Reynolds, M.L. and Young, F.W. (1981) *Introduction to Multidimensional Scaling.* Orlando, FL: Academic Press.

Shohamy, E. (1984) Does the testing method make a difference? The case of reading comprehension. *Language Testing*, 1: 147–70.

Shohamy, E. (1988) A proposed framework for testing the oral language of second/ foreign language learners. *Studies in Second Language Acquisition*, 10: 165–79.

Skehan, P. (1998) *A Cognitive Approach to Language Learning.* Oxford: Oxford University Press.

Snow, R.E., Kyllonen, P.C. and Marshale, B. (1984) The topography of ability and learning correlations. In R.J. Sternberg (ed.) *Advances in the Psychology of Human Intelligence* (pp. 47–103). Hillsdale, NJ: Erlbaum.

Stansfield, C. (1996) *Test Development Handbook: Simulated Oral Proficiency Interview (SOPI).* Washington, DC: Center for Applied Linguistics.

Underhill, N. (1987) *Testing Spoken Language: A Handbook of Oral Testing Techniques.* New York: Cambridge University Press.

Van Lier, L. (1989) Reeling, writhing, drawing, stretching, and fainting in coils: Oral proficiency interviews as conversation. *TESOL Quarterly*, 23: 489–508.

Widdowson, H.G. (1978) *Teaching Language as Communication.* Oxford: Oxford University Press.

Wigglesworth, G. (1997) An investigation of planning time and proficiency level on oral test discourse. *Language Testing*, 14: 85–106.

Willis, J. (1996) *A Framework for Task-based Learning.* London: Longman.

Young, F.W. and Harris, D.F. (1992) Multidimensional scaling. In *SPSS for Windows Professional Statistics, Release 5* (pp. 157–223). Chicago, IL: SPSS Inc.

Afterword: Taking the Curriculum to Task[1]

Christopher N. Candlin

I INTRODUCTORY

The purpose of this edited collection of commissioned papers in the *Applied Linguistics and Language Study Series* has been to provide multiple perspectives on the construct of *task*, drawing on those themes which have had a continuing impact on language education: tasks in relation to teaching, tasks in relation to learning, and tasks in relation to testing. The Introduction to the volume sets out clearly the dimensions of this impact, and how tasks, in their varying interpretations by the participants in these perspectives, teachers, researchers and testers, have been equally variably defined and interpreted. The original papers collected here have engaged themselves with a range of relevant issues surrounding the construct: task definition, the question of the pedagogic validity of tasks in terms of classroom operationalisation, the orientation of tasks to the learner, and the learning validity of tasks in terms of their focus on purpose, form and meaning in classroom interaction, and the potential of tasks as a means of assessing learner performance. All of the papers are grounded in research, make use of a range of methodologies, and are located in a broad set of research sites.

Given the clarity of these papers and the associated editorial apparatus in this collection, it would be otiose in this Afterword to re-canvass their perspectives, and those of other writers cited here, with their distinctive positions on the nature, utility and significance of tasks. In saying so I do not deflect from the spirit of the Introduction in emphasising the point made there that researching language pedagogy is a very long-term project, and no single book can hope to make more than a small contribution to the field. Nonetheless, as those authors in the collection concerned with language learning tasks I co-edited with Dermot Murphy in 1987 also felt (Candlin and Murphy, 1987), it was important then to make a start, and now, thanks to the ensuing wide-reaching research (for some references, see Nunan, 1989, 1991; Crookes and Gass, 1993a, 1993b) and, especially, the innovative contributions collected in this volume, we are much beyond that point.

What I can do here is to return to the spirit of speculation characteristic of that early contribution in 1987. I make no apology for this commitment to speculation. While it is natural to speculate at the outset of enterprises, it is also important to continue to do so, especially when we are some way along the route, if only to check our compasses, as it were, and resight some of our objectives.

What is noticeable about the relatively short history of research into tasks in the context of second language acquisition and pedagogy is how little attention, proportionately speaking, has been devoted to exploring in detail the question of the role that tasks might play beyond the confines of the classroom or other learning environment, in the overall design and construction of an institutionalised language educational curriculum *in macro*, as, for example, in a public secondary or primary school system. By *curriculum* here I am referring, in the more European sense, to the complex of established and ratified guidelines and syllabuses, statements of contents, aims and goals, suggested resources, assessment schemes and systems, modes and models of teaching, in short, whatever is set out, more or less formally, as an approved and legitimated guide to enable, but also to constrain, practices in educational institutions in schooling. This comparative lack of attention to tasks within language education in the context of educational systems is perhaps strange, given that the construct of task has a long history in curriculum theory, stretching back at least to the work of Dewey (1933, 1938) in the United States and that of Stenhouse (1975) in the United Kingdom.

This is not to say that tasks have been ignored as key elements in language pedagogy as a means of structuring thematic content and learner activity, as in the design of curriculum materials (Candlin and Edelhoff, 1982), or as a means of facilitating learner–learner and learner–teacher interaction in the classroom, emphasising both interactional and affective dimensions of communication (Legutke and Thomas, 1991); or as a basis for classroom-level curriculum planning (Prabhu, 1987); or as a means for enhancing experiential learning (Kohonen et al., 2000); or as a stimulus for exploring so-called *contingency* in learners' and teachers' actions (van Lier, 1996) *inter alia*. Indeed, it is most obviously now the case, that writers and publishers of language teaching textbooks have extensively seized on the construct of task as a useful tool for the internal organisation of textbook pedagogic content (Nunan, 1989); in fact, they have gone further and have elevated it to the status of a methodology, fashioning it into the core component of so-called 'task-based (language) learning', which has relatively recently appeared as a kind of latter-day sub-variant of the communicative curriculum (Breen and Candlin, 1980) with a special focus, however, on learners' actions and processes in the classroom. Further, if the role of tasks within the curriculum *in macro* has been under-explored and under-researched, this is also true, though to a lesser extent, in relation to the place and role of tasks in the systematic and sequenced organisation of classroom practice, the curriculum *in micro* as it were, despite the emphasis on task-related classroom-focused research such as that presented in some of the papers in this collection.

In what follows, then, I would like to indicate some of the ways in which this recourse to task, when institutionalised and established within the school curriculum *in macro*, and when drawn upon by teachers *in micro* in their classes, has implications for future emphases and directions in the design and conduct of task-related language acquisitional and language educational research, its questions and its processes. In brief, I want to ask what future research implications might arise from a curriculum and classroom commitment to an engagement with tasks, especially where curriculum and classroom practices in the institutionalised contexts I have indicated have not, by and large, been much influenced so far by the outcomes of task-focused research.

Addressing this issue turns out to be much more difficult than one might think, principally because as far as the matter of placing task as a central construct within the language educational curriculum *in macro* is concerned, there are few examples to my knowledge to which one can refer in the public educational sector. Some examples one can turn to, and ones with which I am personally familiar, are present in, and others alluded to, in a very recent book edited by Breen and Littlejohn (2000), in particular the pioneering and long-standing work in Catalonia by Ramon Ribe and his colleagues (Ribe, 1994, 2000), or by Pnina Linder in the narrower organisational context of the *kibbutzim* schools in Israel (Linder, 2000). I should say that I am excluding here the utilisation and evaluation of tasks in programmes specifically designed and organised for particular user groups, as for example in ESP or LSP programmes. I do so because it seems to me that the commitment of special purpose language teaching to authentication in terms set by external sponsors and their understandings of target behaviours has, to an extent, taken over and absorbed the construct of task from the needs analytical focus of such curricula on what its audiences *do*, in communicative terms, and has led course planners to identify tasks as a way of emulating, simulating and authenticating that work-related activity, rather than espousing the construct as a central design principle because of its perceived socio-cognitive, and more generally educational, orientation and value. Nor am I suggesting, in my reference above to the lack of underpinning research, that those experimental studies involving tasks with small and selective groups, as classically presented in this volume, will not be potentially of considerable value for the design and articulation of curriculum and classroom practices based on their results. Even less am I suggesting in saying this that the sole arbiter of research into language tasks should be the issue of its direct utility or applicability to language education curriculum design and the conduct of classroom activities. Nonetheless, whether explicitly stated or not, it would be jejeune to assume that researchers into tasks, whether from a discourse analytical, SLA or language assessment perspective, are not in part driven by some sense of applicability to those macro and micro curriculum contexts. And, in any case, whether they do or do not, curriculum specialists, administrators and teachers will, in their view quite rightly, look to such research for inspiration or for a warrant, and will wish to draw upon it in their practices. The force of this desire, especially in the climate of popular interest in the construct of task, is to raise the question that there is more than ever an important need *now* to focus on institutionalised practices in language education and their relationship to research results and research planning.

II TASKS AND THE CURRICULUM

As it happens, one key example case of my focus on institutionalised practices is provided by current initiatives and developments in language education in Hong Kong. Let me provide some background. A so-called *Target-Oriented Curriculum* (TOC) has, after a considerable period of discussion and, indeed, ongoing debate, been introduced by the Education Department of the Hong Kong Special Administrative Region (HKSAR) Government in selected primary schools in Hong Kong (though its inception preceded the changeover of sovereignty of Hong Kong to China in 1997). The TOC has particular relevance to the language studies curriculum, English and Chinese, and has been introduced at primary level for these subjects, and for mathematics. Although the TOC has yet to be introduced system-wide in the secondary schools (whether Chinese-medium or English-medium), and, it must be said, there are, and have been, considerable reservations expressed about this extension, the Curriculum Development Institute and Council of Hong Kong prepared curriculum documents in 1999, subsequently ratified and widely distributed, concerning the teaching of English language in secondary schools within a TOC framework (with a supplement for the so-called Advanced Supplementary Level Use of English papers (6th Form in the UK sense)).[2] This document has begun to have some informal impact on secondary level teaching, although it is not as yet mandated as a secondary curriculum for implementation. What is significant for the arguments and illustrations in this Afterword is the central place played by *tasks* in the TOC. Indeed, in casual reference in Hong Kong, there is often an unintended slippage made between a *target*-oriented curriculum and a *task*-oriented curriculum, though this is of course not the appellation of the curriculum documents. In what follows, I draw on these documents to make the connection between tasks-in-curriculum and the calls such system-situated tasks make on task-oriented second language research.

As a way of contextualising this example, let me first outline for readers unfamiliar with Hong Kong or this curriculum the position taken on language learning in these documents, as a backdrop to exploring the orientation they take towards tasks.

Language learning is defined as:

- experiential
- needing to be focused on communicative competence
- prioritised as a learning process
- requiring learners to become independent and to display positive attitudes towards language learning

Language teaching has the goals of:

- helping learners achieve communicative competence, supported by the development of linguistic competence and the mastery of skills and language development strategies

Although familiar enough in current manuals for teacher development in language education, it is important to note that definitions expressed in such a way, and such a statement of language learning and teaching objectives, still display a certain distinctiveness in the world of official second language curriculum documents. Definitions of language learning, and to a lesser degree, perhaps, statements of language teaching objectives, have not so frequently been expressed thus, though we can point to the pioneering work in Europe of the *Rahmenrichtlinien* (curriculum framework) group for secondary levels I and II in the *Gesamtschule* (comprehensive school) in the German state of Hesse in the 1970s and 1980s (Hessische Kultusminister, 1980). Such official curriculum documents have more usually centered themselves on an enumeration of language *content*, to which has been added some reference to desirable target performance skills, though some, like those from Hesse, have also included desirable classroom teaching practices. Something more of the distinctiveness of the HKSAR documents is captured in this extract of a section of the HKSAR documents provided above, where we note a quite contemporary emphasis on language learning as an experiential learning process (Kohonen et al., 2000), on the development of positive motivational attitudes (Dörnyei, 2000), as well as reference to the now more standard, but nonetheless comprehensive, stance taken by the documents on the relationship between language teaching and the development of communicative competence (Breen and Candlin, 1980; Canale and Swain, 1980).

It is proposed that these objectives are to be underwritten by what is referred to as a 'task-based approach'. This is defined in Hong Kong SAR Government (1999a) as follows

The task-based approach aims at providing opportunities for learners to experiment with and explore both spoken and written language through learning activities which are designed to engage learners in the authentic, practical and functional use of language for meaningful purposes. Learners are encouraged to activate and use whatever language they already have in the process of completing a task. The use of tasks will also give a clear and purposeful context for the teaching and learning of grammar and other language features as well as skills. Such language focus components in turn enable learners to construct their knowledge of language structures and functions. All in all, the role of task-based learning is to stimulate a natural desire in learners to improve their language competence by challenging them to complete meaningful tasks. Language use is stimulated and a range of learning opportunities for learners of all levels and abilities are provided. (p. 45)

The document continues:

Effective learning tasks motivate learners by:

- appealing to the imagination
- providing challenge
- developing confidence
- providing a sense of achievement
- expanding interests
- providing enjoyment
- providing learners with opportunities to take responsibility for their own learning (p. 45)

and goes on to say that in the process of accomplishing different learning tasks, learners will:

- develop the skills to manipulate the linguistic system spontaneously and flexibly in order to convey meanings appropriately under different circumstances and to interpret the specific meanings intended in written or spoken texts.
- attain a high degree of linguistic competence and become aware of the social meanings and potential communicative functions of linguistic forms in different situations, and
- develop the study skills and strategies for using language to communicate meanings effectively (p. 46)

Given the more epistemological or research-oriented definitions of task offered by some at least of the researchers and applied linguists as set out in the Introduction to this volume, it is interesting to note the more teacher and teaching-focused definition provided in the curriculum documents. Tasks are defined here as:

activities in which learners are required to draw together for further development a range of elements in their framework of knowledge and skills. They are characterized by an emphasis on activity, participation, flexible differentiation, and communication among participants through a variety of modes and media. (p. 46)

Tasks so defined are said to be characterised by the following features, all of which are illustrated and situated in a quite exemplary and detailed fashion in the Hong Kong document. The intention is to have them serve as a basis for curriculum and syllabus design, and to be realised in classrooms through a commitment to a learning-centred pedagogy, a functional as well as form-focused and text-based model of language (Halliday and Hasan, 1989), and a view of teaching as an instructing, mentoring and facilitating process (see van Lier, 1996):

- a task should have a purpose. It involves learners in using language for what the curriculum document sets out as three so-called 'targets' of the TOC, viz. an interpersonal dimension target (for establishing and maintaining relationships; exchanging ideas and information; and getting things done), a knowledge dimension target (for providing, finding out, interpreting and using information; for exploring, expressing and applying ideas; for solving problems), and, finally, an experience dimension target (for responding and giving expression to real and imaginative experience)

- a task should have a context from which the purpose for using language emerges
- a task should involve learners in a mode of talking and doing
- the purposeful activity in which learners engage in carrying out a task should lead towards a product
- a task should require the learners to draw upon their framework of knowledge and skills (p. 47)

Noteworthy in the document is the quite bold emphasis placed in these features and the characteristics listed below, on the linkages asserted among constructs of authenticity, authentication and acquisition (Breen, 1984; Candlin, 1984). This emphasis already highlights one of the prevailing arguments in the HKSAR document in favour of a task-based curriculum in schooling, namely the implicit claim that language activities associated with tasks have considerable preparatory potential for 'real world' communication. This authentication is typical of a nowadays common utilitarian and ends-focused justification for the English curriculum in schools, especially in foreign and second language contexts, though to be fair, Hong Kong's Department of Education lays an equivalent weight on the development of creativity and 'playfulness' in the curriculum (for some contemporary discussion, see Cook, 2000), especially in lower forms. In any case, such tasks should embody the following characteristics:

- they involve communicative language use in which the learners' attention is focused on meaning rather than on linguistic structures
- they should be authentic and as close as possible to the real world and daily life experience of the learners. Authentic materials should be selected. In addition, the processes through which the learner generates oral and written texts and the things that he/she is required to do with the data should also be authentic and relevant
- they should involve learners in various activities in which they are required to negotiate meaning and make choices in what, when and how to learn
- they should provide opportunities for learners to manipulate and practise specific language features, develop language skills, practise the integrated use of language, acquire language development strategies and use language meaningfully and creatively (p. 47)

It is worth pointing out that elsewhere in the document a distinction is drawn between *exercises* and *tasks*. While tasks are held to '*contain*' the four characteristics above, this is not required of *exercises* which are defined as serving as sequenceable preliminaries to, or supporters of, tasks. In keeping with the defining features advanced in Candlin and Murphy (1987), and in all subsequent writings on the topic, tasks themselves are conceived as being potentially of differential levels of demand on learners, in terms of cognitive load, language difficulty, and conceptual content, and can require variable completion times and be undertaken in a variety of contexts and conditions.

Where the curriculum document focuses on the *purposes* of tasks, as in the list below, it is interesting, in the light of the comment earlier, how the documents adopt a particular ideational and transactional orientation.

Tasks should enable learners to:

- seek information
- process information
- formulate questions and responses
- make connections
- inquire
- observe
- discover
- experiment
- practise
- discuss
- analyze
- reason
- share (p. 49)

The emphasis of such purposes is clearly much less affective and interpersonal than in a parallel inventory to be found in Legutke and Thomas (1991), for example. It may be that this transactional focus is not only driven by post-schooling requirements of communication in the 'real world' but is also in line with the aim of the curriculum documents to require language education-focused tasks to reflect knowledge and skills developed across the curriculum, involving ideas and information from other subjects in both the formal and the informal curriculum. Nonetheless, the curriculum document does ask that tasks involve the personal experiences of the learners, and does target a range of different learning styles and strategies, cognitive, metacognitive, and communicative (Cohen, 1997; Kumaravadivelu, 1991). The educational interests of the authors of the document are most to the fore in their call for tasks to be differentiated and graded for learners of different interests and abilities, and to display a range of different modes of participation and learning procedure, using a range of media. Perhaps surprising in such an official and system-wide document is the view taken of tasks as a kind of 'bankable resource' from which teachers may draw, but also *modify*. This commitment to openness in the curriculum comes close to some of the arguments for a process curriculum called for by Breen (1987) and Candlin (1984), and illustrated more fully in the examples of so-called *negotiated syllabuses* in Breen and Littlejohn (2000). Teachers are enjoined to evaluate tasks for their effectiveness and to experiment with different ways of integrating tasks into larger projects.

Concerning assessment within the curriculum, the document distinguishes between formative and summative assessment and between learning tasks and assessment tasks, offers a range of modes of such assessment practices, and emphasises strongly the importance of criterion-referencing principles as a way of linking performance with the objectives determined for particular teaching tasks. It makes the point:

> To evaluate learner performance against the learning targets, it is important that assessment tasks are used. Assessment tasks resemble learning tasks in that both of them:

- involve the processes of inquiring, reasoning, conceptualizing, communicating and problem-solving
- require learners to activate their knowledge, strategies and skills in purposeful use of English in contexts

The major difference between assessment tasks and learning tasks is that in learning tasks, teachers need to conduct appropriate pre-task, while-task and post-task activities to ensure that learners can complete the tasks satisfactorily. (p. 127)

So much, then, for the general and specific focus on tasks. I have taken some time to highlight and illustrate this curriculum information so as to emphasise that in the case of Hong Kong, and no doubt elsewhere, the construct of task has come to be seen as a powerful element in, and to an extent a driving force for, innovation in the school curriculum for language education. The issue that then arises, and especially in the context of this book, is the degree to which such understandings of the construct and utility of task are warranted by our current state of research, and, more especially, what directions such a deployment of tasks as a guiding curriculum principle might suggest for future curriculum-oriented applied linguistic research. To pose these questions is not to imply that curriculum development is necessarily dependent on research of this kind, though it can hardly not be informed by it, or even to suggest that task-focused applied linguistic research needs to have a curriculum utility. However, to ignore the connection and potential synergy would be perverse. After all, what the TOC in Hong Kong does exemplify is an intense awareness of the curriculum planners of the recent literature in language acquisition and pedagogy and a strong willingness to see a generally held current view of language as communication and of language learning as process, and the classroom as an interactive site of engagement, to permeate its curriculum guidelines.

III   TASK-BASED CURRICULUM-FOCUSED RESEARCH

In his important contributions on the topic, Nunan (1989, 1991, 1993, 1995) provides a highly valuable overview of both task design and second language acquisition research in relation to the construct of task, and in his 1993 paper, especially, rehearses some of the curriculum-related research questions inherent in an orientation of curricula towards a focus on tasks. In a similar way, so do some of the papers in the twin collected volumes edited by Crookes and Gass (1993a, 1993b). The present volume also makes its own important contribution to addressing these curriculum research questions in the works cited in the Introduction and throughout, and, especially, through the specific research reported in its papers. None of these sources, however, specifically addresses the questions that might arise from an actual instance of application in terms of a public curriculum.

Accordingly, what I would like to do is to highlight, somewhat selectively and in point form, some of the issues surrounding research into task design, task operationalisation and task evaluation that seem to arise in connection with curriculum-related decision-making, drawing on a real-world case, namely, that offered above by the particular example of the TOC in Hong Kong. In doing so, let me make it very clear that I am not in any way singling out the TOC for some critical evaluation. It is a very forward-looking and admirably comprehensive document. What it does permit, however, is some exploration of the assumptions and assertions made by curriculum specialists and educational advisers in designing such guidelines, and at the same time provides an indication of where second language acquisition researchers concerned with curriculum issues might want to direct their research planning.

What follows are not questions which are formulated in terms of researchable hypotheses, or indeed necessarily capable of such formulation, though it is to be hoped that some can be. They may be seen, indeed, as somewhat naïve. From my experience in language teacher professional development within a broadly task-based, process- and negotiation-oriented context, however, they are just the kinds of questions that teachers do, or might well, ask in relation to the viability of a task-based curriculum and its underlying constructs. Thus to provide them may assist readers not only in a reflective reading of the papers in this very timely and well-constructed book, and in other sources, but also to identify where curriculum-related task research in language education might be best directed. They may also assist in the negotiation by teachers of those curriculum guidelines within which they have to work, very much in the manner suggested by Candlin (1987), Breen (1987) or in the practical experiences in different educational sectors now more recently exemplified in the case studies provided in Breen and Littlejohn (2000).

A good place to begin is with the definition of tasks. Following the early statements on language learning tasks (Candlin, 1987; Nunan, 1993), the TOC curriculum, as we have seen, sets out its definition of tasks in terms of purposes, inputs and processes, with expected or indicated outcomes, and locates them in particular settings, where participants are invited to engage in a range of roles. The definitions of task usefully provided in the Introduction to this volume help us to conceptualize these distinctive 'task components', as does their use in curriculum guidelines such as those of the TOC. From these components we may identify three overlapping areas within which potentially researchable questions may be asked: questions concerning task *design*, task *operationalisation* and task *evaluation*. I set out below some of these questions, and direct them at each of the areas.

Task design

Central to task design in the TOC is the construct of *purposiveness*. Tasks are identified as having a range of purposes (for example, *seeking information, processing information*, etc). The issue here must be how these purposes are to be distinctively identified in terms of particular task design and how can they be formulated by learners in terms of actionable goals. Specifically,

- Who determines the purposes of tasks, and to what extent can purposes be defined in advance? If learners in a negotiated curriculum (Breen and Candlin, 1980; Breen and Littlejohn, 2000) redefine content during the process of learning, how can task design control content in relation to participants' changing purposes?
- In what ways can task purposes be identified so that learners and teachers can relate these purposes to particular task activities and participant roles?

Associated with purposiveness are other related terms, such as *practicality* and *functionality*, both of which are closely linked in the TOC to the overarching construct of *authenticity*. If tasks are to be 'authentic' and 'close to the real world and the daily life experiences of learners', the issue must be the terms in which these constructs are being defined and in relation to which of the task components. Specifically,

- How is the 'real world' being constructed? In terms of which participants, which roles, which discursive and social relationships?
- What assumptions are being made here between some perceived identification of the social world of the classroom and the learners' social worlds outside the classroom?
- More broadly, if the achievement of authenticity (whatever that may be) is something of a chimera in pedagogic materials, then how can tasks be authenticated in the curriculum, and by whom?

A key concern of the authors of the TOC curriculum, as we have seen, is that tasks should be designed in relation to a number of so-called target dimensions, in their terms *interpersonality, knowledge* and *experience*. The issue that arises here is once more one of realisation. Specifically, questions to ask include:

- How can these target dimensions be described in terms that teachers and learners can comprehend and how can they be defined independently?
- How can the three 'target dimensions' (of tasks within the TOC) be separately targeted within a task, if any activity, or indeed any utterance stimulated by a task, is potentially all-encompassing of all three?

Characteristic of task-based orientations to language teaching and learning is that they be in some sense *learner-oriented*. This is made explicit in the TOC curriculum, as we have seen. The question to raise here is how is this learner-orientation to be defined? Specifically, we may ask:

- What is the focus of the orientation? Is it in terms of developing learner proficiency, encouraging particular learner roles, or facilitating learner engagement?
- If the tasks are to develop learners' meaning-making capacities (as appears to be the case), what is the relationship between this objective and the necessarily concurrent development of learners' language-processing capacity?
- Given that tasks are to be designed to promote learners' overall strategic competence, how is this being defined psycholinguistically and sociolinguistically?

Task operationalisation

Questions concerning task operationalisation have to do with the realisation of the design features of tasks in terms of actual classroom use. They are thus of considerable interest to those whose role it is to enact the curriculum, namely teachers and learners in classroom contexts. The chief questions here focus on the involvement of these key participants in the process, both of task realisation and of necessity, in task design. Specifically, we may ask:

- What might be the effect on learner accomplishment of tasks of a greater or lesser degree of learner involvement in task design?
- If tasks are to involve learners in making choices in what, when, and how to learn, what are the criteria on which those choices are to be made and how can such purposeful choosing be accommodated within the curriculum?
- If tasks characteristically involve learners in 'active participation', how is this participation being defined?

A fundamental question concerning task-based curricula, and one that is addressed very centrally in the papers in this collection, surrounds the relationship between task design, task operationalisation and task performance. Specifically,

- What relationship might there be between varying degrees of task participation and learner performance and learner acquisition of forms and functions of language?
- The activities of tasks are seen as leading to particular communicative (and other) outcomes. How are these products/outcomes being defined? Do they remain stable during the realising of a task or are they redefined in the process?

One of the key incentives for introducing a task-based language learning curriculum, like the TOC, is the perceived positive effect such a curriculum is presumed to have on learner motivation (Dörnyei, 2000). Such a connection may indeed be well-grounded and justified, but issues arise, nevertheless. Specifically, we may ask:

- If 'effective' tasks and their associated characteristics in terms of purposes and activities are held to have a close relationship with motivation, in that they are held to '*challenge, provide imaginative appeal, develop confidence*', how are these attributes of tasks to be defined and operationalised? How can their presence or absence be related to motivation? How can tasks be evaluated a priori against such desiderata?

Central to undertaking the design and operationalisation of any public curriculum in the sense of a planned, institutionally-based programme, is the need to select, to grade and to sequence. The questions we may specifically ask in this context must include:

- How can tasks be selected, graded and sequenced within the curriculum? What would be the criteria for grading and co-ordinating such tasks? What would be the balance, for example, between an externally-motivated selection and sequencing procedure, namely, one based on their perceived out-of-class utility; a class-internal procedural one, based on some linking of skills in the exploitation of some theme; or one more cognitively driven, as in Prabhu's suggestion that tasks be sequenced as a cycle of immediate experience, reflection, abstract conceptualisation and practical action (Prabhu, 1987)?

These are obviously only some of the possibilities. One might, for example, argue for a task sequence in relation to any of the components of a task: its purpose(s), its processes, its outcome(s) and its modes of evaluation. Equally, one might sequence tasks in order to develop the socialisation of the learner within the classroom milieu. There are numerous possibilities and, at present at least, the TOC leaves them open.

Task evaluation

As is clear from the papers in this volume, and from the other sources that are cited here, the literature on task evaluation has primarily addressed two sets of issues: those concerned with evaluating the contributions of tasks to the development of learner cognition and acquisition and those which have been focused on the evaluation of learners' language performance. There are other, perhaps more fundamental questions to be asked concerning the evaluation of tasks, and the relationships between tasks and evaluation. Specifically,

- In relation to the issue of evaluating learner cognition and acquisition, what social factors in terms of learners' backgrounds, schooling, out-of-class socialisation, are being taken into account?
- In relation to the evaluation of learners' language performance, the overwhelming focus of research has been directed at learners' lexico-grammar. Despite an increasing amount of empirical studies in the development of interlanguage pragmatics (Kasper and Rose, 1999), we may ask why has there been little *curriculum-oriented* research which seeks to connect task design and operationalisation with the systematic development of learner discursive strategies and pragmatic behaviour?

As I indicated earlier, these are questions, not a research agenda. Nonetheless, they are suggestive of the research, experimental or, desirably, action-oriented, which needs to be undertaken if the eminently cogent and appealing guidelines for a task-oriented curriculum such as that of the TOC in Hong Kong are to be substantiated and, above all, translated into warranted classroom (inter)action. This seems to me to be the thrust of this imaginative book and its research papers, namely, to develop further a necessary research basis not only for the construct of *task*, but for the warranting of tasks as a central principle in curriculum design, implementation and evaluation. It is to that wider goal that this Afterword is directed.

NOTES

1. I acknowledge here the genial and very relevant title of Patricia Duff's (1986) paper: P. Duff (1986) Another look at interlanguage talk: taking task to task. In R. Day (ed.) *Talking to Learn: Conversation in Second Language Acquisition.* Rowley, MA: Newbury House.
2. Hong Kong SAR Government, Education Department (1998, 1999a, 1999b).

REFERENCES

Breen, M. (1984) Process syllabuses for the language classroom. In C.J. Brumfit (ed.) *General English Syllabus Design.* Oxford: Pergamon Press and the British Council.

Breen, M. (1987) Contemporary paradigms in syllabus design. Parts 1 & 2. *Language Teaching,* 20 (1): 81–92; 20 (2): 157–74.

Breen, M. and Candlin, C.N. (1980) The essentials of a communicative curriculum for language teaching. *Applied Linguistics,* 1 (2): 89–112.

Breen, M. and Littlejohn, A. (eds) (2000) *Classroom Decision-making: Negotiation and Process Syllabuses in Practice.* Cambridge: Cambridge University Press.

Canale, M. and Swain, M. (1980) Theoretical bases of communicative approaches to second language teaching and testing. *Applied Linguistics,* 1: 1–47.

Candlin, C.N. (1984) Syllabus design as a critical process. *Language, Learning and Communication,* 3 (2): 129–45. Also in revised form in C. Brumfit (ed.) *General English Curriculum Design.* ELT Documents No. 118. London: Pergamon Press.

Candlin, C.N. (1987) Towards task-based language learning. In C.N. Candlin and D.F. Murphy (1987).

Candlin, C.N. and Edelhoff, C. (1982) *Challenges: Teachers' Guide.* London: Longman.

Candlin, C.N. and Murphy, D.F. (eds) (1987) *Language Learning Tasks.* Lancaster Practical Papers in English Language Education. Hemel Hempstead: Prentice-Hall.

Cohen, A. (1997) *Strategies in Learning and Using a Second Language.* London: Longman.

Cook, G. (2000) *Language Play, Language Learning.* Oxford: Oxford University Press.

Crookes, G. and Gass, S. (1993a) *Tasks and Language Learning: Integrating Theory and Practice.* Clevedon: Multilingual Matters.

Crookes, G. & Gass, S. (1993b) *Tasks in a Pedagogical Context: Integrating Theory and Practice.* Clevedon: Multilingual Matters.

Dewey, J. (1933) *How We Think.* Boston, MA: D.C. Heath.

Dewey, J. (1938) *Experiences of Education.* New York: Collier Press.

Dörnyei, Z. (2000) *Teaching and Researching Motivation.* London: Longman.

Halliday, M.A.K. and Hasan, R. (1989) *Language, Context and Text: Aspects of Language in a Social-Semiotic Perspective.* Oxford: Oxford University Press.

Hessische Kultusminister, Der (ed.) (1980) *Rahmenrichtlinien: Sekundarstufe 1. Neue Sprachen.* Frankfurt: Diesterweg.

Hong Kong SAR Government, Education Department (1998) *Target-oriented Curriculum Assessment Guidelines for English Language.* Hong Kong: Government Printer.

Hong Kong SAR Government, Education Department (1999a) *Draft Syllabuses for Secondary Schools. English Language (Secondary 1–5).* Hong Kong: Government Printer.

Hong Kong SAR Government, Education Department (1999b) *Syllabuses for Secondary Schools. Use of English. Advanced Supplementary Level.* Hong Kong: Government Printer.

Kasper, G. and Rose, K. (1999) Pragmatics and SLA. *Annual Review of Applied Linguistics*, 19: 81–104.

Kohonen, V., Jaatinen, R., Kaikkonen, P. and Lehtovaara, J. (eds) (2000) *Experiential Learning in Foreign Language Education*. London: Longman.

Kumaravadivelu, B. (1991) Language learning tasks: teacher intention and learner interpretation. *ELT Journal*, 45: 98–107.

Legutke, M. and Thomas, H. (1991) *Process and Experience in the Language Classroom*. London: Longman.

Linder, P. (2000) Is a negotiated syllabus feasible within a national curriculum? In M. Breen and A. Littlejohn (2000).

Nunan, D.N. (1989) *Designing Tasks for the Communicative Curriculum*. Cambridge: Cambridge University Press.

Nunan, D.N. (1991) Communicative tasks and the language curriculum. *TESOL Quarterly*, 25: 279–97.

Nunan, D.N. (1993) Task-based syllabus design: selecting, grading and sequencing tasks. In G. Crookes and S. Gass (1993b).

Nunan, D.N. (1995) Closing the gap between learning and instruction. *TESOL Quarterly*, 20 (1): 133–58.

Prabhu, N.S. (1987) *Second Language Pedagogy*. Oxford: Oxford University Press.

Ribe, R. (1994) *L'ensenyament de la llengua anglesa al cicle escolar secondari (12–18 anys)*. Bellaterra: Publicacions de la Universitat Autonoma de Barcelona.

Ribe, R. (2000) Introducing negotiation processes: an experiment with creative project work. In M. Breen and A. Littlejohn (2000).

Stenhouse, L. (1975) *An Introduction to Curriculum Research and Development*. London: Heinemann.

van Lier, L. (1996) *Interaction in the Language Curriculum: Awareness, Autonomy & Authenticity*. London: Longman.

Index